Queer Japan from the Pacific War to the Internet Age

Kono sekai or *"this world,"* a reference to Japan's diverse queer community.
Calligraphy by Tomoko Aoyama

Queer Japan from the Pacific War to the Internet Age

Mark McLelland

ROWMAN & LITTLEFIELD PUBLISHERS, INC.
Lanham • Boulder • New York • Toronto • Oxford

ROWMAN & LITTLEFIELD PUBLISHERS, INC.

Published in the United States of America
by Rowman & Littlefield Publishers, Inc.
A wholly owned subsidiary of The Rowman & Littlefield Publishing Group, Inc.
4501 Forbes Boulevard, Suite 200, Lanham, MD 20706
www.rowmanlittlefield.com

P.O. Box 317, Oxford OX2 9RU, UK

British Library Cataloguing in Publication Information Available

Library of Congress Cataloging-in-Publication Data

McLelland, Mark J.
Queer Japan from the Pacific war to the internet age / Mark McLelland.
p. cm.— (Asian voices)
Includes bibliographical references and index.
ISBN 0-7425-3786-2 (cloth : alk. paper)—ISBN 0-7425-3787-0 (pbk. : alk. paper)
1. Homosexuality—Japan. 2. Japan—Social conditions—1945- I. Title.
II. Series: Asian voices (Rowman and Littlefield, Inc.).
HQ76.3.J3M35 2005
306.76′6′0952—dc22 2004022480

Printed in the United States of America

∞ ™ The paper used in this publication meets the minimum requirements of American National Standard for Information Sciences—Permanence of Paper for Printed Library Materials, ANSI/NISO Z39.48-1992.

Contents

Illustrations

Acknowledgments

Important though my intellectual debts are to many friends and colleagues, this book could never have come about except through the generous financial support of the Australian Research Council and smaller grants from the University of Queensland and the University of California at Santa Barbara's Center for the Study of Sexual Minorities in the Military, all of which enabled me to gather the enormous archive of Japanese-language material upon which this study is based. Gathering this material was made much easier by the efforts of Hitoshi Ishida, who worked for a time as my research assistant in Japan and spent many long hours standing at the photocopier, and by my brother-in-law Mitsuru Sakuraba, who always seemed happy, on request, to use his credit card for the acquisition of a variety of perverse materials. My sister Susan must be thanked too, for stocking the refrigerator with alcohol (although the cupboards were usually bare) during the many times I stayed at their Tokyo apartment while conducting research in Japan. I am also deeply indebted to the members of Chuo University's Japan Postwar Transgender Study Association, who allowed me to raid their archives, and also to the staff of Tokyo's Fūzoku Shiryōkan. Many friends and mentors on Japan's gay scene, too, have been unstintingly generous in chatting with me about the project in a variety of Ni-chōme bars. During the writing process the text itself was read and critiqued by numerous friends and colleagues; I am particularly indebted to Darren Aoki, Peter Cryle, Hitoshi Ishida, Vera Mackie, Fran Martin, Takanori Murakami, James Welker and series editor Mark Selden for their comments, criticisms and suggestions. Thanks also to Tomoko Aoyama for providing the calligraphy. Finally, I must thank my cats Alasdair and Alysha, whose constant demands for attention gave me other things to think about while writing this book.

A NOTE ON LANGUAGE

All Japanese names occur in Japanese order, that is, surname first. The correct reading of Japanese names, particularly pen names, is often problematic, and great care has been taken to provide accurate readings. However, even the catalogue of the National Diet Library has been known to provide inaccurate readings of obscure authors, and it is likely that there are inaccuracies in my transcription of some of the contributors to the "perverse press" genre of the 1950s. Where possible I have followed the National Diet Library transcriptions, except in cases where these transcriptions diverge from pronunciations designated in the publications themselves.

I have used macrons to designate long vowels in my transcriptions of cited Japanese terminology and also of personal names, but I have not used macrons for any terms that are commonly rendered in English, especially place names such as Tokyo and period titles such as Taisho and Showa.

Introduction

This book offers an introduction to some of the individuals, communities and cultures that have emerged in the postwar period within the context of what in Japanese is frequently referred to as *kono sekai*. The term means "this world," and it has been used since at least the end of the Second World War to refer to a wide variety of sexual subcultures. "How did you discover this world?" or "How long have you been on this path?" are questions frequently heard even today in Japan's gay, lesbian and transgender bars, in magazine and documentary interviews with members of sexual minorities and on sex-related sites on the Internet. The term can be used broadly to refer to a wide variety of nonheterosexual and gender-variant practices and identities and, depending on the context, could cover gay men, lesbians and transgender individuals; it can also be used more specifically to refer to one subculture—for instance, male cross-dressers.

Although the scope of *kono sekai* is very broad, finding a single adjective in Japanese that can be used to speak of diverse nonheterosexual individuals is more difficult. In Japanese *gei* (gay) has always referred exclusively to homosexual men, as has the term *homosekusharu* (homosexual). In recent years *kuia* (queer) has gained some currency, but is mainly used by more academic or activist-oriented denizens of *kono sekai* and is not much understood by those outside these groups. The English word queer does, however, resonate with a Japanese rubric for discussing "abnormal" *(ijō* or *abunōmaru)* sexuality, very common in the postwar press—*hentai seiyoku*—which can be nicely rendered as "queer sexual desires." Although *hentai,* meaning (sexually) perverse, queer or strange, has had a largely pejorative nuance, there are recent examples of it being deployed in a more playful sense, as in *Bessatsu Takarajima*'s (1991) collection of interviews and investigative reports on Japanese sexual subcultures entitled *"Hentai-san ga iku"* (There goes Mr. or Ms. Queer). More recently it was appropriated by Fushimi Noriaki, one of Japan's leading gay writers and critics, for the title of a collection on gay salarymen—"*Hentai suru sararii-man*"—"salarymen doing queer" (Fushimi 2000). Indeed, Fushimi himself has pointed out how close queer and *hentai* are in meaning; in 2003 he went on to release a collection of interviews with a wide range of sex and gender nonconformists entitled *Hentai (kuia) nyūmon* (A *hentai* [queer] introduction), where he uses the terms interchangeably. It is primarily in this sense, then, as a translation of the Japanese term *hentai*, that I use the English term "queer" to describe a range of nonheterosexual and gender-variant identities, practices and communities that have come into being in Japan in the postwar period.

However, my use of queer also references "queer theory," especially the manner in which queer theory critiques fixed identities. Drawing upon an explanation offered by Duggan and Hunter (1995: 196–7), queer theory can be understood as an approach that challenges sexual identity categories in three main ways. Firstly, queer theory is extremely skeptical of humanist narratives positing the progress of the self and of history and purporting to tell the story of the heroic progress of lesbian and gay liberation against the forces of repression. Queer theory also critiques empiricist methodologies that claim to represent directly the "reality of experience" and to relate, simply and objectively, what happened, when and why. Finally, queer theory offers a critique of identity categories that are presented as stable, unitary and "authentic," or as offering special insight into the underlying "truth" about the self. Like Ken Plummer, in this book I am more interested in how sexual stories are used and the cultural work that they do than in whether they offer accurate renditions of individuals' experiences. As Plummer notes, "The truth of these tales may not be the issue: the work they do in the lending of coherence to a life and its problems is what matters" (1995: 173).

This book is also intended as a contribution to the ongoing elaboration of the history of sexuality, a project that until very recently, in English-language scholarship at least, has almost entirely been developed in relation to Europe, North America and former European colonies. Although strong and enduring cultural connections between these societies may sustain and enable the fiction of a singular history of sexuality, close investigation reveals that sexuality is not a unitary phenomenon, subject only to minor local inflections or elaborations. So, rather than offering a history of the development of an already preconceived group of "sexual minorities" in Japan, I am more interested in exploring the emergence of those cultural factors that enabled individuals who experienced a wide range of *hentai seiyoku* or "queer desires" both to conceive of themselves and be conceived of by others as distinct kinds of people.

As outlined, my project is not to recover underlying identities that have always existed, albeit under different names, but, as is common in studies of sexuality situated in the humanities, to trace those factors that have led to sexuality being constituted in some ways and not others in particular space-time conjunctures. Since the early 1980s an important body of work has emerged that, drawing upon theoretical innovations made by Michel Foucault, Jeffrey Weeks and others, persuasively argues that sexuality is not a universally present biological or psychological reality but is itself a cultural product, or rather "the set of effects produced in bodies, behaviors, and social relations by a certain deployment deriving from a complex political technology" (Foucault 1990: 127). If sexuality is a product rather than a cause, a project rather than an essence, then it follows that different political technologies, functioning in different contexts, will result in different effects. Foucault notes that this is certainly the case across class lines, stating, "This deployment does not operate in symmetrical fashion with respect to the social classes, and consequently . . . it does not produce the same effects in them," and concluding that "we must say that there is a bourgeois sexuality and that there are class sexualities" (1990: 127). Much subsequent work has highlighted other differences that exist both within and between cultures, including those nominally grouped together as part of "the east" and "the west." However, these divisions need to be treated with caution.

The history outlined here is one of both continuities and fractures and of indigenous ideas that continued to exist alongside foreign borrowings. As discussed in detail in following chapters, it was not the case that an already constituted "Japanese sexuality" was transformed through influence from "the west" either during the opening of Japan in the Meiji period (1868–1912) or during the Allied occupation following the war. Rather, from the end of the nineteenth century, the very notion of the sexual as a distinct realm of human consciousness and experience was being constituted simultaneously in different societies as modernization, including capitalism and colonialism, accelerated the movement of new ideas, cultural practices and people across borders. As Dikotter says in relation to changing understandings of sexuality in Republican China, these transformations were "not so much a 'shock of encounters' between 'East' and 'West' . . . but rather the emergence of a plurality of intertwined modernities that have diverse origins and many directions" (1995: 12).

Since the Meiji period, Japanese society has been engaged in a complex negotiation with ideas deriving from the west in the realm of sexuality as much as in such other fields as government, education, technology or science. This process has often been understood in a rather polarized manner, with a backward Japan borrowing extensively from an advanced west. Yet Japan's use of "the west" has been both strategic and rhetorical. As Fruhstuck points out, "'the West' was used as a synonym for certain claims to truth and the importance of scientific knowledge in general"

(2003: 80). The manner in which these claims were made often did more to support the views of local Japanese intellectuals than to give an accurate account of the western originals. It is important to remember also that "the west" was deployed in different ways by various interest groups in Japan, as a cause of consternation by traditionalists and a rallying flag for reformers (Robertson 1999: 24). Japan was also far from passive in relation to the nations of the west but "envisioned itself as a full participant in the industrializing, mass militarizing, nationalizing world" by appropriating European discourses and then strategically deploying these discourses so as to position itself as a "modern" nation in its relations both with its neighbors and the west (Dudden 1999: 168).

Any process of cross-cultural comparison is therefore fraught with difficulties, especially when it takes the categories and modes of analysis characteristic of a particular epoch (the present) or location (the west) as its starting point. Cryle (2001: 20), for instance, warns of the tendency toward "transhistorical reductiveness" in accounts that attempt to decode the sexual discourse of previous eras. It is also important to be aware of a similar tendency toward *transcultural reductiveness*, a tendency to locate the sexual ideas and practices of "other" societies along a continuum of sameness or difference from those of the west. This has been a particular problem for a kind of gay and lesbian scholarship that, in its enthusiasm for the liberatory potential of western lesbian and gay movements, seeks to discover and nurture these categories in societies outside the west.

Any researcher whose intellectual project involves the investigation of the cultures of the non-west, who is based in an institution in the anglophone world, and whose scholarly activities are conducted through the English language is faced with serious problems when attempting to give an account of cultural difference. In order to guard against the reduction of other sexual modalities into a discourse that has a very specific history and role within anglophone cultures, Cryle calls for "a close hermeneutical reflection about our own situated capacity to know" (2001: 12). He presciently points out "the 'we' of modernity" (2001: 20) is already a particular mode of subjectivity, enabled in large part by the very elaboration of a field of relations and experiences that have coalesced to become a person's "sexuality" and that it is therefore difficult for us to give an account of systems of desire not easily reduced to what Pflugfelder describes as "the currently canonical trinity of 'homosexuality,' 'heterosexuality,' and 'bisexuality'" (1999: 5). This situation is complicated further by the fact that there are also multiple modernities (Sakai and Hanawa 2001: ix) and that consequently the "we" of anglophone societies such as the UK, the United States, and Australia and the "*ware-ware*" (we Japanese) of contemporary Japan are voiced from different locations and necessarily have different resonances.

One of the most persistent strands in postwar sexual discourse in the west has been discussion of sexual liberation, a process that, climaxing sometime in the late 1960s, has supposedly resulted in the forces of freedom gaining the upper hand over the forces of repression. During this period we have seen the rapid elaboration of a range of "sexual identities" and, increasingly, micro-identities, as individuals and communities attempt to define ever more precisely the nature of their sexual beings. Yet many scholars and activists alike have viewed this process with skepticism. At a recent conference on sexuality and human rights, Mark Johnson commented:

> Individuals are increasingly subjected to, and colonized by, discourses of identity (be it ethnic, national, gender, or sexual) to the extent that the compulsion to identify oneself as something or other is now becoming almost hegemonic, and all action or behaviour is read in terms of the occupation or transgression of this or that identity. (2000: 371)

One unfortunate consequence of the prioritizing of sexual identities in the west has been that societies outside the west have been seen as somehow less "liberated"—that is, as behind the west in their support for and cognizance of these categories, categories that are taken at face value as both transcultural and somehow necessary.

In the case of Japan, this tendency is apparent in the commentaries of Francis Conlan, the translator of *Coming Out in Japan* (Itō and Yanase 2000), and Barbara Summerhawk, one of the translators and editors of *Queer Japan* (1998). Through making available to English readers texts that offer, for the first time, first-person narratives from sexual minority groups in Japan, these commentators have played an important role in interpreting these narratives for western readers. For instance, Conlan tells us in the front matter of *Coming Out in Japan* that Japanese people are characterized by their "Confucianist mentality, which favours uniformity and authoritarianism," and that "traditionally held conservative, mainstream attitudes are so deeply ingrained in the Japanese psyche that they are virtually sacred." Needless to say, these "feudal values" are the main reason that nonconformity is "held in contempt" and that "bringing about social change is even more difficult in Japan than in the west" (Itō and Yanase 2000: ix–xvii). Explaining Japanese people's supposed negative attitude toward homosexuality in terms of their "feudal" mentality is particularly ironic given that male-male sexual relations were not only common throughout Japan's feudal period (1600–1867) but were, in fact, highly valued in certain circumstances (Pflugfelder 1999; Ikegami 1995; Leupp 1995). Indeed, as the first chapter in this book shows, antagonism toward same-sex sexuality is a characteristic of *modern* Japan and is deeply tied in with notions of "civilization and enlightenment" that Japan appropriated from the west during its period of rapid modernization in the Meiji (1868–1912) and Taisho (1912–1925) periods.

Perhaps most tellingly, however, Conlan comments that during a recent trip to Japan he was struck by "the imbalance between levels of technology and social attitudes," the latter having moved forward in Japan, if at all, "by a negligible amount." Here, Conlan is basically arguing that Japan, despite its status as a technological superpower, lags behind the west in terms of social and moral development, an approach typical of what Fabian has termed "the all-pervading denial of coevalness" (1983: 35) underlying western encounters with "other" societies—an assumption that he refers to as "the West-and-the-Rest complex" (1983: 155).

Summerhawk, in her introduction to *Queer Japan*, relies upon rhetorical strategies similar to Conlan's in developing her argument positioning sexual minorities in Japan as the hapless victims of a repressive regime. In Summerhawk's Japan, even heterosexuals who fail to conform find themselves excluded from society: "Not being the traditional patriarch or the submissive wife puts one on the outside of a society very structured in its interrelated sets of obligations and responsibilities" (1998: 6). In making such judgments, Summerhawk relies on "normative and naturalized perceptions of American 'we-ness'" (Yoneyama 1999: 72)—Japan is perversely "other" to an idealized American society in which husbands are never patriarchs and wives are far from submissive. The same process of homogenization characteristic of Conlan's text is apparent when Summerhawk invokes what "we" already "know" about Japan rather than engaging with actual demographic trends within Japanese society—trends that, unsurprisingly, have much in common with those in other advanced postindustrial democracies.

Summerhawk informs us that "a majority of Japanese gay men live in contradiction, a constant struggle with the inner self, even to the point of cutting off emotions and the denial of their own oppression" (1998: 10–11). Summerhawk's willingness here to speak for "a majority of Japanese gay men," whose experience she subsumes under the sign of "oppression," invites comparison to that of some western feminists who have been criticized for their reductive accounts of the complex lives of women in postcolonial nations, as discussed by Mohanty (1984), among others. The result of this strategy is that those who fall outside the identity model are disenfranchised, their experience silenced by the criticism that they are "in denial."

The unfortunate result of the rhetorical strategies engaged in by both these translators is that lesbian and gay activists in Japan whose mode of self-presentation closely accords with that of similarly "out" gay people in the nations of the west are spoken of as somehow being in advance of their closeted peers. It is no surprise that the mode of subjectivity that is highlighted as the most "authentic" (and therefore progressive) by both Conlan and Summerhawk is that of the "out" gay person and that this state is pictured in evolutionary terms—a state supposedly achieved by gay people in the west toward which Japanese people are still inching. Summerhawk states that "Itoh [*sic*] and his partner Yanase represent . . . a role model for other gay men [and] a source of 'hopes and dreams'" (1998: 14), suggesting elsewhere that they have "mapped a way" for others to follow. Conlan's preface to *Coming Out in Japan* also speaks of Itō and Yanase's story as "courageous, inspiring and necessary" and as "a manual for others to follow" (Itō and Yanase 2000: 1). The result of Conlan and Summerhawk's approach is that the superiority of the west is once again underlined—or, as Sakai points out, "the West" again functions "as a synonym for modernity and progress, as a projected trajectory for the subject's self-transcendence" (2001: 84).

My critique of Conlan's and Summerhawk's approach is somewhat regretful given that both are clearly well intentioned, one might even say impassioned, in their attempts to give voice to lesbian- and gay-identified Japanese whose existence has largely been passed over in silence by "Japanese Studies" as it is taught in western academic institutions. However, I am not alone in expressing skepticism toward the supposed liberatory potential of lesbian and gay identities, particularly when those identities are posited as the endpoint of a long and difficult journey, which is often described as the process of "coming out." Like Paul Robinson, I am skeptical about the movement from diversity to uniformity apparent in how homosexual desire has recently been explained, discussed and represented, culminating in the postwar period in the "coming-out story." Robinson argues that "coming out" has become the controlling factor in the narrative structure of the "gay life" and represents a kind of conversion narrative of "phoniness versus authenticity, nothingness versus life" (1999: 393). It is clearly important when presenting accounts of historical and cultural diversity that these are not presented as simple stories of evolution or revolution, according to which current terminologies and practices are always better.

As outlined above, both Conlan's and Summerhawk's accounts of the emergence of lesbian and gay sensibilities in Japan rely on metaphors of the journey—from oppression to freedom, from darkness to light. The "map" and "manual" metaphors too suggest that "sexual identity formation" is a journey or a process with clearly discernible stages—we can either flounder around lost on our own or follow in the footsteps of the mapmakers, or refer to the manuals left by those who have boldly gone on before us. Central to this typography, one might even say cartography, is the modernist story outlined earlier—one that sees sexuality as in a continual, if precarious, push against the forces of repression toward a state of liberation.

The story told in the following chapters does not chart the triumphal progress of Japan's sexual minorities from the shadows and ruins of war. There was no Stonewall Revolution in Japan, no iconic event that represents a turning point (no matter how imaginary) in this journey. This book is written contra Conlan, Summerhawk and others who assume sex to be "a brave but thwarted energy waiting for release or authentic self expression" (Butler 1990: 95). Instead, my focus is on the changing nature of narratives of nonheterosexual "queer" or "perverse" desires *(hentai seiyoku)* that have been voiced in a variety of media in Japan since the early 1930s and on relating these to wider social attitudes and events that enabled such stories to be told. The approach I take is broadly genealogical in the Foucauldian sense, in that I have attempted to recover the "subjugated knowledges" (Foucault 2003: 7) of a range of queer individuals and communities who have left a record of their thoughts, behaviors and practices in the postwar period. Given the very different social climate in postwar Japan and the anglophone societies of the west, particularly relating to the expression of "sexual perversity," the Japanese popular media of the '50s and '60s are replete with accounts of perverse desire—yet little use has so far been made of this "buried and disqualified" knowledge (Foucault 2003: 8).

Given my genealogical approach, which pays close attention to the particularity of local knowledges, the problem of nomenclature is paramount in a survey such as this. To talk about "sexual minorities" in the immediate postwar period is already to invoke an anachronism that obscures rather than helps focus this investigation. How is one to avoid a hermeneutic circle that cannot but read contemporary categories and modes of organization back into a time and culture where they have no place? I have therefore tried to prioritize Japanese over English terminology. The problem remains, however, as to what extent, and how exactly, Japanese terms should be translated into English. As Sakai and Hanawa point out, "Modernity . . . cannot be considered unless in reference to translation" (2003: ix), but translation is always only approximate, particularly in the case of Japan's postwar sexual culture, when so many terms, both indigenous and foreign derived, are themselves used so inconsistently.

There are many difficulties inherent in approximating Japanese nuances—even of terms that may once have come from English (or from German, French or Latin) but that in the Japanese context have taken on very different meanings and associations. To mention but two particularly troublesome examples: *sodomia* is not reducible to the English "sodomite" but was taken up for a time in the immediate postwar years as a general label designating men interested in a range of same-sex sexual interactions; *gei* too, in the postwar context, designated a commercial transgender identity quite distinct from that emerging in the nascent "gay" communities of New York or San Francisco. As Jackson points out in his discussion of "gay" identities in Bangkok, "the internationalization of the originally English label 'gay' masks the persistence of different worlds of homosexual meaning in culturally distinct societies" (2003: 152). In order to divest loanwords of their cultural baggage, I have therefore consistently romanized Japanese pronunciations of foreign terms as opposed to reverting to their original derivations, so as to emphasize that in the case of intercultural borrowing, homophones are seldom synonyms.

Other terms, such as "homosexuality," which I prefer to the cumbersome "same-sex sexuality," should also be read as if in quotes. This is because general terms such as "homosexuality" or "the homosexual"—which bring together in one conceptual rubric a wide variety of same-sex acts, performed by men with men and women with women, irrespective of gender identity or a participant's "active" or "passive" role—coalesced in Europe earlier than they did in Japan. As Jackson points out, in Europe at the end of the nineteenth century there developed "new, highly intrusive forms of religious, legal and biomedical power over human sexuality" (2003: 152), the result of which was "less a principle of inhibition than an inciting and multiplying mechanism" (Foucault 1990: 46). This convergence of state, religious and medical power did not eventuate in the same manner in Asian societies. In Japan, where homosexual acts remained unregulated by law, Buddhist and Shinto leaders failed to interest themselves in same-sex sexuality, and where psychiatry had less influence on medical discourse, "sexual identities" did not coalesce into fixed patterns till much later.

Even in the postwar press, no single term had yet emerged that could be used to describe adequately both male and female homosexuals—as, for example, "gay people" does in English—or to designate a category such as "gay men," which can refer equally to drag queens, butch clones or closeted public servants. Although the translation of "homosexuality" into the Sino-Japanese characters *dōseiai* (same-sex love) had already taken place at the beginning of the twentieth century, its use was limited and it was not generally invoked as a self-referent. In the 1950s, for instance, women sexually interested in other women were spoken of as practitioners of "Lesbos love" *(resubosu ai)* and occasionally as "female homos" *(josei no homo),* whereas homosexual men were grouped together under the loanword *sodomia* or the traditional term for male-male eroticism, *nanshoku*. However, more important than these general rubrics were specific terms that designated an individual's role within the sexual encounter—whether they were *danshō* (cross-dressing male prostitutes), *onē* (big sisters), *pede* (pedophiles), *tachi* (tops), *neko* (bottoms), or *donden*—that is, "reversibles," who would go either way.

With the above in mind, something ought to be said about the organization of this book. The book's original focus was to have been the Internet and the role this new technology has played in bringing together and giving voice to an enormous number of sex- and gender-variant individuals. Prior to the advent of this new medium, it was difficult for queer people—whether Japanese or foreign—not already networked with these communities to gain information about them and practically impossible for those not resident in Japan. Yet, early in the research I became dissatisfied with this seemingly obvious assumption. A chance encounter with a stack of postwar "perverse magazines" revealed to me a large body of writing, much in the first person, about "queer desires" that began as early as 1946 and continued until the development of niche media for homosexual men, and slightly later for lesbian women, in the early 1970s. What I had thought was a new development in Japan—a medium that enabled the widespread dissemination of first-person narratives about sexual minorities—was already in place in the immediate postwar years, far earlier than similar media developed in anglophone societies. Though print media clearly lack the scope of the Internet, particularly in such a wired society as Japan, my assumption that queer networking before the Internet had been very limited and that what had existed would prove difficult and laborious to uncover was clearly mistaken. In fact, as chapter 2 shows, the amount of material available is so enormous that it is quite impossible to do it justice in a single monograph.

Although the immediate postwar period would have been a tidy point at which to commence this narrative, particularly as Pflugfelder's (1999) exemplary history of Japanese male same-sex sexuality stops at this juncture, it soon became clear that starting with the war's end had its own problems, since the particularities of postwar sexual experience could not be adequately investigated without at least some reference to Japan during wartime. But when did Japan's war begin, exactly? With the bombing of Pearl Harbor in 1941? With Japan's war against China in 1937? Or with Japan's annexation of Manchuria in 1931? This latter event, which set Japan on the warpath, was the start of what Japanese historians have termed the "15-year war," and it is from this point that I decided to open the narrative, although the need for further contextualization required some reference to sexual ideas and practices that had come even before.

Despite the fact that the book's title suggests a straightforward chronological narrative, after a process of trial and error it became apparent that it would make more sense if the chapters were organized around certain themes within a looser chronological framework. Chapter 1, for instance, opens with a discussion of the emergence of the category of sexuality within Japanese discourse. Consideration is then given to how increased state intervention in the personal lives of individuals during Japan's 15-year war impacted upon gender and sexual experience, leading toward both a reductive heteronormativity in discourse about sex and a polarization of gender roles. The chapter goes on to discuss how war mobilization resulted, paradoxically, in increasingly homosocial situations that both encouraged and facilitated homosexual interaction, and how the exigencies of war required both men and women to take on gender roles at variance with official ideologies.

The manner in which Japan's defeat at the end of the Pacific War and the ensuing occupation by Allied forces served to discredit imperialist ideologies regulating sex and gender while opening up new commercial spaces for heterosexual and homosexual expression is the topic of chapter 2. The chapter looks at the inquiry into perverse desire that took place in "perverse magazines" *(hentai zasshi)* of the 1950s and '60s, focusing particularly on the connection made between male homosexuality and feminization. Although this research tended to treat perverse desires as a form of arrested development, the discursive space of "perverse desires research" provided a context in which the experience of actual individuals with "abnormal" sexual interests could interact with and challenge the explanatory framework provided by experts. Significantly, at this time, such topics as male homosexuality and cross-dressing, or cross-dressing and sadomasochism, which today are conceived as separate sexual phenomena, were tied in with heterosexual acts (including sadomasochism, swinging, scatology and voyeurism). Despite being presented as deviant, these acts were also the source of considerable fascination for both writers (who included many amateurs as well as "experts") and readers. These magazines did not present a variety of distinct "sexualities" but rather a perverse paradigm based on an all-encompassing interest in queer desire and its diverse manifestations.

Chapter 3 charts the progress of the *gei bōi,* who emerged in the late 1950s as the most visible representative of male homosexuality in popular culture. Unlike more masculine-identified American gay men who were emerging in places such as New York and San Francisco at precisely the same time, in Japan *gei bōi* were contained within a transgender paradigm closely associated with the entertainment world. The ability of some transgenders to cross over into mainstream entertainment did much to establish transgenderism as the main paradigm through which same-sex desire was understood at this time; the popularity of such performers resulted in a process of "touristization," in which previously subcultural bars, clubs and cabarets began to cater to a more mainstream clientele. Though there was little interaction between homosexual men and homosexual women, the new cultural prominence of the *gei bōi* also affected how same-sex-desiring women were perceived with such parallel transgender categories for women as "brother girls" and "male-dressing beauties" developing in Japan's entertainment world in the 1960s.

The gradual process whereby male homosexuality was separated from the general category of "perverse desire" and from the transgender paradigm of homosexual identity prevalent in the entertainment world is outlined in chapter 4, which looks at the growing division between the worlds of the *homo*—that is, masculine-identified homosexual men—and the *gei bōi*. While in the 1950s and '60s a variety of sexual acts and practices had been bundled together under the term "perverse desires," the decline of the perverse magazines in the 1970s can be attributed to the evolving distinction between sexual practices like sadomasochism (conceived of as an act or play) and more ontological states, such as homosexuality, which increasingly came to be interpreted as subjective and essential aspects of the person. The most important evidence of this trend was the establishment in 1971 of the commercial publication *Barazoku*, which was aimed at a male homosexual market and which sparked a rapid increase in both the volume and the range of publications aimed at masculine-identified homosexual men.

Although a strong and identifiable *homo* culture had developed in Japan by the end of the 1970s, it was still in many ways quite distinct from that of Anglophone gay cultures of the period. Chapter 5 looks at the changes in the Japanese homosexual world that enabled the term "gay" (or *gei*) to begin to be used by Japanese homosexual men with political, not transgender, connotations. However, the fact that gay was not used in Japanese in this manner until the end of the 1970s does not mean that Japan was behind the United States or Europe in terms of activism. In fact, Tōgō Ken, Japan's first openly homosexual politician, began campaigning for minority sexuality rights as early as 1971. Yet his personal and campaign style had little in common with the fundamentalism characteristic of anglophone lesbian and gay activism of the time but was remarkably similar to recent queer activist approaches. The chapter suggests that despite the founding of western-style lesbian and gay organizations in the mid-1980s, the more inclusive (and arguably more radical) queer style of activism and identification pioneered by Tōgō lives on and has the wider constituency. It is argued that the Internet has been particularly important in creating a new space for queer desire to be articulated and for new alliances to be formed.

Chapter 6 looks at the further dissociation of transgendered men from the world of male homosexuals and the recent emergence of the category of transsexual. Although bars and social organizations catering specifically to the needs of male transgenders could be found in Tokyo as early as the mid-1950s, it was not until the late 1970s that amateur cross-dressing clubs were established that enabled a larger number of men to experiment with their transgender desires. The early '80s saw the rapid development of media directed at male cross-dressers that enabled the foundation of regional, national and international transgender networks even before the advent of the Internet facilitated this process. While the category *gei bōi* had been the most visible homosexual and transgender category since the war, in the 1980s there was a proliferation in transgender identities that enabled the dissociation of the category *gei* from transgender performance. The gradual dissociation of homosexuality from transgenderism also facilitated the emergence of the transsexual—that is, an individual who, after receiving corrective surgery, was able to reenter society as a "normal" member of the other sex. However, the development of medical categories of transgender identity that took for granted the naturalness of gender categories such as male and female has not been welcomed by all. By the end of the 1990s the Internet had become a forum for lively debate over the meaning, use and control of all sexual and gender identity categories, with a new focus on the emergence of the *tōjisha*, or the "person [directly] concerned," as the final arbiter of truth about the self.

Given the plurality of the debate over sex and gender issues now taking place in Japan, the book closes not with a conclusion but with an afterword suggesting some avenues for further research and exploration.

1

Heteronormativity on the Road to War

The telling of any story is fraught with the issue of where to begin. I had hoped to start this book with Japan's defeat at the end of the Second World War, but it became clear early on in the research that immediate postwar developments could not be understood without reference to what had come before, particularly the social ideologies and experiences that most Japanese people had been subject to during Japan's long, 15-year period of regional conflict. Yet even this periodization has its problems, as there was no clear break in attitudes toward sexuality between Japan of the 1930s and Japan of the 1920s. As in any society, different parts of the population moved at different speeds; attitudes among men and women, city and rural dwellers, and among the different classes changed at different rates and in relation to different factors.

I therefore decided to open this chapter not with any specific event but with a more general overview of the development of the notion of "sexuality" as a distinct realm of human experience in Japanese popular discourse. After a brief inquiry into Edo period (1600–1867) ways of categorizing individuals' (mainly men's) sex lives, I go on to look at how in Meiji Japan, in a process that was unfolding simultaneously in both the United States and Europe at this time, the notion of sexuality developed in tandem with an increase in public media for discussing and dissecting it. I note how privileged men, who had previously had a range of sexual options, increasingly found themselves constrained by emerging notions of "normal" and "perverse" desires. Gradually, elite men's sexual energies were channeled into heterosexual and, at least potentially, reproductive sexual acts. Women too were caught up in this movement, but as outlined below, sexual propriety for women was very much predicated on class; elite women were expected to contain their desires within marriage, whereas lower-class women were expected to sell sexual (as well as other forms of) labor.

Ironically, the gender polarity and heteronormativity stressed in official ideology during the march toward war in the 1930s was paralleled by increasing homosociality (sex-segregation) as men were drafted into the armed forces and large numbers of women moved into the factories to take their place. These social arrangements created all kinds of homoerotic alliances that were difficult for the authorities to control. Men and women also found themselves adopting a variety of gendered and sexual stances in relation to each other and the state, not all of which were in accord with official values.

NANSHOKU, JOSHOKU AND LOVE BETWEEN WOMEN

During the Edo period there was no necessary connection made between gender and sexual preference, because men, samurai in particular, were able to engage in both same- and opposite-sex affairs. Same-sex relationships were governed by a code of ethics described as *nanshoku* (male eroticism) or *shudō* (the way of youths), in the context of which elite men were able to pursue boys and young men who had not yet undergone their coming-of-age ceremonies, as well as transgender males of all ages from the lower classes who worked as actors and prostitutes (Pflugfelder 1999; Leupp 1995). The latter group included *onnagata,* or female-role players, from the kabuki theater as well as *kagema,* or transgender prostitutes.

Male homosexuality in Japan had long been associated with both transgender performance and prostitution, associations that were to remain strong in the modern period. De Becker notes how some establishments in Yoshiwara, Tokyo's main brothel district, "hired and offered to their patrons the services of attractive boys in the same manner as the regular brothels dealt in women" (1905: 369). These establishments had been so popular during the Edo period that some Japanese historians, somewhat implausibly, suggest that they had a retarding effect upon population growth (Kuno 1937: 367–8). Although popularly referred to as *kodomo-ya,* or "children's houses," the brothels also employed young men who catered to a female clientele, including, it was rumored, ladies-in-waiting from the shogun's harem (Kuno 1937: 367). While many of the young boys (referred to as *butai-ko,* or "stage children") had ostensibly been placed in these establishments to receive training to appear on stage, most simply waited on the guests and offered them sexual services. Both *onnagata* and *kagema* were understood to have become transgendered for professional purposes—that is, to earn a living—and while they would offer sexual services to other men (and occasionally women), their transgender performance said nothing about their own sexual preferences.

The other paradigm within which male homosexual relationships took place was age related, tracing its origins back to Buddhist monasteries in the Heian period (794–1185), where adult monks could establish sexual relationships with young child acolytes known as *chigo*. This practice supposedly derived from China, and like other borrowings from the continent, it "was seen as part of a civilizing process" (Faure 1998: 227). Unlike in the Christian world, where "sodomy" was perceived as a serious sin, sometimes punished at the stake, Japanese Buddhism not only tolerated intergenerational relationships between monks and boys but even offered doctrinal support for them (Faure 1998: 213).

Due to the fact that many samurai were educated in the monasteries, the "way of youths" also became popular among Japan's military elite. Within this system, an adult, known as a *nenja*, or "man who loves," could court and become the lover of a youth known as a *chigo* (page) or *wakashū* (youth) who had not yet undergone the coming-of-age ceremony and had his forelocks shaved (Furukawa 1994: 100). At this time *nanshoku* (eroticism between men) and *joshoku* (eroticism between men and women) were not seen as mutually incompatible; neither *nenja* nor *wakashū* were yet, in Foucault's terms, seen as distinct "species" (1990: 43). Similarly, transgender performers such as *onnagata* and *kagema* were seen not as distinct personality types, still less as deviant "sexualities," but as occupational categories.

Edo-period sexual culture was phallocentric and organized around an active/passive polarity—that is, one sexual act was of overwhelming significance: penetration by a penis. The partner who penetrated the body of his lover was invariably the elder partner in an intergenerational relationship or the male partner in transgender relationships or relationships with women. Given the prominence that "lesbian love" was to achieve in male pornography in the postwar years, there is surprisingly little representation of women's same-sex desire in Edo-period culture. Although instances of same-sex sexual acts between women are recorded in a variety of literary, artistic and other sources, such acts were not codified into a *dō*, or "way," of loving, and there is little discussion of (or terminology for) specific roles adopted by women. The polarized, role-based style that structured sexual interactions between men seems not to have been reduplicated in relationships between women, although, as Leupp (1998) points out, many of the incidents involving women's same-sex love in the literature do involve women of different status, such as mistress and servant or paying client and courtesan. Significantly, while *nanshoku*, made up of the characters for "man" and "eroticism," was a general term covering a variety of forms of love practiced between men, *joshoku*, made up of the characters for "woman" and "eroticism," actually referred to love relationships between *men* and women. No concept existed at this time that referred in a general sense to women's same-sex love (Wu 2002: 68), and there was no way of cognitively linking both male and female "homosexuality."

Compared with numerous literary sources discussing sexual and romantic affairs between men (Miller 1996; Ihara Saikaku [1687] 1990; Watanabe and Iwata 1989), incidents involving women are far fewer, and no texts that take the love between women as their central theme seem to have been written during this era. However, the fact that women did desire and provide sexual pleasure for other women was acknowledged, particularly in erotic woodblock prints known as *shunga*. Most (but not all) of these illustrations showing women pleasuring each other were created by male artists and were most probably enjoyed by a male clientele. Further underlining the phallocentrism of the culture, they usually portray the use of dildos as penis substitutes. Dildos were commercially available in sex shops in both Edo and Osaka. The fact that catalogues describing *tagaigata* or dildos "for mutual pleasure" write the term "mutual" with nonstandard characters, including two "woman" *(onna)* radicals (Leupp 1998: 24), suggests that women purchased these devices and used them together. Whether desire between women was always mediated by a penis substitute is impossible to deduce from surviving representations; cunnilingus between women, like fellatio between men, for example, is never depicted in erotic artwork of the period (Leupp 1998: 34).

THE EMERGENCE OF "SEXUALITY"

The Meiji period (1868–1912), during which Japan was opened to western influence, coincided with the development of European sexological discourse. The closing decades of the nineteenth century, a period in which the new field of sexology was being widely elaborated in German medical circles, was also a time in which Japanese intellectuals were traveling to and borrowing extensively from Germany. Between 1870 and 1905, a total of 448 Japanese students attended Berlin University alone, of whom 30 percent read law and 42 percent medicine (Martin 1995: 27). In fact, since the opening of Japan, "Western medicine had been brought to Japan almost exclusively by German doctors, and the faculty of medicine at Tokyo University was in the hands of German professors and their Japanese students," among whom German, not Japanese, was the daily means of communication (Martin 1995: 44–5). The early prestige of German models and the fact that the circulation of more recent anglophone ideas was restricted during the Pacific War enabled German paradigms and terminology to live on well into Japan's postwar period.

However, the frequent reference to German and other "western" scholars and theories should not be understood as a wholesale adoption of these approaches by Japanese intellectuals but rather as an authenticating strategy on the part of Japanese writers who used the cultural capital of foreign ideas in support of their own theories. The deployment of foreign references in a text was often a rhetorical strategy wherein "references to the order of things in the West . . . served primarily to underscore the Japanese authors' own opinions" (Fruhstuck 2003: 79). The fact that German ideas existed alongside native categories that were themselves being deployed in new ways and in different contexts is an example of the already hybridized nature of Japanese sexual culture at the beginning of the twentieth century, illustrating Fran Martin's contention that sexual discourse in modern societies is unavoidably "polyglottic and translational" (2003: 249).

One of the most important intellectuals who deployed both native and foreign ideas about sexuality in his writing was the novelist Mori Ōgai, a military doctor who had spent four years as a student in Berlin. He published a wide range of articles on sexual issues; these writings constituted one of the main conduits through which the categories devised by German sexologists such as Krafft-Ebing[1] were disseminated into Japanese and via Japanese into Chinese (Yokota-Murakami 1998: 199, n. 8). There is clear evidence of German influence in Ōgai's autobiographical novel *Vita Sexualis,* published in 1909 (and banned by the authorities one month after release); the title alone echoes Krafft-Ebing's own *Psychopathia Sexualis,* and the narrator of the novel describes the development of his sex life in terms not dissimilar to those of a classic case study.

Ōgai was writing at precisely the time that *seiyoku* (sexual appetite or desire) was beginning to be elucidated as a factor behind character development in Japanese fiction, and his novel is one of the first to take the "sexuality" of its protagonist as its central theme. Although the term *seiyoku* was already in use in medical literature by the middle of the Meiji period, its wider dissemination was accelerated by the adoption of the term by fiction writers such as Ōgai, as well as others associated with the naturalist school in the first decade of the twentieth century. *Seiyoku* first appeared with this new connotation in Shōgakkan's *Great Japanese Dictionary,* published in 1907 (Yokota-Murakami 1998: 133).

The adoption of sexuality as a topic for novelistic treatment was significant in that it allowed the depiction of a new dimension of interiority, a hidden realm of desire in need of confession by the protagonist and elaboration by the author. Yokota-Murakami comments, "What is sexual thus emerges exactly as something that is private, that which has to be concealed, and therefore, to be revealed" (1998: 132). Sexuality was constituted via new narrative structures; in Plummer's (1995) terms, it became a "sexual story" that needed to be confessed or told because it was a privileged site for understanding or revealing the self. This new kind of sexual literature was quite different from what Yokota-Murakami describes as the "anatomical approach" (1998: 136) characteristic of earlier erotic writing, which was more concerned with sexual acts than interior identities. As a "fundamental" aspect of human nature, an individual's sexuality thus became a key means of understanding the kind of person he or she was. Yokota-Murakami notes how it was precisely at this time that individuals who had a predilection for certain sexual acts (such as peeping) began to be defined in terms of those predilections, as characterizing specific types of persons. Using peeping as his example, he notes that

> what distinguishes *debakame-shugi* (or, voyeurism) from the traditional forms of "peeping" such as *kaimami* (a mere glimpse: occasional glimpses that princes and courtiers obtained of the courtly ladies who were enclosed by curtains and screens) is the ontological status the former gives to one who peeps. (1998: 143)

The elaboration of a realm of sexuality led to the designation of normal *(seijō)* and perverse *(ijō)* forms of sexuality and, accordingly, people. Indeed, from the end of the Meiji period, drawing upon theorists such as Freud, discussions of "perverse" or "queer" desire *(hentai seiyoku)* began to circulate in popular magazines that advocated the improvement of public morals in pursuit of "civilization and enlightenment"—a popular slogan of the period (Matsuzawa 1997: 54–5). In particular, the previous discourse of *nanshoku* and the transgender practices associated with male prostitution were portrayed as feudal, incompatible with "civilized morality," and something that ought to be eradicated.

Although the exact date of the introduction of the concept remains unclear, by the early Taisho period (1912–1925) *dōseiai*, or same-sex love, had emerged as an approximate translation of the European concept of "homosexuality" (Furukawa 1994). For the first time in Japanese a category became available within which a variety of female-female same-sex acts could be grouped; it also became possible to speak of both male and female same-sex desire as dimensions of the same phenomenon (Wu 2002: 68). While both male-male and female-female same-sex practices were considered equally perverse, there was a qualitative difference between them in that same-sex love between women was considered to be more psychological, emotional and spiritual, whereas men's desires were considered more carnal. As a consequence, *dōseiai* tended to be used much more in relation to female same-sex love. In part, this was an accident of the translation of "homosexual" as *dōseiai,* since *ai,* the character chosen to represent "love," was more emotional in tone than *koi,* an alternative character that had a stronger erotic charge (Furukawa 1994). This "love" between members of the same sex seemed to describe well the widely reported schoolgirl crushes that occurred in the dormitories of Japan's new educational establishments for girls. Spoken of as "S" relationships, in which the *S* stood for *shōjo* (girl), sister or even sex, these crushes, albeit considered morbid, were not taken too seriously, since they were regarded as temporary aberrations, something that the girls would outgrow (Robertson 1998: 68). Although the association of female same-sex love with the poet Sappho and the island of Lesbos was widely recognized (*Hentai shiryō* 1928: 73; Curran and Welker in press; see also figure 1.1 below), the *katakana* version of the noun "lesbian" *(resubian* or *rezubian)* did not become current until the early 1960s, making it difficult to speak of lesbian identities in the prewar period.

Despite the fact that *dōseiai* was originally a focus for discussions of female-female love, men's same-sex attraction increasingly became subsumed under the label. However, the long emphasis on the carnal nature of men's desire meant that *nanshoku* remained the primary term for male-male sexuality well into the postwar period. As will be discussed in subsequent chapters, it was not until the mid-1960s that *nanshoku* and its derivatives were finally eclipsed by more recent terms as *homo* (from *homosekushuaru*) and *gei* (gay).

Another factor leading to the narrowing of sexual identification and practice in the early modern period was the Meiji state's endorsement of the "modern family," which held love and fidelity between husband and wife to be the "pinnacle of reason and emotion," or indeed the greatest pleasure in human life. In this system, the family was viewed as the core unit of social stability and progress and the training ground for an individual's entire moral education (Fruhstuck 2003: 75). The patriarchal family unit also functioned metonymically as part of a state-sponsored ideology that posited Japan itself as a "family state" *(kazoku kokka)* with the emperor as the father of the nation. The ideology underpinning the new "imagined community" (Anderson 1983) of the Japanese nation increasingly came to be organized around the notion of bloodline *(kettō),* resulting in what Robertson has termed a dominant and modern cultural ideal of "ethnic national endogamy" (2002: 192). Since sex was the process through which the bloodline was passed on and if properly managed could be "improved," or if left to chance could be "diluted" or, worse, "polluted," Japanese citizens were encouraged to think more instrumentally about the deployment of their reproductive potential.

Figure 1.1 "Lesbische Liebe" (lesbian love). *Hentai shiryō* (Perverse materials), January 1928

However, increased public discussion of sexual matters and state support of eugenic and sexological interventions into people's private lives did not always result in the "improving" behavior desired by the ideologues. People's interest in sexual matters was often as prurient as it was scientific. The new delineation of "normal" sexual attitudes and practices meant that attention also had to be paid to the perverse other—that is, practices and people that the healthy citizens needed to avoid.

JAPAN'S "PERVERSE" CULTURE

During the early Showa period (1926–1989), Japan developed a significant publications industry devoted to the discussion of sexuality—in the 1920s at least ten journals were founded that focused, in particular, upon perverse sexuality. These included *Hentai shiryō* (Perverse material, 1926), *Kāma shasutora* (*Kāma shastra*, 1927), *Kisho* (Strange book, 1928) and *Gurotesuku* (Grotesque, 1928). These journals specializing in sexual knowledge, as well as articles and advice pages contributed to newspapers and magazines by a newly emerging class of sexual "experts," frequently discussed "perverse sexuality," albeit usually diagnosed as a problem. The result was that *hentai,* signifying sexual interests that were understood to be "queer" or "perverse," became a widely recognized term (Matsuzawa 1997: 55). The sexological journals offered readers the opportunity to write in and describe their own perverse desires in the hope that expert advice might remedy their condition. One unforeseen side-effect of this process was that the perverse themselves were given a voice. The journals ensured that "concepts and theories that in scientific language might be too difficult and abstract for the common reader were recast into the form of confession and 'expert' responses in advice columns" (Fruhstuck 2000), resulting in the widespread popularization of sexological "knowledge."

The experts who wrote these articles and analyzed the perverse desires of their correspondents did so in a popular medium that appealed to a readership far wider than the medical community. As Fruhstuck points out, by the middle of the Taisho period rising literacy rates and the proliferation of cheap newspapers and magazines meant that reading had become a favorite leisure activity of the working classes, allowing a "low scientific culture" to develop (2003: 103). Although Meiji-period sexology had been the province of the elite, the Taisho period saw what Miyazawa describes as a "*hentai* boom" (1997: 55), the first of several explosions of interest in perverse sexuality that were to sweep the Japanese media over the next half-century.

Precisely how this new, popular audience received and understood the sexological magazines is difficult to ascertain, but Pflugfelder suggests that the readership was "clearly more attracted than repelled by the 'perverse' nature of their contents" (1999: 287). Pflugfelder describes how "the discourse on 'perversion' transformed the sexual behavior of others into a spectacle for consumption as well as a vehicle for self-understanding" (1999: 289) and provided both writers and readers with a new kind of narrative pleasure. Indeed, the perverse press is best understood in relation to the wider cultural phenomenon known as *ero-guro-nansensu,* or "erotic grotesque nonsense," which was prominent in the popular culture of the late 1920s (Bessatsu Taiyō 1997: 44–5, 132; Matsuzawa 1997:

55–6; Roden 1990). While the strictly supervised brothel districts were recognized as safe spaces for the "traditional" Japanese practice of prostitution, other institutions, such as cafés and dance halls, were sites for less restrained, "foreign" or "French-style" modes of interaction between waitresses and clients (Garon 1999: 108) or, worse, between "modern boys" *(mobo)* and "modern girls" *(moga)* who socialized together away from the prying eyes of the family. This frivolous scene, one in which women participated with some autonomy, was considered a dangerous foreign development. The *moga* were one instance of the general category "problem women"—that is, women who failed to conform to a narrow, codified model of femaleness and who had caused consternation in Japan's press since the turn of the century (Robertson 1999: 2).

Donald Roden (1990) has pointed out that the 1920s was a decade characterized by an iconoclastic spirit and a fascination with gender ambivalence in many of the world's capitals, including Berlin, Paris, New York and Tokyo.[2] This interest was evident not only in the prevalence of cabaret and other stage acts, including the all-female Takarazuka revue (Robertson 1998; Roden 1990: 47–8), but also in the avant-garde art world. It was during the 1920s that the prominent Japanese theater and art group MAVO began to play with cross-dressing in its stage and installation work (Weisenfeld 2002). Radical political groups too, such as the feminist organization Seitō-sha, were experimenting with a variety of hetero- and homosexual relationships (Wu 2003: 78–9; Curran and Welker in press). By this time, Japan was already implicated in wider social movements that were affecting notions of sexual identity and gender performance throughout the world. As Pflugfelder comments:

> Japanese popular culture had become embedded by the early twentieth century in a global context wherein related (though never entirely identical) sociocultural phenomena were shared among industrial capitalist societies and discourses flowed with relative ease across national borders. (1999: 290)

During this period, Japanese print culture was preoccupied with *ryōki,* a new compound word made up of the characters "hunt" and "strange," which can be translated as "hunting for the bizarre" or "curiosity seeking." The term *ryōki* first appeared in dictionaries in the early 1930s and, as Angles points out, "involved a scopophilic desire to uncover strange and bizarre 'curiosities,' especially ones having to do with the erotic, so that the onlooker might experience a degree of precarious excitement and even titillation" (2003: 183). One such magazine was *Decameron,* a classic erotic-grotesque publication that scoured the globe for strange stories, discussing the demimonde in Paris and Shanghai, bizarre sex customs from anthropological records, and news-related articles such as the latest double love-suicides.[3] This magazine was well illustrated and included old European erotic engravings as well as anthropological photographs, primarily of grotesque body modifications. It even featured a "nonsense room" (the title in English), where short articles of spurious sexual interest were printed. Homosexuality was also discussed in the magazine. The April 1931 edition featured a discussion of the love life of Greek hero Alcibiades, and passing mention was made of Japanese cross-dressing prostitutes, referred to as *kagema,* as well as of lesbianism. *Hentai shiryō* (also published under the Latin title *Materia Curiosa*) was similar, discussing a wide range of sexual topics including phallic worship, flagellation, and fellatio, and offering descriptions of bizarre sexual initiations picked up from anthropological studies. The magazines did not segregate either male or female homosexuality but discussed same-sex love alongside a range of other perverse phenomena, such as fetishism and sadomasochism, the result of which was to suggest that sexual perversion was both multiple and widespread.

Roden refers to the irony inherent in the Taisho popularization of sexology, which, ostensibly, warned readers about the dangers of perversion and encouraged correct sexual knowledge and practices. Yet, despite the fact that *hentai* (perverse) was often invoked as the opposite of *jōtai* (normal)—it was perversion, not normality, that was obsessively enumerated in popular sexology texts, thus giving "the impression not only that 'perversion' was ubiquitous, but that the connotations of the term were not entirely negative" (Pflugfelder 1999: 287). Public interest in perversity fed demand for increasingly detailed and lurid descriptions, and "what started out as prescriptive literature quickly lost the blessings of educators and police and thus descended into the underground culture" (Roden 1990: 46). Indeed, the very act of *ryōki,* or seeking out curiosities, came to be viewed as pathological by some educators. Angles notes growing concern expressed over the *ryōkibyō kanja,* or "patient with curiosity-hunting disease," who was defined as a

> perverse entity who seeks out extraordinary stimulation and feels an interest in things that go beyond common sense. They are people for whom strolling in the Ginza, unemployment anxiety, the cinema, cafes and such do not provide enough stimulation; therefore they hunt about wildly in all directions. (2003: 184)

Despite the discourse prevalent in sexological publications situating homosexuality on the strange or perverse side of the sexual spectrum, it does seem to have been widely practiced, especially in the dormitories of Japan's middle and high schools. In large part this was encouraged by the "taboo on social intercourse between the sexes" that was rigorously enforced among middle-class and elite girls and boys (Dore 1999: 159). Girls' secret "S" relationships have already been mentioned; boys too seem to have been keen on same-sex crushes, albeit of a more carnal nature. Roden notes how the dormitory system that housed younger and older boys together encouraged homosexual predation, especially in the context of "storms," wherein senior boys would gang together to raid the sleeping quarters of the freshmen (1980: 37, 141–2). These activities, although not endorsed by the school authorities, were regarded as the regrettable result of youthful exuberance rather than as the expression of sexual pathology. Indeed, in what Roden refers to as "pre-Freudian" days, the fun that students had with their roommates could more easily be "glossed over as 'innocent' or playful" (1980: 179). When penalties were handed out, they were not harsh. For instance, in his autobiography socialist Ōsugi Sakae, whose previous dalliances had been with girls, mentions that he was introduced to homosexuality while studying at cadet school at the turn of the century. Ōsugi's turn of phrase is interesting here, as he refers not to *nanshoku* but "the vices of *bushidō*" (the way of the warrior), suggesting that the long association of homosexual attraction with the military caste in Japan remained prominent well into the Meiji period (see also Ujiie 1995). The main vice of *bushidō* was joining the junior boys in their beds after lights-out (Ōsugi 1992: 65, 68). This "amusement" *(asobi)* resulted in a ten-day confinement in the guardhouse when Ōsugi was caught in the act by the sergeant on night duty (1992: 77). When he was later expelled from the academy, it was not for his pursuit of young lovers, however, but for the wounding of a fellow student with a knife in a fight.

How homosexual interaction was understood by the students themselves at this time can be glimpsed from a letter received by Kabiya Kazuhiko (1962e: 124–5) during the middle 1920s.[4] (Kabiya was an "expert" on homosexual matters who contributed scholarly articles to sexological magazines both before and after the war and whose work is discussed in greater detail in subsequent chapters.) The letter was from a 35-year-old man who was reflecting on relationships that had taken place at middle school when he was 15 years old, sometime around 1905. He mentions that at this time "anal sex was emphasized among students in general"[5] and that older students might have two or three younger lovers, known as *chigo-san*, originally a term referring to the young pages who attended senior monks and samurai. *Chigo* had long been the object of romantic affection. Yet although such "beautiful boys" *(bishōnen)* were much prized, this term does not seem to have connoted effeminacy, since the author stresses that he was a keen sportsman—he mentions enjoying swimming, riding, racing and playing baseball.

During his first year of middle school, at age 15, he "was loved" *(aisare-*

mashita) by a senior classman from whom he "received baptism by sprinkling" *(senrei wo ukete)* twice a week.[6] Intriguingly, fidelity seems not to have been expected by either party; three other junior students were also regular receivers of the senior's sprinklings, although the writer believes himself to have been the most loved. The writer also mentions that he was simultaneously engaged in relations with three classmates from the same year with whom he practiced "mutual lewdness between the thighs," five upper-classmen in relation to whom he was loved "passively" and five lower-classmen "with whom I, of course, was active." These relationships seem to have been clearly age structured, with the "active" (that is, penetrative) partner being the older, the "passive" (or penetrated) partner the younger. In the case of same-age cohorts, anal sex was not practiced, the more "mutual" practice of interfemoral (between the thighs) sex being preferred. The reason the writer approached Kabiya for advice was not that he considered his student experiences, which he narrates in a matter-of-fact manner, problematic, but the fact that he had maintained a predilection for the passive role in anal sex well into adult life, a taste that was difficult to satisfy now that his previous partners were all married.

However, as Angles (2003) is careful to point out, this rigidly codified and age-graded pursuit of younger boys by older ones, despite widespread evidence for its occurrence, is not the only model through which same-sex love was expressed in boys' schools and colleges. He notes the emergence in the early Taisho period of a more egalitarian style of male love centering on appreciation of male beauty rather than sexual predation, as discussed in the literary work of Murayama Kaita, Edogawa Ranpo, Inagaki Taruho and Kawabata Yasunari, all of school age during the late Meiji. The emergence of such sentiments was part of the "revolution of emotion" *(kanjō kakumei)*, which saw writers expressing more personal and intimate feelings that were in stark contrast to the rigid, public, Confucian-inspired notions of duty and propriety underpinning official Meiji discourse. These authors, in focusing upon the lover's appreciation of the beloved's beauty and emphasizing the innocence of the latter, made a distinction between this kind of "spiritual" love and the more carnal interests expressed in school dormitories. This maneuver was not specific to the love of boys but, as Yokota-Murakami points out, was symptomatic of the diffusion of the concept of romantic love *(ren'ai)* in Japanese society more generally. Traditionally, love stories had not made sharp distinctions between emotional and physical attraction, but from the end of the Meiji period romantic love gradually came to be seen as spiritual in nature, a "moral achievement," incompatible with base, carnal instincts. Taisho thinkers argued that the biological instinct needed to be sublimated into the kind of love *(ren'ai)* "which foregrounds moral affections, sacrifice, and spiritual affection" (Yokota-Murakami 1998: 162). Stories featuring this kind of spiritual affinity were common in popular boys' magazines of the period such as *Nippon shōnen* (Japan's boys) and *Shōnen kurabu* (Boys' club), illustrated by Takabatake Kashō, an artist who specialized in depictions of beautiful boys (Bessatsu Taiyō 1995). Many of these stories featured an older boy who took a younger boy under his wing; samurai tales often featured scenes of boys fighting and dying together. Angles suggests that this widespread "appreciation of boyish beauty" was an important factor in literary discourse at the time and functioned as a counter discourse to the *hentai seiyoku* code, which, in emphasizing carnality, viewed male-male love as a perversion of desire (2003: 17–8). During the war years, romantic love, described as *sen'yū*, or love between comrades, was to emerge as an important narrative device for describing the affection that developed between veterans and young recruits in the homosocial environment of the battlefield.

The most widely read and influential sexological work of the Taisho period was *Hentai seiyokuron* (Theory of deviant sexual desire), first published in 1915 and constantly reprinted over the next decade. In these pages the military was identified as another institution particularly susceptible to the spread of homosexuality (Roden 1990: 45–6). During the Meiji period, the practice of *nanshoku* seems to have lived on especially among men from Satsuma, who were well represented among the military elite (Watanabe and Iwata 1989: 122). Mori Ōgai mentions the strong predilection toward boy love demonstrated by students from this area of Kyushu, referring to them as "hard-liners" *(kōha)* because of their antipathy toward the "softies" *(nanpa)* who preferred to play around with women (1971: 118–9). The tolerance of homosexual play among "campus roughnecks" on the understanding that "homosexuality arouses vigor" seems to have been a bone of contention among students whose inclinations were more toward women. One writer to a school magazine in 1902 complained that "a number of my fellow students have been punished for displaying an interest in women. But I have not heard of any punishment for those who engage in violent homosexual assaults" (cited in Roden 1980: 188). This student seems to have felt himself discriminated against on account of his heterosexual tastes. Indeed, newspaper reports at the turn of the century often expressed concern at the vogue for homosexual relationships among students in Tokyo, one writer suggesting that the danger of molestation was so great that "adolescent boys cannot go out at night" (cited in Watanabe and Iwata 1989: 122). Hyperbolic though this may seem, novelist Tanizaki Jun'ichirō, who was a young boy during this period, wrote in his memoirs about his fear of being abducted on his way home from the bathhouse by "young delinquents who liked to pursue still younger boys" (1988: 64).

Despite the facts that Tokyo University was the center of German influence in medicine and social and political theory and that students brought up in Tokyo were strongly influenced by these foreign ideas, students from Kyushu were still under the sway of the previous "hard-liner" *(kōha)* code, which cautioned against the potentially effeminizing consequences of sensual contact with women (Furukawa 1994: 101). In the Satsuma district, there had been a long tradition of adolescent males joining young men's groups, which took part in such tasks as community policing and defense. During this time, all contact with women was disparaged but affairs with *bishōnen,* or "beautiful boys," were common. The imperial navy, in particular, contained many men from the Satsuma area and was reputed to consider the beauty of potential recruits among other factors. Writing in 1912, essayist Ozaki Shirō mentions that "the Japanese navy does not employ those who are not good-looking. Those cadets who are employed are disciplined to be loyal and brave. And so I recommend the *bishōnen* of the navy as representative of Japan" (cited in Furukawa 1994: 103–4). Other commentators dealt with this observation less favorably, one journalist nicknaming the Japanese navy the "buggery fleet" on account of the recruitment policy of its Satsuma-born minister, who rewarded his *bishōnen* schoolmates with top posts (cited in Pflugfelder 1999: 211).

Tanizaki describes how as a nine-year-old he was once abducted by a drunken army officer who carried him about town. He managed to escape only when the officer, who had stopped by the roadside to urinate, was questioned by a policeman. He also mentions that "a pederastic taste for handsome little boys was on the increase in Tokyo toward the end of the century, perhaps due to the strong influence of Kyushu politicians from the southern Satsuma domains, a traditional hotbed of such practices" (1988: 44). The fact that many police officers were also from Satsuma meant that rowdiness occasioned by fights over the affections of boys tended to go unpunished.

Homoeroticism was particularly pronounced during the Russo-Japanese war of 1904–1905. In his memoirs, published in 1905, Basil Chamberlain remarks on the "frank and intimate" relationship between soldiers and officers, noting how newcomers to Japan were frequently bewildered by the sight of "two or three soldiers strolling along hand in hand, as if they were Dresden shepherdesses" (1905: 44). However, Watanabe argues that the end of the Russo-Japanese conflict in 1905 saw a sea change in attitudes toward homosexuality in the military (Watanabe and Iwata 1989: 124), as the traditional code associating male-male love with martial valor was overwritten by the notion of homosexual pathology and attitudes became increasingly intolerant. Public references to homosexual relations among the military became taboo, and newspapers quashed reports about love suicides among men in the armed forces for fear of drawing the ire of officials (Pflugfelder 1999: 328).

The association between homosexuality and military life was not, however, peculiar to Japan. In the first decades of the twentieth century, German society was also rocked by a series of scandals, particularly the Eulenburg affair of 1907; the investigation into the latter alleged that "champagne orgies" between officers and enlisted men were common (Spencer 1995: 314–5). The German army continued to be implicated in homosexual scandals until the rise of Hitler's National Socialist party in the early 1930s. Ernst Roehm, head of Hitler's paramilitary force known as the SA, or Brown Shirts, was widely known to be homosexual and carried on his affairs with impunity. However, in 1934, Roehm was murdered, along with 2,000 other Brown Shirts, during the infamous Night of the Long Knives. His demise ushered in an era of fierce Nazi persecution of sexual minorities, during which many individuals were interned in concentration camps from which they never emerged (Plant 1986). However, the long tradition validating homosexual love within the context of military life in Japan, and the fact that unlike in Germany (and most of the rest of Europe) homosexual acts between men were not illegal at this time, meant that the Japanese armed forces never moved to excise homosexuality from the ranks, preferring instead to tolerate it behind a wall of silence.[7]

While the intergenerational pattern of homosexual behavior characteristic of *shudō*, or the way of boys, carried on well into the Meiji period in the homosocial environments of schools, colleges and military academies, the transgender paradigm of male prostitution seems also to have survived, albeit underground. As mentioned, male prostitution had taken place in brothels located in specific areas of Japan's major cities from the middle years of the Edo period. The Tempō Reforms (1841–1843) had, however, targeted male prostitution in particular; by the beginning of the Meiji period, recognizable male brothels that plied their trade openly had already disappeared (Furukawa 1994: 105), and *kagema* were seen as relics of the Edo period. However, Furukawa notes that in the gender-bending environment of the Taisho period there was increasing media discussion of the "new *kagema*," cross-dressing male prostitutes who sought customers in central Tokyo's Hibiya Park, behind the Kannon Temple in Asakusa and around the new kabuki theater in the Ginza. There existed also several large-scale prostitution organizations based in Asakusa. Furukawa mentions 30 main and ten smaller inns that employed more than 50 *kagema* between them (1994: 107). Newspaper reports also mention a large ring of over 300 *kagema* working in Fukuoka in Kyushu.

Although the continuation of homosexual interaction organized around age and gender difference is conspicuous in the early modern period in Japan, it would be mistaken to think that this situation was unique. At the same time in Europe and America, too, homosexual interactions took place in terms of gender and age-related systems. For instance, the intergenerational model of homosexual interaction was that of an elite or at least middle-class practice looking back to ancient Greece for validation of relationships between adult males and younger men (Dowling 1994). Within this system, the youth and beauty of the "passive" partner (the beloved) and the ability of the older, more educated partner to act as a mentor were important aspects of the attraction. Such a relationship developed between Japanese poet (and later professor of English at Keio University) Noguchi Yonejirō[8] and the American writer Charles Stoddard, whose friend and lover Noguchi became while studying in the United States at the close of the nineteenth century (Sueyoshi 2002). Their relationship, which Noguchi discussed freely in both his letters and diaries of the period, evinces the blending of the elite Euro-American tradition of romantic friendship, fin-de-siècle Bohemian culture, Greek-inspired ideals of mentorship and Japanese paradigms of intergenerational sex.

Within working-class culture in both Europe and the United States, masculine-identified adult males were free to engage in sexual liaisons with effeminate homosexual men, known as "faeries," without their own masculine gender role being brought into question. Known as "trade," masculine men could act as the "inserters" in relationships with effeminate men without any compromise of their masculine status (Chauncey 1994: 258). In the west, however, these earlier paradigms were giving way to a more egalitarian understanding of homosexuality in which both partners were equally adult and equally masculine—a process that was not to take place in Japan to the same extent until well after the war.

In response to the relatively open discussion of sexual matters and widespread, if covert, homosexual behavior, Japan's descent into militarism in the early 1930s saw the government tighten its hold on sexual discourse and practice. Japan's escalating conflict with China beginning in 1931 and its withdrawal from the League of Nations in 1933 ushered in a period of government repression that sought to mobilize the nation as a whole for the war effort. One result was an increasing didacticism on the part of the nation's leaders and further attempts to bring the media under direct state control. As Dore points out, "Not even Victorian England produced such large numbers of moralizers, or gave them such complete control of the police forces, the means of education, and the organs of public opinion" (1999: 162). Consequently, just as the press had been placed under state supervision, by the late 1930s film too was being purged of "frivolous activities" and deployed as a means for the promulgation of official ideology regarding sex and gender (Standish 2000: 34).

Although public interest in perverse sexuality probably did not diminish, it became more difficult for writers to justify their interest in this topic during wartime, and those considered to have transgressed public morals *(fūzoku)* could find themselves in trouble with the police. As the government introduced increasingly severe austerity measures and the price of paper soared, writers whose work was not directly supportive of the war effort ran the risk of seeming unpatriotic. Finally, the outbreak of general war with China in 1937 saw the suspension of publications of a sexual and frivolous nature altogether. From this point on the government controlled the paper supply, allocating stocks on the basis of a publication's "quality"—that is, the extent to which it endorsed official ideologies. A 1940 cabinet report stated that "the best policy is to abolish harmful and useless newspapers and magazines and to support the development of healthy newspapers and magazines which are equipped to aid the government as it moves toward its national destiny" (cited in Mitchell 1983: 311), a policy easily achieved, given the government's control of paper supplies. Having silenced the sexology press, the government instructed agencies such as the Special Higher Police (Tokubetsu kōtō keisatsu) to restrict also the dissemination of birth-control information and to disrupt the meetings of sexologists who offered advice on birth control or suggested that such nonreproductive practices as masturbation might be harmless (Fruhstuck 2000). Open discussion of sexuality thus largely ceased during the war years.

HETERONORMATIVITY ON THE ROAD TO WAR

Japan's 15-year war, as it is sometimes referred to by historians, was characterized by increasing state surveillance of and interference in the personal lives of the Japanese population. Igarashi points out how the wartime regime attempted to create obedient and patriotic bodies by forging ties between nationalist ideology and bodily functions, asserting that Japanese bodies were "at the heart of nationalist discourse" (2000: 51). At this time, Japan shared with European nations, particularly Nazi Germany, an interest in "race improvement"; both the state and the media were proactively engaged in promulgating eugenicist policies (Fruhstuck 2003). Robertson notes how even ordinary Japanese were subjected to a regime of "spiritual hygiene and thought control," for, like Japan's colonial subjects, "Japanese too had to be physically and mentally colonized and assimilated into the cultural machinery of New Japan" (2001: 26).

One result of this discourse was an increased polarity in gender roles, resulting in women being cast solely as mothers, whose purpose was to breed sons for the empire, and men being regarded as fighting machines, part of the national body (Low 2003). Women, who had no political agency, were particularly constrained by this ideology. The most important role for women—that of "good wife, wise mother" *(ryōsai kenbo)*—was actively promoted by government policies, media reports and social pressure. Indeed, the government went so far as to introduce eugenic policies to ensure maximum reproduction, encouraging women to "*umeyo fuyaseyo*" (bear children and multiply). Healthy-baby contests were held across Japan, and awards were made to families with more than ten children (Fruhstuck 2003: 167; Robertson 2002: 199). Given that reports on family planning and the sale of contraceptives were illegal, sexual activity, for bourgeois women at least, was organized entirely around reproduction.

However, not all women's bodies were deemed suitable vessels for reproduction (Igarashi 2000: 49). Popular media throughout the 1930s exalted marriage and fecundity only for "superior persons," calling for "the segregation and sterilization of so-called abnormal persons, namely the mentally infirm, physically handicapped and sexually alternative" (Robertson 2001: 24). Indeed, legislation like the 1940 National Eugenics Law *(Kokumin Yūsei Hō)* was introduced allowing the government to sterilize certain types of undesirable bodies, such as those suffering from hereditary diseases (Fruhstuck 2003: 166–7; Mackie 2003: 112). The law also forbade medical procedures that would result in the sterilization of otherwise healthy persons—a regulation that was to have unforeseen implications for Japanese transsexuals in the postwar period (McLelland 2004).[9]

State surveillance of individual bodies was achieved through neighborhood and village associations, membership in which was necessary in order to receive rations of food and clothing. Also, as the war progressed and an increasing number of adult men were drafted and sent overseas, teenage children, particularly boys, were recruited to work in the factories, where they were subject to a "protective guidance network" of men and older boys who drilled them in both physical and mental hygiene. The boys lived communally in dormitories, where they were constantly subjected to "surveillance, military drill, and spiritual indoctrination"; "hard core" *(kōha)* groups of youths would patrol entertainment areas "beating students who appeared to be shirking their duties" (Ambaras 2004: 41).

During the war years, many women and women's organizations too were co-opted by the state to police the behavior of other women, children and elderly men who remained at home. Rather than resisting this appropriation, many women, having previously been denied any political agency, actively embraced the opportunity to command a greater role in the public sphere and eagerly campaigned against such anti-patriotic behavior as smoking, drinking, attending dance halls, perming the hair or wearing "gaudy clothes" (Garon 1997: 144). Dour matrons could be found standing outside railway stations berating women they considered overdressed and insisting that they adopt a more sober appearance in support of the war effort. In an attempt to enforce more thrifty attitudes, "embarrassing photographs of conspicuous consumers on shopping sprees were published in the newspapers" (Robertson 2001: 26). Such surveillance made it essential to maintain proper personal decorum. The maintenance of personal hygiene, bodily health and proper deportment became state requirements, since any individual who succumbed to either mental or physical disability risked being segregated in institutions where, toward the end of the war when food supplies were scarce, starvation often occurred. As Igarashi notes, "members of Japanese society were ordered to adjust their bodies and thought to accord with state requirements. When this was not possible, their bodies were mercilessly discarded" (2000: 51).

Despite intensive state interest in the sexual life of the populace, little attempt was made to confine men's sexual expression to monogamous marriage. A number of state-led interventions acknowledged that men's sexuality needed a variety of outlets and that chastity before marriage and continence within it were unachievable goals for most men. Despite the fact that the revised Civil Code of 1898 had overturned the rights of concubines and instituted monogamy (Dore 1999: 160), there was a significant imbalance in the response to sexual infidelities by husbands and wives, respectively. Adultery by husbands was not considered grounds for divorce; there were no legal issues at stake unless the husband's infidelities were with another married woman. Wives, however, could be divorced for adultery and even face prison sentences for infidelity (Garon 1997: 99). That the practice of punishing only wives involved in adulterous affairs was underpinned by government policy is clear from the forced resignation of Takikawa Yukitori, a law professor at Kyoto Imperial University, whose 1932 book *Keihō tokuhon* (Criminal law handbook) had criticized the manner in which wives were singled out for punishment in adulterous affairs, arguing that neither partner should face legal proceedings (Mitchell 1983: 273).

As Dore points out, there was a "tacit approval of male sexual freedom, but a strict localization of the opportunities for sexual stimulation and enjoyment to brothel or semi-brothel districts whose existence was justified as an essential means of preserving the purity of the home" (1999: 159). The most important concession to men's perceived sexual needs was therefore the fact that prostitution was a legal trade recognized and regulated by the government, which required both brothel owners and prostitutes to register and apply for a license to practice. Licensed prostitution had been a prominent aspect of the entertainment industry in Japan and an important money earner for poor families since the early years of the Tokugawa period. During this time, it was often the fate of young girls from poor rural families to be sold for an up-front fee to procurers or directly to brothels. As in Europe at this time, the political and economic elite "assumed that their social inferiors were inclined towards wantonness, and that peasant women's virtue was for sale" (Leupp 2003: 48). Indeed, the lower classes in Japan, who represented the large majority of the population, were much less concerned than the ruling classes with controlling sexual behavior, and among them "no special value seems to have attached to virginity, and there was no specific concept of, or opprobrium attached to, bastardy" (Leupp 2003: 48). While the chastity of daughters of the samurai and rich merchants represented substantial cultural capital, since these daughters were important items of exchange between families who controlled political and economic resources, elite and peasant alike "seem to have taken the prostitution of humble women and girls for granted" (Leupp 2003: 48). Not much changed with Japan's opening to the west. At the beginning of the Meiji era, prostitution was not one of the "feudal practices" from which the new state saw fit to distance itself, although indenture contracts were banned in 1872 and in 1900 the prostitution of girls under the age of 18 was made illegal (Leupp 2003: 190). Licensed prostitution remained an important part of the economy of the major cities, and individual prostitutes, who were often sent to work in brothels abroad, "played an important role in the maintenance, survival and material development of the local communities they left behind" (Mihalopoulos 1993: 42).

The number of licensed prostitutes in prewar Japan peaked in 1916 and remained at a level of about 50,000 throughout the 1920s and early 1930s. Prostitutes worked in a total of 550 licensed areas spread throughout Japan but mostly in port cities and big towns and near military garrisons (Garon 1997: 94). Prime reasons for the official endorsement of prostitution were the prevention of venereal disease, since the health of licensed prostitutes was more easily monitored, and the protection of "daughters of good families" by ensuring that men's natural sexual needs were satisfied by women from the lower orders. Changes in social demographics also convinced government officials of the necessity for organized prostitution. Widespread migration from the countryside by men in search of work saw the male population of the cities grow, while the conscription of men into the armed forces delayed the average marriage age and separated husbands from their wives.

Certainly, the brothels were well attended, approximately 30 million customers visiting them in 1937, an enormous figure given that the male population aged 16 and over was only 21 million in 1935 (Garon 1999:

104). Although small but influential lobby groups, mainly drawing support from Christian and women's organizations, continued to pressure the government to abolish prostitution, it was never in the interest of the state to restrict men's access to prostitutes. When a bill aimed at prohibiting licensed prostitution was introduced to the Lower House in 1931, Diet member Yamazaki Dennosuke

> responded with a speech laced with obscenities and graphic language. Since lust was absolute, he argued, to try to repress it would only bring on masturbation, the chief cause of respiratory problems. Besides, he continued, was it not true that some of the "gentlemen" in the Lower House kept concubines? Would this practice, too, be abolished? he asked mockingly. (Garon 1997: 105–6)

The ideology underlying state-sponsored prostitution drew upon a hydraulic model of male sexuality that saw the male body as a machine driven by physical forces that needed proper management so as to maintain proper functioning. A Bureau of Hygiene official commented in 1900 that "the male body needed to satisfy sexual lust to maintain itself, just as a train would come to a halt if it did not burn coal" (Garon 1999: 101). While the male body was seen as a steam train, other metaphors posited brothels themselves as "breakwaters" or "public latrines" (Garon 1999: 100) preventing male sexuality from bursting out in inappropriate ways or being directed toward the wrong kind of person, particularly "daughters of good families."

Lower-class women were considered morally and intellectually inferior by the ruling classes, and increasingly they came to be seen as the bearers of suspect genes. However, their sexual labor was willingly exploited, since it served to drain off men's excess sexual energies while also providing much-needed income for their poor rural families. Women from more privileged backgrounds, on the other hand, were idealized as good wives and wise mothers whose war effort was increasingly identified with the conception, birth and rearing of children. Indeed, propaganda literature referred to particularly fecund women as constituting a "fertile womb battalion" (Robertson 2002: 199). As in Europe, this focus on the reproductive capacity of middle-class women's bodies was closely "linked to the process of growth and establishment of bourgeois hegemony" (Foucault 1990: 125), in which "a preoccupation with heredity" (Foucault 1990: 124) emerged as a central concern. The result was a system in which the bourgeois female body was "required to assume maternity as the essence of itself and the law of its desire" (Butler 1990: 92). Elite and middle-class women came to be seen as the managers of "human resources" in a very literal sense. Yet rather than resisting this discourse that reduced them to the status of reproductive machinery, many women's leaders supported the notion that children were "public goods" whose management was women's responsibility (Ueno 1996). Women's activists such as Hiratsuka Raichō themselves deployed the argument that the purpose of sexuality was to bear children and that the sexual activities of the population should be correctly managed since eugenics raised the "public value" of reproduction (Fruhstuck 2003: 125).

Under pre-Meiji Confucian ideology, women had been conceived of as "borrowed wombs" whose purpose was to incubate the life-giving seed provided by the male and thus bear new male heirs who would ensure the continuation of the patrilineal line. In imperial Japan, however, women's active agency in reproduction was acknowledged alongside that of men, and women found that their role as the bearers of future imperial citizens gave them greater "cultural capital" (Fruhstuck 2003: 119) at a time when the government was taking an unprecedented interest in the reproductive capacities of the population. Through bearing more children, women were able to "improve their status as imperial subjects and by the same token further the expansion of the empire" (Fruhstuck 2003: 119). Hence, some campaigners for women's suffrage hoped that their eager and active support of the war effort would result in a greater public role for women in Japanese society. Indeed, as Maeda (1999) points out, the acknowledgment of women's importance as defenders of the "home front" did result in increased power and autonomy for some women, who "found joy and excitement in their activities in support of the war."[10]

Throughout the 1930s and early 1940s, the government's pronatalist policies and its support for registered prostitution resulted in sexuality becoming increasingly heteronormative for both men and women. Lower-class women were recruited to staff Japan's many brothels, while women from "good families" were allowed no sexual activity outside of marriage. Men too were caught up in debates about the proper deployment of sexuality. Family planning and advertisements for contraceptive devices were banned, but the authorities tolerated advertisements for medicines purporting to increase male potency or cure such common ailments as nocturnal emissions and premature ejaculation. These advertisements often featured female faces or other body parts, reinforcing the assumption that "men's sexual desire was to be shared with women" (Fruhstuck 2003: 172), particularly wives, whom husbands were encouraged to dutifully impregnate. Condom advertisements were also permitted, although it was their "hygienic" potential that was stressed, not their contraceptive function (Fruhstuck 2003: 146), suggesting that they were intended for extramarital activities.

In the homosocial environment of the armed forces especially, Japanese men were encouraged to express themselves heterosexually through government-sponsored military brothels, euphemistically known as "comfort stations" *(ianjo),* in which women from Japan's colonies were forced to serve as prostitutes. Back home, prostitution had been seen as the unfortunate fate of women from poor backgrounds obliged to provide sexual labor to support their families. By draining off men's excessive lust, as we have seen, these poor women were expected to protect the daughters of the middle and upper classes, whose destiny was to become future wives and mothers. However, if bourgeois Japanese women were idealized, the bodies of women from Japan's colonies were mercilessly exploited in what Shibata (1999) argues were "mass rape camps." Although the existence of the comfort system was not widely known by civilians in Japan, the general inequitableness in the treatment of Japanese and non-Japanese women went largely unquestioned by Japanese women themselves, among whom there was a "ready acceptance" of nationalist sentiments that relegated non-Japanese women within the empire to a subordinate status (Maeda 1999). Japanese women of the middle and ruling classes tended not to identify with other women across class or race lines, since, as Foucault has pointed out, implicit in the bourgeois construction of sexuality was "a dynamic racism, a racism of expansion" (1990: 125) obsessed with the notion of "blood." This resulted in what Foucault terms "a 'class' body" organized around concern with its own "health, hygiene, descent and race" (1990: 124). Although poor and foreign women had a role to play in the state management of male sexuality, their suspect blood needed to be kept from polluting that of the ruling classes. Abortion and contraception were anathema within the context of the bourgeois family, but in the comfort stations and brothels dire methods were employed to prevent the conception or birth of children.

The hydraulic model of male sexuality described the sex act in purely physiological terms and assumed that any blockage in the natural flow of men's sexual energies would cause physical and mental debility (Suzuki 2001: 99–103). Accordingly, regular sex was necessary in order to properly regulate male desire, and Japanese soldiers "were socialised into a particularly aggressive form of masculine sexuality" (Mackie 2003: 110) that took a functional view of the female body. There was no notion that women might have autonomous sexual feelings or desires; women's bodies were objects to be used by men. Elite women existed to bear new citizens for the empire, whereas Japanese women from poor backgrounds and women from the colonies were for draining off the excess and potentially destabilizing sexual energies of Japanese men.

The fact that one brand of condom handed out to the soldiers was named "attack number one" *(totsugeki ichiban)* is indicative of the extent to which the military model of male sexuality was imbued with violence (Fruhstuck 2003; 41; Kanō 1993: 42). Widespread distribution of condoms to Japanese soldiers began in 1931, at the beginning of Japan's campaign in China. Soldiers were issued "hygiene matchboxes" containing two condoms whenever they left their base, and from this point on condoms were classified as "munitions of war." In 1942 as many as 32 million condoms were distributed to the Japanese forces, a ration of 20 per man (Fruhstuck 2003: 40). The military's widespread encouragement of condom use was not a matter of consideration for the women abused by the soldiers but solely of limiting the spread of venereal diseases among the ranks.

Hence, as Fruhstuck points out, "prostitution within and outside of the military was geared toward the functionality of male sexuality through the use of female bodies in order to secure the power system within the military and over the empire" (2003: 37). The Japanese imperial army's invasion, subjugation and exploitation of foreign territories could be comprehended metonymically through the exploitation of the women of these defeated nations, women whose bodies were yet another resource to be used in the interests of Japanese expansionism. This official ideology endorsing men's "natural desires" and sustaining their control over and use of (non-Japanese) women's bodies seems to have been accepted by many of the soldiers themselves; one ex-soldier reflected in his memoirs that

> on a battlefield, in order for a man to be "useful," it is necessary to maintain a healthy body and an aggressive mind. Managing sexual desire harmonizes body and mind, and lubricates war operation. It is natural and necessary for military leaders to establish comfort stations. (cited in Shibata 1999: 62)

The idea that male desire, unless carefully managed, would burst out in violent and unpredictable ways was deeply ingrained. In Kobayashi Masaki's 1959–1961 trilogy of antiwar films *Ningen no jōken* (The human condition), the ultimate humiliation faced by the hero, Kaji, and his small band of surviving soldiers retreating across Manchuria is to look on impotently as Japanese women are abducted and raped by the invading Soviet army. Indeed, in preparation for the imminent arrival of U.S. forces in Japan, the Japanese government, assuming that the Americans would use Japanese women in much the same way that Japanese soldiers had used the women of the colonies, organized the Recreation and Amusement Association—yet another euphemism for state-sponsored prostitution—in the hope that the foreign invaders' sexual predations could be contained. This time poor and destitute Japanese women were recruited to act as a "female floodwall" *(onna no bōhatei)*, which, it was hoped, would prevent the corruption of more respectable women (Molasky 2001: 105).

Despite the active role the Japanese military took in facilitating soldiers' access to women, there were scant references to the sexuality of Japanese soldiers published during the war years. Any mention of "soldiers' sexuality and its distortion, deflection, and sublimation on the battlefield" (Rosenfeld 2002: 92) was suppressed either by military censors or through self-censorship on the part of writers. The existence of comfort stations and the widespread abuse of non-Japanese women throughout the colonies hardly supported the official rationale behind Japan's colonial endeavor—the ridding of the region of western influence and the creation of a Greater East Asia Co-Prosperity Sphere, and it is not surprising that the comfort system was barely mentioned in press releases, government reports, or literary accounts of battlefield life. Although the exploitation of native women, if more widely known, would have undermined Japan's rhetoric of Asian liberation, other, more equitable, relationships between Japanese men and women of the colonies that could have been exploited as propaganda were also censored. Popular wartime novelist Hino Ashihei remembers that the military refused to allow him to comment on soldiers' sexual lives. When he introduced a love story between a Japanese soldier and a Chinese girl in his novel *Hana to heitai* (Flowers and soldiers), which was being serialized in the *Asahi* newspaper, he received a telegram from the general headquarters demanding to know how he intended to develop the story. He took the hint and curtailed the development of this subplot in later installments (Rosenfeld 2002: 96). Japanese women too were deterred from marrying men from the colonies, including Korean nationals who had been brought to Japan as laborers following Japan's annexation of the peninsula in 1910. Such interracial relationships threatened the imagined hierarchy that positioned the Japanese as the leaders of Asia and fueled anxieties about "the dilution and vitiation of the Japanese race" (Robertson 2001: 5; 2002: 205).

However, after the war many men who had served in the military wrote accounts of their wartime experiences, including their sexual aspects. In discussing this literature, Kanō suggests that most authors shirked any individual responsibility for wartime rape or the use of "comfort" facilities into which women had been forcibly recruited, pointing out that "the only evils in this way of thinking become 'war' and 'the military'" (1993: 41). To this extent, these narratives have much in common with official accounts of the war, which are characterized by a "victim consciousness" positing Japanese people themselves as victims (of a global economic conspiracy, of ultranationalist militarists or of atomic bombing) and failing to consider the immense hardships visited upon Japan's colonial subjects (Figal 1996; Gluck 1993). Even personal war narratives tend to follow this trend; Figal points to stories of the *jibunshi*, or "self-history," genre, "where undeniable wartime privation and a sense of helplessness prevail over adequate exposition of active war support'' (1996: 919). This mentality helps explain the surprisingly nonchalant manner in which wartime sexual atrocities could be narrated and, importantly, received by the reading public, which regarded such actions as regrettable but unavoidable during wartime. For instance, Kanō cites a passage in which a Japanese army surgeon relates a visit to a comfort station:

> Each corps was assigned a day to visit [the comfort station]. When the day for our surgical corps came, 35 applicant soldiers and I packed two lunches each and departed. . . . There were seven huts with straw mats instead of doors. We ate lunch, and then the soldiers lined up by platoon in front of the drapes. It took an average of five minutes per soldier. It looked as if we were waiting in line for a public toilet, but all the soldiers were satisfied when they returned to base. (cited in Kanō 1993: 42)

The reference to the public toilet is significant, it being a common metaphor for brothels, which were understood as places where men could evacuate their excess desire. Indeed, the term ''hygienic public bathroom'' was a euphemism sometimes used to describe comfort women by Japanese soldiers (Shin and Cho 1996: 53)—''hygienic'' because, unlike unsupervised prostitutes, the military enforced a strict health code on brothel workers so as to prevent the spread of venereal disease. Soldiers were thus encouraged to think of the bodies of prostitutes as little more than ''semen toilets'' (Suzuki 2001: 103). Wartime author Tamura Tajirō employed a related if more decorous metaphor when he referred to comfort stations as ''laundry rooms'' staffed by ''laundry women'' whose purpose was to cleanse men of their pent-up desires. He writes, ''Just as one washes a pile of dirty clothes at the cleaners, so the soldiers came here to launder their flesh, to launder their souls'' (cited in Kerkham 2001: 316). Curiously absent in these accounts is any discussion of pleasure—presumably because of the dangerous individualism inherent in pleasuring the body. Women's bodies were viewed as mere instruments men used in order to rid themselves of unruly desires, desires that were themselves seen as solipsistic, something in need of periodic evacuation so that soldiers could focus their attention on the war effort, without distraction. Little room was left for romance, or indeed for human feelings of any kind.

While the disciplinary regime controlling the bodies of civilians, particularly those of subject peoples, was harsh, the military was marked by severe repression of its own soldiers. As well as being subject to a fierce physical training regimen, soldiers were indoctrinated through frequent recitations of the ''Imperial Precepts to Soldiers,'' the purpose of which was to ''instill virtues of loyalty to the emperor and love of the country''

(Fruhstuck 2003: 33). Brutal and hierarchical, the military was an environment where an order from one's superior officer was treated as an order direct from the emperor himself. The bodies and minds of soldiers who failed to make the grade were subject to harsh and violent humiliation. Igarashi cites the memoirs of photographer Fukushima Kikujirō, whose patriotism was destroyed upon his induction into the army, where he witnessed soldiers who could not properly recite the Imperial Precepts beaten to a bloody pulp and the dead bodies of deserters kicked "until the bellies were ruptured and the internal organs burst out" (2000: 51).

LOVERS IN ARMS

The above account has stressed how both male and female sexuality became increasingly heteronormative during the period leading to the outbreak of war. Yet this process resulted in demographic changes that were actually counterproductive in terms of the policies meant to normalize and contain sexuality. Although the ideology of the period was relentlessly heterosexual and pronatal, actual social organization became increasingly homosocial. As the 1930s progressed, greater numbers of men were drafted into the military, delaying the marriage of bachelors and separating married men from their wives, thereby encouraging the development of greater intimacy between men. At the same time, unmarried women moved to take the place of these men in the factories and other industries. One of the results of this separation between the sexes was what Standish has, in relation to films of the period, referred to as "the death of romance" (2000: 51)—since romantic love between a man and a woman was seen as incompatible with the "heroic masculinity" demanded by the war effort. Standish points out how in Japanese films of the early 1940s "women were marginalized if not deleted from the narrative completely" (2000: 53). The result was that "the underlying text inherent in the images of masculinity dominating Japanese films of the late 1930s and early 1940s was a discourse of sexual repression" (2000: 51) in which men's romantic love for women was displaced by a "homosocial brotherhood." Film heroines, when they appeared at all, were depicted as sublimating their romantic feelings for men into a "love of country" (2000: 63).

Given Japan's long association of militarism with male-male desire (Ujiie 1995), it might be supposed that the Japanese military would have been a site for homosexual activity, just as it had been during the Russo-Japanese War some 30 years previously. Some accounts published after the war indeed suggest that the homosocial environment of the military led to unexpected relationships, especially between senior and junior soldiers and between Japanese soldiers and men of the colonies.

Sexual violence by the Japanese armed forces against women of the colonies has been well documented, and we know also of a few incidents in which homosexual rape was perpetrated by Japanese soldiers. An example was that described by Philippine "comfort gay" Walter Dempster, whose life was featured in a recent documentary film.[11] According to postwar accounts, homosexual rape also occurred between soldiers, especially as ever younger men were drafted into the armed forces as the war progressed. As outlined below, there are various accounts of army officers taking a special interest in the handsome young recruits who served them as orderlies. This interest was not always welcomed by the younger men.

Isolde Standish discusses a series of films made during wartime in which military institutions were represented as "offer[ing] a sense of masculine fellowship and community symbolized in spectacular shots of massed gym exercises and marching formations" (2000: 66). In these productions *sen'yūai* (comradely love) was emphasized to an extent not paralleled in similar propaganda films created by the Allies. Kobayashi Masaki's postwar film trilogy *Ningen no jōken* (The human condition), however, offers quite a different take on life in such institutions, particularly for those who failed to adequately embody military masculinity. A scene from part 2 of the trilogy, *The Road to Eternity,* suggests the atmosphere of sexual violence that could arise in the rigidly hierarchical, homosocial environment of the barracks. Kobayashi depicts how Obara, a weak and listless new recruit who has failed a training exercise, is forced by more senior members of the squadron to mimic the seductive antics of a prostitute soliciting customers. Later that night the recruit commits suicide. Although the scene shies away from a climax of homosexual rape, the atmosphere of sexual violence is palpable; the film depicts how powerless junior men were to resist the demands of their seniors. Some media accounts (see Ashidate 1960) also point to how other powerless figures, in this case prisoners suspected of collaborating with the enemy, were subject to sexual torture and even anal rape. Such incidents raise the question of how male homosocial desire was experienced, mediated and expressed during wartime.

As mentioned earlier, the military authorities were "quite aware of the explosive danger of pent-up sexual energies and employed or allowed various strategies to respond to the soldiers' desires" (Rosenfeld 2002: 98), the most prominent of these strategies being ensuring soldiers' access to female prostitutes. The following account of a visit to a comfort station by a company of soldiers suggests how men's homosocial desire might have been contained by the sexual use of women:

> Right after the long battle, we rushed to the women while holding our crotches. When we arrived at their place, we waited very anxiously in line, waiting to be relieved from the extreme tension from the war by unbuttoning our pants and dangling our loincloths in front of each other. (cited in Shibata 1999: 54)

However, various postwar accounts, with varying degrees of explicitness, suggest that male homosocial desire may have been within a military context as unruly a force as was heterosexual desire. Rosenfeld draws attention to an incident described in a postwar story published by popular war novelist Hino Ashihei, whose wartime writings had been extremely reticent about sexual matters. In *Seishun to deinei* (Youth and mud), serialized from 1948, Hino describes the retreat of a squadron of Japanese soldiers through the jungle of Burma, where, on account of the humid conditions and their lack of salt supplies, the men become debilitated. In order not to lose all the salt from their bodies, the men are instructed to lick the sweat from their skin after exercising. One soldier, witnessing the glistening body of his comrade, cannot restrain his passion and leaps on him. The story continues:

> Tamaru pressed his face against his comrade's back. His tongue ran over the rough undulation of ribs. Then he felt some new salty substance on his lips pressed against Komiyama's back. It was his own tears, but he did not realize it, and thought confusedly that he had sucked too hard, and this new bitter liquid had come from inside his comrade's body. In ecstasy, he sipped the bitter liquid, wailing and collapsed on top of his friend. (cited in Rosenfeld 2002: 98)

Since this homoerotic passage is, apparently, unique in Hino's work, Rosenfeld prefers to read it as "a reversal or distortion of the presentation of *heitai* [soldier] relationships as noble and admirable" (2002: 98) rather than as a description of an actual homoerotic incident between men at war (although he does not disavow that possibility). However, multiple examples of homoerotic incidents and situations described in postwar writings about the war articulate homosexual desire in less ambiguous ways.

War is a time of considerable tension between official attempts at creating social cohesion through ideology and propaganda and the unavoidable social violence, displacements and upheavals that affect much of the population. Studies by Berube (1990), Jivani (1997: 55–86), Wotherspoon (1986: 36–7, 47–9) and others have shown how the war years provided increased opportunity for homosexual networking and contact in the United States, the UK and Australia. The mass mobilization and sexual segregation of men and women in the armed forces in particular provided same-sex-desiring men and women with opportunities to make contact and develop relationships. Furthermore, many individuals who otherwise would not have engaged in same-sex sexual activity found it convenient to take part in "situational" homosexual acts in these homosocial environments. Invoking the hydraulic model of male sexuality discussed earlier, postwar reports in Japan refer to such homosexual activity as *seiyoku no hakeguchi*—that is, outlets or release valves for sexual desire.

In the U.S. forces official policies forbade the induction of self-confessed homosexuals and mandated the removal of men and women found to have engaged in homosexual acts, but these policies had the actual effect of heightening and strengthening homosexual identity and community (Berube 1990). Furthermore, attitudes varied widely, with many men whose daily survival seemed insecure adopting a live-and-let-live attitude toward the homosexual relationships that were known to be taking place around them. Unfortunately, attitudes toward homosexuality adopted by the imperial armed forces during Japan's 15-year period of conflict have not been researched. There are, however, many avenues of investigation that could be productively pursued. For instance, the numerous accounts of wartime experience written by Japanese ex-soldiers in the postwar period could reveal incidents that would throw light on attitudes toward same-sex sexual interaction in the military. Also, despite the highly heteronormative and pronatal stance adopted by the government during the war years, some intriguing accounts of homosexual feelings and experience on the battlefront are documented in Japan's postwar press. (See figure 1.2.)

As described in detail in the next chapter, very soon after the war, particularly during the period between the immediate end of the war and 1955, the Japanese press saw a boom in erotic publications. Numerous magazines, featuring a wide range of articles, turned their attention to human sexual customs, and, as might be expected given the intense and often traumatic nature of wartime experience, many stories and letters recount in a confessional tone incidents from readers' own lives during the war. Letters columns in particular long continued to print confessions from men whose sex lives had been indelibly marked by incidents they had experienced during the war. Given the highly hierarchical nature of prewar Japanese society, many of these stories explore the psychology of sadomasochism (see for example Ashidate 1960; Akasaka 1952) or present wartime sexuality in terms of pathology (Ashio 1953). However, there also exist other stories, particularly those detailing homosexual love affairs, written from the perspective of both junior (Ryūta 1954) and senior (Morii 1952) partners, that are tinged with regret and nostalgia.

Take for example this short piece entitled "Homosexuality on the

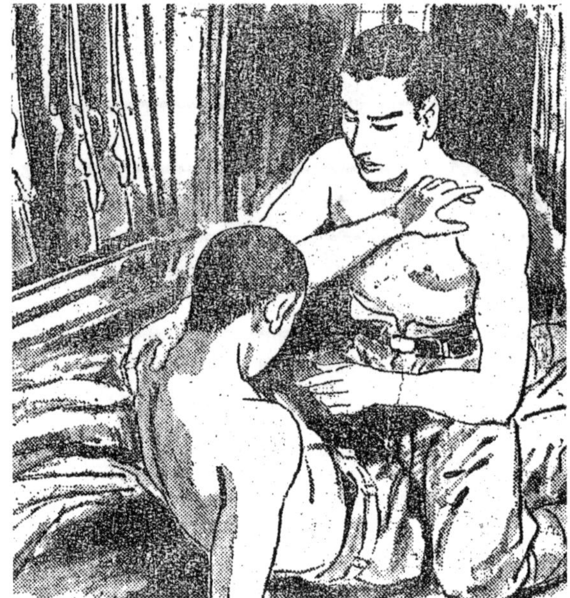

Figure 1.2 "*Danshō* in military uniform." ***Shinsō jitsuwa*** **(True tales), May 1947**

battlefront," which appeared in the sex-customs magazine *Kitan kurabu* in 1952.

> Homosexuality *(dōseiai)* on the battlefield, deriving from the love between comrades *(sen'yūai)*, becomes the foundation of a strong esprit de corps; in a life played out against a bleak backdrop, it frequently has a revitalizing effect. The special effects of this pure, platonic homosexual love between comrades are a demonstration of self-sacrifice and also a spirit of resolute, reckless bravery; this disposition among soldiers can be said to be great.
>
> Apart from this pure, spiritual union there is homosexuality as a substitute for women, an outlet for sexual desire *(seiyoku no hakeguchi)*, and it is also the case that homosexuality can be triggered by the presence of perfectly feminine youths. . . . Relationships between officers and privates, older and younger soldiers, these kinds of human relationships opposite to nature (*han shizenna*) are exposed against the backdrop of war and are unavoidable.
>
> As far as possible, veteran officers choose for their orderlies soldiers who are beautiful youths *(bishōnen)* and soldiers standing on sentry duty want to choose intimate friends from among themselves. In the midst of a male only group, how is it that feminised young men *(joseika shita danshi)* come to be so esteemed? This is a secret known to all who have experienced military life even once. (Asakura 1952: 6)

This passage rehearses ideas of the self-sacrificing nature of male love, a conspicuous narrative of the earlier *bushidō* code (Ujiie 1995; Watanabe and Iwata 1989: 122; Mishima 1977), alongside the more contemporary understanding of homosexual relations as "opposite to nature." The writer's conclusions that in the extreme environment of the battlefront these feelings are "unavoidable" and indeed may actually prove useful to the war effort were echoed by other commentators reflecting on homosexuality and war. Ōgiya (1953: 158), for instance, draws a parallel between the need for comfort women and the inevitable and unavoidable attraction felt by older soldiers toward "beautiful male youths" in the ranks, mentioning that older and younger soldiers in relationships were referred to as brothers-in-law *(giri ani-otōto)*. Such comments suggest that official narratives that were strictly heteronormative in tone do not accurately reflect the realities of wartime experience.

The above writers evince a long-held Japanese attitude that homoeroticism is a widespread response to be expected in homosocial environments and not a pathology particular to specific individuals. Indeed, Pflugfelder suggests that Japan's "relatively benign" stance toward male-male sexuality during wartime was a result of "the greater compatibility of male-male erotic behavior with hegemonic masculinity within the prevailing gender system" (1999: 327). Unlike policies enacted by Japan's ally Nazi Germany, there was no organized campaign to eradicate homosexuality from society; unlike the situation in the United States, there were no campaigns directed at removing "sexual deviants" from the armed forces. In fact, male-male sexual interaction remained unregulated by law throughout Japan's years of militarism; postwar accounts of homosexual relations during wartime suggest that certain modes of homosexual interaction were tolerated within the military, particularly between senior and junior men.

It is difficult to know how much to read into postwar accounts of homosexual interaction in the Japanese armed forces. Perhaps, as Berube (1990) argues in the case of the U.S. forces, the kind of treatment that known homosexual men might receive was highly context specific and dependent upon a number of factors, not least how well the war was going at any particular point, as well as the temperament of individual officers and the general level of camaraderie among the troops. However, there are accounts suggesting that not only homosexual activity but homosexual relationships were accepted to a certain extent within the Japanese military.

One article with the title "A sojourn into male-male eroticism: *sodomia* notes" (Kondō 1954), printed in *Fūzoku kurabu* in 1954, tells of the author's early "baptism" into sodomy at age nine and his casual encounters with other males at school and later as a university student in Tokyo. It was not until he was inducted into the army and sent to serve in Manchuria, however, that he discovered his first "homosexual partner" *(homo no aite),* a corporal named Suda. Despite the fact that Suda had a fearsome reputation within the squadron, the author found himself "spoiled" *(kawaii gatte)* by the corporal, who never asked him to participate in the harsh labor that was the usual lot of new recruits. One evening, after a banquet, when most of the soldiers in the barracks had left to enjoy themselves at the local comfort station, the author found himself pulled into an empty room by Suda, who confessed his love for him and pleaded for his love in return. The two then spent the night together in the same bed, with the result that "given the narrowness of our quarters, the relationship between me and Corporal Suda immediately began to be talked about throughout the squadron." This seems not to have been a cause of concern for Suda, however, since from that point on "every night he would get into bed beside me and hold me to him and not let me go." The author goes on to state that no one was especially surprised by this development, since homosexuality *(nanshoku)* was a fad *(hayari)* throughout the squadron; the barracks had the atmosphere of a homosexual club *(nanshoku kurabu).* After Suda was transferred to another unit, the author had two more long-term relationships with other soldiers before returning to Tokyo at the end of the war to marry a woman chosen for him by his mother.

It is, of course, difficult to take such stories at face value, and it is hard at this remove to know the extent to which such narratives are based on fact or on fantasy. These stories of wartime love were sometimes offered voluntarily by readers, but others were written by semiprofessional writers who made spare cash by running off articles for the plethora of "perverse sexuality" magazines that sprang up after the war. As products of popular culture the purpose of which was to entertain, these magazines were hardly concerned about establishing the veracity of the tales they reproduced. Any researcher who tries to distinguish between factual and fantasy incidents in this vast literature is therefore faced with the dilemma reported by Ken Plummer, who in the 1970s had to file away unused a decade's worth of sexual stories he had collected from a wide range of informants since he was unable to know what in them was true, what was wishful thinking and what was pure fantasy. Plummer later went back to this material but from a different angle. He notes that the "truth" of a story is not always its most salient feature but that

> the telling of stories can ultimately move beyond the life of a person or a community, and beyond an informational educational role, and become a clue to the wider symbolic workings of whole cultures. The stories told in daily lives flow from the culture and back into it: they are major resources for comprehending a culture and its dynamics, values and changes. (Plummer 1995: 176)

In dealing with this literature, I make no attempt to weed out the fantastic from the authentic but argue instead that all stories are scripted within the terms of specific narrative frames and that the manner in which a story is framed, as much as the veracity of its contents, can tell us about the wider workings of a culture. Below I look at two stories in detail, one published in 1953 that details the sadomasochistic relationship that developed between a Japanese officer and his young orderly stationed in Japan at the end of the war, and another published in 1954 that discusses the love relationship that developed between an invalided Japanese soldier and a male Indonesian servant who tended him.

The first article, entitled "Recollections of my time in the army" (Morihara 1953), appeared in *Kitan kurabu*, the longest-lived of the perverse magazines, published between 1952 and 1974. As described in detail in the next chapter, the main interest of this magazine was sadomasochism, predominantly of a heterosexual nature, although articles on cross-dressing and male and female homosexuality were often included. This particular article is interesting since it is accompanied by a photograph. The author describes how he enjoys looking at the many photographs of women in sadomasochistic poses published in the magazine but notes that photographs of men are rarely included. He goes on to explain that he happens to have in his possession a large collection of sadomasochistic male photographs and relates how he came by them.

The author, an ex-army officer who at the end of the war was stationed in Japan, explains that a naked and bound youth photographed outside in a field is his orderly, who first entered his service in the summer of 1944. Reminding readers that "at that time in the Japanese military there was no such thing as human rights and terrible things *(hidoi koto)* took place on impulse" (note the passive voice here—a common distancing technique in postwar narratives), the author confesses that "I discovered a sadistic *(sadisuchikku)* place in my heart." The object of his sadistic attentions was a young soldier who had been drafted while in the midst of his studies of literature at an imperial university. Unsure quite why he chose this soldier among others to be his orderly, the author puts it down to the fact that his sadistic instincts were aroused by the young man's privileged background and "noble" face.

Officers and their orderlies lived in very close quarters, as it was important that the young men be at their seniors' beck and call at all times. This provided the author with many opportunities to "spoil" *(kawaigatte yarimasu)* his young servant, by allowing him into the officers' accommodation (which was heated in winter) and giving him better food rations than the other soldiers. He goes on to relate how "given this relationship I think it was a natural development for us to enter into homosexuality *(dōseiai)*." However, the relationship described in the article was mediated not so much through physical contact as through the camera lens. The officer would use his orderly as a model for his photographic hobby, most shots being taken outdoors and with the young man naked. The orderly would be ordered to strip and would then be bound in a variety of poses (the one photograph included shows him standing, back to the camera, bound to a tree with his arms above his head). The couple would then later look at the photographs together, the younger man apparently narcissistically enjoying the attention of the older man. However, these photo sessions became increasingly brutal, with the orderly forced to remain naked for long periods in freezing winter weather; at one stage the officer whipped the young man's behind with his pistol. These photo sessions apparently resulted in numerous prints; the author's stated purpose in writing the article was to seek opportunities to publish them, partly in the hope that his ex-orderly would see them and make contact with him again. The author says he has been unable to forget the young man and thinks of him "like a child." He says "I would like us to meet again democratically *(minshuteki)* and continue our relationship."

This story is interesting for a number of reasons, not least because it refers to photographic evidence of a homoerotic relationship that (ostensibly) took place in the armed forces. Although only one picture was printed alongside the article, a note from the editor explains that the author had supplied six photographs but space restrictions made it impossible to use more. The article itself was also shortened, perhaps because homosexual stories were not expected to be of interest to the mainstream of the magazine's readers.

Of interest also is the manner in which the story picks up several themes from the article cited above on homosexuality on the battlefront. Here is one instance of a codependent relationship between an officer and orderly, the kind of relationship described as "unavoidable" given the homosocial nature of military life. It also echoes themes explored earlier, particularly the hierarchical nature of the military and the manner in which subordinates—both male and female—were used by those above them. Perhaps most interesting, though, is the contrast between wartime relationships, where there was no concept of "human rights," and the postwar situation, in which people could meet "democratically." Given that prior to the war's end homosexual relationships in Japan had been organized hierarchically in terms of age and gender difference, it is significant that the author looks forward to a new mode of homosexual interaction, one that can take place along more egalitarian lines.

If accounts of homosexual relations between members of the Japanese military are common in the postwar press, there are fewer descriptions of homosexual contact between soldiers and the men of subject nations. As outlined above, heterosexual contact between Japanese men and women of the colonies was widespread and institutionalized, but in terms of public discourse, it was barely referred to. In large part this was due to anxieties about the corruption of the Japanese bloodline by children of mixed race, who would have disrupted the racial hierarchy. The sexual dynamic between Japanese men and the women of subject nations was one of exploitation—comfort women were recruited from these nations and deployed in the service of Japanese military expansionism in much the same manner that the natural resources of these countries were appropriated for Japanese ends. But what of the relationship between the Japanese military and the men of the colonies? Was there also a sexual dynamic at work here?

Robertson's (1998) discussion of the first Japanese-Philippine propaganda film, *Dawn of Freedom* (*Ano hata wo ute*), produced in 1943, suggests that there were homoerotic undercurrents in Japan's relation to the men of subject nations. The film includes a depiction of a farewell scene between a Filipino officer and his Japanese soldier friend; it is "shot like a love scene." While neither can understand the other's language, the two stare lovingly into each other's eyes, making their sentiments clear. Following Markus Nones, Robertson notes that "obviously homoerotic, *Dawn of Freedom* comes close to bringing male homosexuality and the desire of the 'other' to light" (1998: 103). Quite how widespread this "desire of the other" was is difficult to evaluate, but one article describing a same-sex love affair that took place during the Japanese occupation of Indonesia suggests how unexpected relationships could develop between Japanese military men and the men of subject nations.

Entitled "Coconut Oil"[12] and published in *Fūzoku kagaku* (Namiki 1954), one of the more short-lived sex-customs magazines, the article describes a relationship between a young invalided Japanese soldier and an even younger Indonesian servant. Quite unlike the story related above, this account is written in an elegiac, even rapturous manner; the love between the soldier and the servant boy has eclipsed in the writer's memory all other details about the war. The account opens with the words, "A beautiful native boy came toward me bearing a clay pot full of thick, amber liquid. Oh, how the feel of the liquid—coconut oil—transfixes me even now." It continues in this vein, tinged with regret and nostalgia.

The author describes how in 1944, after having graduated from an agricultural college at the age of 19, he was sent to Sumatra as an apprentice in a Japanese firm responsible for increasing agricultural production in the region. However, after only a short time as an office worker he was drafted into the army, where he underwent training in the jungle. The poor conditions, rough work and unfamiliar climate proved very debilitating, and the author came down with malaria. He was hospitalized for several months. During this time, his fever was often so high that he was unable to rise even to visit the toilet; he lost a great deal of weight, leading to further debilitation. Throughout his illness he was attended by a young 16-year-old Javanese boy named Tora, with whom he developed a friendship.

Initially it seems to have been Tora who was attracted, explaining to the author in his broken Japanese that "older brother, you are different from other Japanese." The reason Tora gave for this observation was that unlike his fellow soldiers, the author did not speak to him in a loud, threatening manner, and that his demeanor was more polite. The author confesses that it was not his intention to behave in such a polite manner; his apparent meekness was due to his weak condition. Nevertheless, Tora seems to have taken a special interest in the young soldier and gone out of his way to care for him.

Given the long period that he had been an invalid, the author's muscles had wasted, and he experienced cramps and pains. At the army doctor's suggestion, Tora began to give the author a daily massage; it was at this point that the author began to notice something special in the way Tora related to him. The author recounts the first massage session in this way:

> Soon after [the visit from the doctor], Tora came along smiling, carrying a clay pot full of a sticky amber liquid.
>
> "What's that?" I asked.
>
> "It's coconut oil" he replied. . . .
>
> Tora told me to get naked and lie with my face down, then he began to pour the coconut oil on my back, buttocks and thighs. When I told him that the doctor had said he was an excellent masseur, he said "that's right" in a happy voice. . . . Then, after turning over, Tora mounted my chest with his back to my face and began massaging downwards from my chest. I realized he was massaging with extra care and I thought this a little odd. I was about to tell him to stop but remembering the way he had looked after me, I just bit my tongue and watched Tora's round buttocks moving up and down in front of my face. Up until that point, despite the fact that Tora had been caring for me even to the extent of carrying away my urine in an old beer bottle, I hadn't felt anything special for him, but now under his soft touch, I found myself escaping into a dream world.

Despite the fact that the author's pain soon began to subside, the daily massage sessions continued and became "half play" *(hanbun wa asobi)*, "play" being a term that in Japanese strongly connotes sexual interaction. Indeed, the author eagerly anticipated the massage sessions, in which he would "experience such pleasure that I forgot everything." The "play" gradually became more overtly sexual, and Tora would come to join the soldier on his bed during the day and "entwine my body like a snake." It is at this point in the narrative that the author reminisces, "Actually, I have once had a woman." He goes on to describe how before leaving Tokyo he had been dragged against his will to visit a harborside prostitute by his drunken coworkers. He remembered the seedy room and the witchlike face of the prostitute caked in makeup, regretting that he had come to know women in this manner. His interaction with Tora was "totally different"; unlike the ugly, dry body of the woman, the soft, youthful Javanese boy seems "like a female leopard," and he cherishes their time spent together. Indeed, he begins to think that it would be bearable for him to die in Sumatra without the knowledge of his family in Japan, since Tora had become "the only family and lover for me."

However, with the sudden end of the war, locally recruited servants like Tora were immediately released. Much to the author's regret, Tora disappeared overnight without saying goodbye, leaving the soldier feeling lonely and abandoned. Yet just before the author was to be shipped back to Japan, Tora suddenly reappeared and they were able to make a hurried farewell, but largely a silent one, since neither was able to speak much for fear of bursting into tears. After Tora made a final salute they parted, the author musing that "our separation seemed somehow untrue given the extent to which we had given our bodies and souls to each other."

Writing ten years after these events purportedly took place, the author is led to wonder,

> Wasn't this all just a dream, the result of a malarial fever? The rubber forest, the hospital ward made from reeds, the sound of the breeze in the trees, the cries of unfamiliar birds, when I think of these things now, they feel far off and child-like. Even Tora's figure which I ought not to forget seems vague to me now. But there is one thing that I clearly remember—coconut oil—with its distinct feel and aroma.

While the accounts concerning Corporal Suda and the sadomasochistic relationship between the officer and his orderly discussed earlier rehearse familiar themes from the traditional *nanshoku* code—the age difference between the two parties, the disparity in power relations between lover and beloved and the sometimes unwilling acquiescence of the younger partner—"Coconut Oil" draws upon the alternative, more mutual discourse of love between beautiful boys discussed by Angles (2003). In this account, the age difference is only three years, and the seduction comes not from the elder but the younger partner. It is only after the relationship has begun that the Japanese soldier begins to appreciate the feline beauty of the younger man and is unwittingly drawn into a deep emotional involvement. If the hierarchical relationships between veteran soldiers and recruits can be seen as supporting the war effort, providing a convenient means for the senior partner to evacuate his desire while reinforcing the subordination of the younger partner, "Coconut Oil" is deeply troubling to this system. In this story the war is reduced to a backdrop against which the real drama—the unfolding relationship between Japanese soldier and Indonesian boy—is played out. Becoming "the only family and lover" for the author, Tora breaks down the familiar Japanese dichotomies of inside and outside, both replacing the narrator's biological family and supplanting the emperor and the imperial project as the author's emotional focus. Of the three stories, then, this tale of interracial attraction is most subversive.

However, despite participating in different modes of homosexual interaction, none of the protagonists in the stories outlined above can usefully be described as "homosexual," let alone "gay," and it is doubtful that these figures can be incorporated in an unfolding narrative of Japanese gay history. Rather, the stories describe the peculiar, unexpected, spontaneous nature of the relationships that can develop between men during wartime, relationships that the authorities would have found difficult to discipline or prevent. These stories and others like them are quite unlike the "coming out" narratives that Berube (1990), Robinson (1999) and others have suggested began to proliferate in the United States and other western societies as a consequence of the Second World War. As mentioned, the concept of "the homosexual" had already taken shape in anglophone societies by the beginning of the conflict; there were various attempts by U.S. and other Allied officials to identify and exclude both male and female homosexuals from the ranks, thus inadvertently advertising the very identity category that they wished to excise. "The homosexual" as an identity was not, however, well recognized in Japanese popular discourse at this time, and the next chapter will explore the parameters within which male homosexual conduct and identity could be articulated in the early postwar period.

CONCLUSION

This chapter has described how Japanese society became increasingly heteronormative and how gender roles for both men and women were further polarized as a result of Japan's descent into militarism. Yet, ironically, while the militarist state had by 1937 set in place a formidable regimen of ideological control, various factors necessitated by the war effort itself worked against the very gender categories that the government was attempting to instill. Firstly, despite pronatal government policies, the increasing drafting of men into the armed forces removed husbands from wives and delayed the opportunity for marriage for many other younger men. Romantic love was portrayed as a distraction for men, who were encouraged to heroically disregard such personal concerns. Despite the provision of prostitution facilities to "comfort" these men and make their sacrifice more bearable, the homosocial environment of the barracks and the battlefield proved conducive to unforeseen homoerotic and homosexual bonds. In Japan, however, the Pacific War does not seem to have served as a catalyst for the development of homosexual identities and communities to the extent that historians such as Berube (1990) have suggested was the result of mass mobilization in anglophone societies during the Second World War. Although homosexual behavior may have been widespread, there was as yet no single category as reductive as the English term "the homosexual" that could serve as a focus for government repression or for self-identification and group solidarity.

Furthermore, the war effort also served to break down gender distinctions, as various sumptuary regulations forbade women from accentuating their feminine appearance—wearing clothes that were too showy, applying lipstick or other cosmetics and curling the hair were all frowned upon. As austerity measures took hold and it became difficult to find more-feminine clothes, women increasingly wore a style of baggy pants, known as *monpe,* producing a more masculinized appearance. Also, despite official government ideology that promoted women as the literal bearers of "human resources" (Mackie 2003: 113), the mass mobilization of the male population as part of Japan's military expansionism led to serious labor shortages in home industries that had previously been dominated by men. From the late 1930s, single women were increasingly recruited into transport and heavy industry. Married women, whose job it was to produce more children, were also encouraged to produce more foodstuffs through tilling the land and gathering seafood (Mackie 2003: 113). Finally, in 1944, as Japan's defeat came to seem inevitable, both women and children were encouraged to take up arms to defend the homeland in case of invasion. One powerful image of the closing months of the war was of short-haired, trouser-clad women brandishing bamboo spears in preparation for a final desperate battle against the invaders. By this time the official segregation of gender roles had all but collapsed, women having literally become the defenders of the home front.

While internal contradictions between official ideology and the necessities of life during wartime meant that gender ideologies and actual gender roles were already in conflict, it needs to be remembered that by the war's end there had been about 1,800,000 Japanese casualties and that 40 percent of the built-up area of 66 of Japan's largest cities lay in ruins. Infrastructure had collapsed, and much of the population was faced with starvation. In addition, over six million Japanese soldiers and civilians were stranded overseas, many in internment camps (Molasky 2001: 8).

Where Allied nations saw their success in the war as a vindication of their social systems and ideologies, Japan's shocking defeat resulted in widespread disillusionment among the Japanese with previous paradigms, practices and moral codes. Indeed, as Dore comments, "the confusion which followed the defeat was catastrophic to the old morality. In some cases it was catastrophic to moral restraint of any kind" (1999: 162). It was in this context of widespread social confusion that a new kind of sexual culture rapidly emerged, as is described in the next chapter.

NOTES

1. Krafft-Ebing's *Psychopathia Sexualis* was first translated into Japanese in 1894.

2. Garon (1999: 109), for instance, draws attention to a 1931 advertisement for a book entitled *Tōkyō ero on parēdo* (Tokyo eros on parade), which claimed to be the definitive guide to sex establishments in Tokyo. Intriguingly, the ad appeared in the in-house journal of the Home Ministry, opposite a notice for a new legal dictionary.

3. Love suicides in which both partners died together were both a popular romantic trope in Japanese literature and a real-life strategy for many couples whose love was doomed owing to the impossibility of social validation of the relationship—particularly the case with same-sex partners. See Robertson (1999) for a discussion of the phenomenon.

4. Having lost the envelope, Kabiya is unsure of the precise date.

5. Literally *"okama ga kōchō sarete"*; *okama*, a slang term for the anus, featured in the phrase *okama wo horu* or "digging a hole," a reference to anal sex.

6. The baptism metaphor for initiation into (passive) homosexual sex was quite common, appearing also in the postwar literature. See for example Kondō (1954: 143), who "received baptism into sodomy *(sodomii)* at age nine."

7. On this point it is interesting to consider a reader's response to an article on homosexuality published in the UK's *Times Educational Supplement* in 1957. The writer comments, "When I was a boy at one of the major public schools in the thirties, I used to be amazed at the successful barrier of silence which separated our widespread homosexual practices from the world outside our school houses, and at the almost Masonic secrecy about the whole business which was observed by men who had been through the school and who must have known what went on" (cited in Westwood 1960: 26). Silence about homosexual affairs clearly cannot be taken as an indication of their absence.

8. Today Noguchi Yonejirō is better known as the father of sculptor and artist Noguchi Isamu.

9. Article 16, Paragraph 1, required doctors to get the opinion of other doctors and submit a report to the administrative office before performing any "operation to render reproduction impossible" (see Norgren 2001: 144). The same prohibition was expressed in Article 28 of the postwar *Yūsei Hogo Hō*, or "Eugenic Protection Law" (see my discussion in chapter 6).

10. An example of such pleasure in power can be seen in Kobayashi's 1959 film *Ningen no jōken,* in which the Japanese matron of a Manchurian hospital for the war wounded sadistically enjoys bullying both male patients and female staff.

11. Gil M. Portes (dir.). 2000. *Markova: Comfort Gay*. During the Japanese occupation of the Philippines, Dempster was working in a club as a *bakla,* or transgender entertainer, when he and his fellow performers were invited to a hotel by a group of Japanese officers unaware that they were biological males. Upon discovering the sex of the performers, the officers took Dempster and his companions to an army barracks, where they were serially raped by the soldiers. Dempster claims to have then been detained for the next five months and been forced to clean and cook for the soldiers as well as provide sexual services before finally managing to escape.

12. The title in Japanese is "Miniya karapa," which is a Japanization of the Indonesian term for coconut oil—*minyak kelapa*. I am grateful to Helen Creese for pointing this out.

2

Japan's Postwar Perverse Culture

A new sexual culture arose surprisingly quickly after Japan's defeat and occupation by U.S. forces. Street prostitutes sprang up everywhere "like bamboo shoots after the rain," and there was a boom in the peddling of amateur pornography (Shimokawa 1995a: 172). Intellectuals like Sakaguchi Ango[1] wrote about the sense of "release" *(kaihō)* at the war's end from hegemonic gender and sexual norms that Japanese people had experienced. Jay Rubin points out that "the Japanese were sick to death of being preached at constantly to be good, frugal, hardworking, and self-sacrificing" and were consequently attracted to "a decadence that was simply the antithesis of prewar wholesomeness" (1985: 80). Many people were keen to forget the past and looked forward to the beginning of a new and newly private life in which eroticism was flaunted as an important symbol of liberation.

The immediate postwar years saw the development of a *kasutori* (low-grade, pulp)[2] culture that Dower describes as "a commercial world dominated by sexually oriented entertainments and a veritable cascade of pulp literature" (2000: 148). Japanese writers were now free to dispense with the "wholesome" preoccupations of earlier literature and instead explore more "decadent" themes (Rubin 1985: 72–3), including a whole genre of "carnal literature" *(nikutai bungaku)* in which the physicality of the body was emphasized over more ideological concerns (Kerkham 2001: 325–35; Igarashi 2000: 55–61). As Igarashi points out, for many survivors, their bodies were the only possession they had managed to preserve from the destruction of the war; Japan's burned-out cities became sites for celebration of the "raw, erotic energy of Japanese bodies" (2000: 48). He notes how some workers celebrated the end of the war by staging "wild parties" in which they listened to jazz songs and women wore lipstick—emblems of the decadent west that had been prohibited during the war.

One had only to glance at the covers of the *kasutori* press to understand that there had been a radical break from the past. Women's bodies were prominently displayed in a manner that would have been inconceivable before the war. The covers alone of magazines such as *Venus, Sekai no onna* (World women), *Jitsuwa romansu* (True romance stories), *Wink, Lucky* and *Happy* were testament to a new sexual regime that was challenging previous notions about the sanctity of Japanese womanhood. Traditional Japanese notions of feminine beauty gave way to increasingly westernized representations, as evidenced by the photographs and illustrations contained in the *kasutori* press. Dower notes that

> from this time on, the idealized western female figure, long limbed and amply proportioned, became an object of male lust—and an ideal for young Japanese women to emulate. . . . Being tall and amply bosomed were new criteria for feminine beauty. (2000: 149–52)

The *kasutori* press reflected and also accelerated an increasing trend toward the westernization of women's bodies, encouraging the adoption of fashions that had been forbidden during the war. These included the dyeing and perming of hair, increased use of cosmetics and the wearing of such clothes as close-fitting blouses, skirts and tights emphasizing parts of the female anatomy—breasts and legs—that had been hidden by traditional clothing, such as the kimono, or the baggy *monpe* pants of the war years. (See figure 2.1.) This "liberation" of Japanese women from traditional codes of feminine propriety was, however, double-edged, since female bodies were "immediately caught up in market forces that offered them to male desire at a price" (Igarashi 2000: 58). In the immediate postwar years, it was members of the occupation forces who had privileged access to Japanese women's (and sometimes men's) bodies.

American soldiers were the source of the much coveted signifiers of female modernity, leading to many relationships between occupation personnel and local women. Some Japanese women were driven by economic necessity to become the "temporary wives" of Allied officers, women known as "only-san," since they were contracted to only one man. Others, known as "butterflies," entered into agreements with several soldiers at a time, and a still larger number of street prostitutes catered to occupation soldiers indiscriminately (Tanaka 2002: 165). During the war, as we have seen, Japanese men, as members of the imperial forces, had imposed themselves on the bodies of women from subject nations through military brothels known as "comfort stations" (Shibata 1999); the sight of Japanese women in the embrace of foreign men was for

Figure 2.1 Advertisement for a permanent wave at a Ginza hair salon. ***Shinsō jitsuwa*** **(True tales), May 1947**

many a stunning symbol of Japan's defeat and humiliation. Some young Japanese men and boys too found it expedient to sleep with the former enemy in hope of financial gain or preferential treatment in job applications. No doubt many men were coerced, just as many women were. One young man, for instance, wrote of the fear he experienced when he was taken off the train by an occupation officer, led to a nearby hotel, stripped, made love to and then sent on his way with a 1,000-yen bill in his pocket (Wada 1953).

To some extent it was Japanese men who were most disadvantaged by the new regime and whose self-esteem was most damaged by Japan's defeat and occupation (Iwamoto 2002; Molasky 2001).[3] Recalling his wartime experience, one middle-aged Japanese man put it this way: "For all

Japan's men losing the war meant losing their balls'' (Koga 1973). Mochizuki Mamoru, a psychologist, went so far as to state that Japanese men had ''lost faith in their masculinity and superiority over women because of the Occupation experience,'' arguing that Japanese men were turning sissy and that the new American fashions they had adopted were actually the fashions of American gay men *(gei bōi)* (1955: 152–5).

The occupation also brought to Japan many American women, who offered a range of new models for female behavior that would have been unthinkable during the war years. The ''liberated American woman'' became for many Japanese women emblems of gender equality (Bardsley 1999: 18) and represented a threat to traditional Japanese male privilege. Indeed, one commentator suggested that postwar equality between men and women was leading to an increase in the popularity of male homosexuality *(danshoku ryūkō)*, since many men, spurned by newly liberated women, found they ''got on better'' with other men (*Fūzoku zōshi* 1954: 104).

The sudden transformation in Japanese women's appearance, their new gender roles, and the widespread depiction of women in the erotic embrace of foreign men were all startling changes. It was, after all, only during the occupation that the open portrayal of kissing became possible in Japan. Unlike the United States, where the (heterosexual) screen kiss was a staple of Hollywood romance, the public representation of kissing (in the movies, in magazines or on the street) had been censored in the prewar period. Kissing was not understood as a mark of affection but as an intimate and intensely sexual act and did not become a widespread erotic practice for dating couples until after the war (de Vos 1973: 273), when it was humorously referred to as a symbol of democracy (Yamamoto and Ozawa 1975: 83).

Before the war any overt display of public affection between the sexes, even between man and wife, had been considered risqué (Dore 1999: 159). However, American service personnel did much to challenge these notions of unacceptable behavior by conspicuously strolling down the streets with their Japanese female companions, known as *panpan* girls, or canoodling with them in parks, train stations and other public areas (Yamamoto 1976: 150–1; Yamamoto and Ozawa 1975: 83). One bystander, a middle-school boy at the time, recalls how he suddenly became conscious of sex as he ''looked on with envious eyes at *panpan* girls in bright red lipstick strolling around town clasped in the embrace of American soldiers'' (Yajima 2000: 9). Public sexuality was suddenly visible and acceptable in a manner not seen prior to the war's end, and ''petting'' *(pettingu)* couples were conspicuous features of parks and shrine precincts (*Hyakuman nin no yoru* 1963c: 152–3). Strip shows too were ubiquitous and remained so for many years, and female nudity continued to be displayed in popular media to an extent impossible in anglophone publications of the period. (See figures 2.2 and 2.3.)

Igarashi points out how, for some, "sexual enjoyment marked the postwar liberation of Japanese bodies and expressed defiance of the regulatory regime that demanded bodily sacrifices" (2000: 55). While in the prewar period interaction between men and women had been extremely circumscribed and the modern custom of dating practically unknown, after the war young heterosexual couples began to experiment sexually much more. The *kasutori* press commented on the popularity of such sexual behaviors as petting and "necking," noting how practices that had previously taken place as a prelude to intercourse within marriage were now being adopted as recreational activities by young people generally (Ōta and Kabiya 1954). Marriage in Japan had long been viewed as an institution the purpose of which was procreation and child rearing, but the new postwar environment saw a greater emphasis placed on fulfilling the emotional and sexual needs of the couple, which resulted in a demand for information about sexual practice and pleasure. Dutch gynecologist Theodoor Van de Velde's international best-selling sex guide *Ideal Marriage,* which had previously been banned, was translated into Japa-

Figure 2.2 Children look at a placard advertising a strip show in Asakusa, Tokyo. *Fūzoku kagaku* (Sex-customs science), December 1954

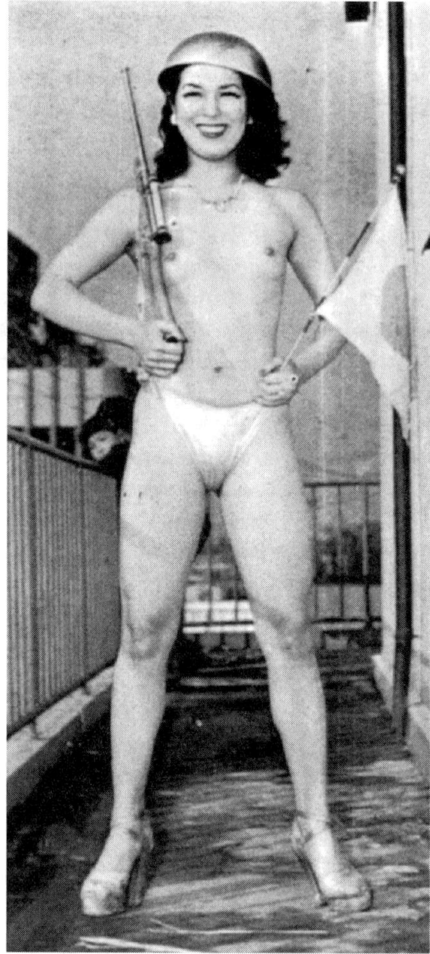

Figure 2.3 Female model in military pose. *Fūzoku kagaku* (Sex-customs science), December 1954

nese as early as 1946, under the title *Kanzen naru kekkon* (Perfect marriage). The book, soon released in cheap pirated versions, placed great emphasis on foreplay and the role of oral-genital contact, and it was to have a major impact on sexual discourse over the next decade (Yamamoto and Ozawa 1975: 85–6).

This visibility of "dating" couples on the streets of Japan's cities resulted in the popularization of a (significantly foreign) term describing the modern couple—*abekku*—from the French *avec* ("with"). One magazine that pioneered this new mode of coupledom was itself entitled *Abekku,* whereas others used the traditional term for a married couple, *fūfu* (literally husband and wife) but modified it to reflect the new values. These magazines included *Modan fūfu seikatsu* (Modern married-couple lifestyle), *Shin fūfu* (New married-couple) or *Kanzen naru fūfu no seikatsu* (Complete married-couple lifestyle) (Fukushima 1987: 90–1). Such *kasutori* magazines were replete with articles offering advice to the modern couple on the art of hand-holding, kissing and more *nikutaiteki* (carnal) pursuits, such as petting and foreplay. Often the discussion was pitched in terms of sex education; indeed, such was the level of ignorance about sexual matters among previously sheltered young women that some writers felt it necessary to point out that kissing did not lead to pregnancy (Yamamoto 1976: 54). During the war years, official ideology had taught that indulging in sex for purely personal pleasure was "irresponsible"; the government had introduced strict bans on abortion and the dissemination of family planning literature, which meant that information about sexuality had been difficult to obtain. However, in postwar publications contraception was discussed outside of the eugenics paradigm that had dominated sex education before the war, and it was now possible to represent sex in terms of pleasure not duty.

Although the war years had witnessed in the United States a loosening of sexual mores that had provided a major impetus toward the development of homosexual identity and community (Berube 1990), the postwar period saw the reassertion of "traditional" values and a rapid escalation in the surveillance and control of dissident sexualities (Canaday 2003; D'Emilio 1992). There had been intermittent attempts to rid the ranks of gay men and lesbians during wartime, and these efforts intensified after the war's end. Pat Bond, for instance, tells of her experience in the Women's Army Corps during Japan's occupation:

> They started an incredible witch hunt in Tokyo. It was really unbelievable—sending 500 women home for dishonorable discharges. Every day there were court martials and trials. I don't know any women from that era who didn't get dishonorable discharges. (Mariposa Film Group 1977)

In Japan, however, it was the postwar period that witnessed a loosening of traditional sex and gender ideologies, resulting in an endorsement of "curiosity seeking" in sexual matters and a less judgmental attitude in the popular press toward homosexuality and other nonprocreative acts. The comparatively open atmosphere surrounding sexual discussion in the popular culture of postwar Japan was also enabled by other factors. Where the Allied victory over Japan and Germany had done much to bolster America's sense of superiority and the conviction that its political institutions and social systems were right and just, Japan's defeat resulted in widespread disorientation and a rejection of the ideals of the past, including a questioning of narrow gender norms and restrictive sexual practices. As Dore comments:

> The paralysis of government that followed the defeat in 1945 removed the props of the old morality. It did more. The connection between the unique Japaneseness of Japanese family life and sex morality, and the unique Japaneseness of Japan's military supremacy, her glorious traditions and her magnificent future destiny, had been too explicitly pointed out by the prewar moralists for the discrediting of the latter not to have disastrous effects on the former. (1999: 162)

The widespread use of terms such as "new" and "modern" in Japanese postwar culture indicates not so much a chronological separation from the past as an ideological one—many Japanese people were in the business of refashioning themselves by rejecting the narrowness of the past. The rhetorical space occupied by emerging homosexual categories in Japan was therefore very different from that embodied by the figure of "the homosexual" in western cultures, as described below.

THE "PERVERSE" PRESS

Various *kasutori* magazines containing many sex-themed articles of a less than educational nature were referred to as *ryōki*, or "curiosity seeking," and had much in common with the prewar fad for publications specializing in erotic, grotesque nonsense (Bessatsu Taiyō 1997: 198–9; Fukushima 1987: 92–3). Developing out of these fly-by-night publications, from the early 1950s a range of more high-brow magazines appeared that allowed readers to indulge their interest in queer or perverse desires *(hentai seiyoku)*. Of particular interest is the freedom with which these magazines discussed people who in English were politely spoken of as "sex deviants" or "sex variants" but in common parlance were more usually referred to as "queers" or "perverts."

In the English-speaking world, discussion of any kind of nonheterosexual practice was at this time extremely circumscribed by censorship. Outside of medical or criminological literature, where homosexuals in particular were objectified and discussed entirely in terms of deviance/punishment or diagnosis/cure, there was little scope for the public airing of sexual issues.[4] This only became worse in the 1950s under the Joseph McCarthy campaigns, which politicized homosexuality—associating it with communism (Canaday 2003: 355; Spencer 1995: 356–7).[5] Indeed, the editors of *ONE*, the first homophile publication, founded in 1953 in Los

Angeles, were investigated by the FBI for supposed communist affiliation (Streitmatter 1995: 32). The FBI regularly attended homophile conventions throughout the 1950s and '60s and kept up its surveillance of community publications. Any material that put forward a nonpathological view of male or female homosexuality thus had to run a gauntlet of "customs, post office, and federal, state, and local law enforcement officials" (Stein 2000: 239). As well as investigating suspect sexual minorities within the United States, authorities were also proactive in guarding the borders of the country against sexual deviants. Immigration legislation like the 1952 McCarran-Walter Act denied visas to immigrants who were "psychopathic personalities" (Canaday 2003: 355–9), a category interpreted to include "sexual deviants." This act was also used to deport immigrants already residing in the United States who had been arrested on gross indecency charges involving same-sex partners, on the grounds that these individuals had failed to disclose their status as "sex perverts" when originally applying to enter the country. The influence of the Cold War served only to intensify this suppression of homosexuality, not just in the United States but throughout Anglo-Saxon societies, including the UK and Australia.[6]

Curiously, given the efforts the U.S. forces had made to identify and expel both male and female homosexuals (Berube 1990) and the censorship of film and literature that included reference to "sex deviants," the occupation authorities were largely uninterested in monitoring the sexual content of Japanese media. Jay Rubin notes that the Civil Censorship Detachment "had no concern with material that was obscene or pornographic, providing that material was not detrimental to Occupation objectives" (1988: 170). Hence, it was possible for new kinds of sex-related Japanese publications to be considerably more frank than prewar magazines, or indeed, than any publications existing in English at this time.

In the United States, it was difficult not only to publish magazines that took a nonjudgmental stance on human sexual diversity but also to send them through the mail to subscribers, because of the postal service's stance against the dissemination of "obscene" literature. For instance, the U.S. mail seized all copies of the October 1953 issue of the homophile newsletter *ONE*, calling it "obscene, lewd, lascivious and filthy." This objection seems to have been based mainly on the magazine's inclusion of an advertisement featuring a handsome man modeling silk pajamas (Streitmatter 1995: 32). It was not until 1958 that the U.S. Supreme Court finally "established that the subject of homosexuality is not, per se, obscene" (Streitmatter 1995: 35).

Hence, while the immediate postwar years were in many ways a progressive period in Japan, noticeably so for women[7] and sexual minorities,[8] the same period in the United States was "one of the most regressive eras in the history of gay Americans" (Streitmatter 1995: 17), as it was for sexual minorities throughout the English-speaking world. Writers for Japan's perverse press often commented on the American attitude toward homosexuality, finding it odd that a society that prided itself on its supposedly equitable treatment of men and women and that proclaimed itself on a mission to "democratize" Japan should maintain such harsh legal and social sanctions against male homosexuality. As one writer commented, "Japan was heaven for American homosexuals" (Oka 1953: 100). Indeed, during the early 1950s American GIs could be found looking for sex in Tokyo's centrally located Hibiya Park, where many Japanese boys who "chased after foreign ass" gathered (Oka 1953: 100).[9] American military officers in particular were much in demand, since it was possible for young Japanese men to receive grants for foreign study through their mediation or be taken back to the United States as "houseboys" (Mishima 1968: 149). However, the military police apparently patrolled Hibiya Park, on the lookout for "intimate liaisons" between Japanese youths and members of the occupation forces, and any soldier found in a compromising position was immediately repatriated (Ōgiya 1953: 159). The Japanese police were, on the contrary, uninterested in these after-hours assignations and would have been unable to arrest the Japanese partners anyway, "since there were no laws by which they might crack down" (Mishima 1968: 56).

While public discourse about homosexuality was limited by censorship in the United States, the freedom of association of homosexuals was also severely restricted. For instance, in California in the 1950s the Alcoholic Beverage Control Board collapsed the difference between homosexual identity and conduct when it suggested that any behavior signifying homosexual status—such as touching, same-sex dancing, limp wrists, high-pitched voices, or the wearing of female clothing or mannish attire (in the case of women)—was evidence of a bar's dubious character and grounds for closing it. Indeed, bar raids and arrests were numerous in many cities throughout the United States and other anglophone countries in the 1950s and '60s; many bars installed warning systems, such as bells or flashing lights, "at which sign all customers are to make certain that no one is standing too close to his neighbor" (Achilles 1967: 232). It was not until 1967 that a landmark ruling by the New Jersey Supreme Court "unanimously upheld the rights of lesbians and gay men to congregate in bars" (Stein 2000: 282). In the UK, where all sexual acts between men, even in private, were illegal, homosexuals fared little better, and the police employed a variety of means to entrap and convict suspects (Westwood 1960: 137–42). The open discussion of gay bars and their clientele that took place in Japan's perverse press was therefore unparalleled in

English-speaking countries, where any public disclosure of the subculture would have led to police investigation, intervention and arrests.

It was not until the early 1960s in the United States and elsewhere that more socially progressive accounts of sexual variety were able to be published[10] and not until the 1970s that gay people began to associate without fear of police harassment. The Japanese perverse press of the 1950s, in contrast, offers a remarkable resource for the study of postwar minority sexualities, a source unparalleled in English and probably in any other language in the world. Indeed, these "perverse," "abnormal," or "mania" magazines, as they were variously termed, had an extremely wide range of interests and, purporting to offer true accounts, drew upon anecdotes from Japan's feudal past as well as stories from European and Asian societies, often relying on anthropological reports. Significantly, these early magazines did not segregate the material into hetero- or homosexual-themed publications, as became standard in the 1970s, but featured a wide range of perverse acts and queer desires, including practically any type of sexual activity other than "ordinary sex *(futsū no sekkusu)* between a man and a woman" (Shimokawa 1995b: 53). The longest-lived was *Kitan kurabu* (Strange-talk club), published between 1952 and 1975; though mainly focusing on sadomasochism (Kitahara and Saotome 2003; Matsuzawa 1997: 60–2), it included discussions and illustrations of a range of "abnormal" *(abunōmaru)* topics including homosexuality and male and female cross-dressing. Other magazines that included information about homosexuality and transgender phenomena were *Ningen tankyū* (Human research; 1950–1953),[11] *Amatoria* (1951–1955), *Fūzoku kagaku* (Sex-customs science; 1953–1955), *Fūzoku zōshi* (Sex-customs storybook; 1953–1955), *Ura mado* (Rear window; 1956–1965) and *Fūzoku kitan* (Strange talk about sex customs; 1960–1974).[12]

The "experts" who wrote for the perverse magazines of the 1950s were different from those writing in the prewar sexological publications, in that fewer claimed any kind of medical or psychiatric training. Referred to as *sensei*,[13] many writers were more literary in bent, and their authority derived from their extensive reading about both Japanese and foreign *fūzoku*,[14] or "sexual customs," which included such psychoanalytic and sexological works as Kinsey's (1948) *Sexual Behavior in the Human Male*, which had been translated into Japanese in 1950, as well as anthropological, historical and literary treatises. For instance, one typical roundtable discussion on "perverse sexuality" printed in the December 1953 edition of *Fūzoku zōshi* illustrates the diversity of perspectives on offer—it took place between a medical professor, a "sex critic" *(sei hyōronka)*, a scholar of French literature and a journalist. This diversity meant that no single mode of analysis, such as psychoanalytic theory, established itself as normative, leading to a more open, hybrid climate for debate.

While a familiar repertoire of theories from sexology and psychoanalysis, such as "inversion," "arrested development," "fetishism," "narcissism" and "penis envy," were rehearsed in these articles, more literary theories deriving from writers like André Gide, D. H. Lawrence and Jean Genet were also discussed, as was the occurrence of homosexuality among men of cultural "genius," such as Michelangelo, Oscar Wilde, Paul Verlaine and Arthur Rimbaud (Yanagiya 1953; Iwakura 1951; Nakano 1951). Thus, unlike in the anglophone press, where homosexuality was liable to be read in terms of cultural degeneracy, many articles in Japan's perverse press associated male homosexuality in particular with periods of high cultural attainment, such as classical Greece, the medieval Arab world, Renaissance Italy and Genroku Japan.[15]

Indeed, the discourse on male homosexuality in Japan's perverse press was quite unlike the sociopsychiatric literature then current in the United States, "in which homosexuality [was] presented as a 'sickness' and the major task of experts [was] presented as the uncovering of its epidemiology, etiology and cure" (Warren 1979: 224). Rather than dealing with perverse sexuality as a pathological condition that was of interest only to medical, legal and religious authorities, several early 1950s publications attempted to frame their discussion in broader, more cultural terms. *Ningen tankyū* acknowledged on its cover that it offered articles on "sexual science for cultured persons *(bunkajin),*" pointing out in an editorial that so long as sex education remained incomplete, sex could never be truly "liberated." *Fūzoku kagaku* too offered its readers "a unique gathering of sex-customs researchers," and, in an attempt to benefit from the new cachet of the English language, it also featured the line "For your sexual customs study" on many of its covers. *Fūzoku zōshi* also described itself on the cover as "a new interest magazine for contemporary persons," suggesting that its subject matter should be of concern to all modern-thinking people. In fact, many contributors to these magazines referred to themselves and their readers as members of the "intelligentsia" *(interi),* among whom interest in sexual perversity was held to be particularly keen. These figures included such literary luminaries as Mishima Yukio and Edogawa Ranpo, who were frequent visitors to Tokyo's developing homosexual bar scene. Ranpo, whose early fiction featured many incidents of male-male desire (Angles 2003), had also been a sponsor of Iwata Jun'ichi, a prewar researcher into Japan's homosexual past, and sometimes contributed his own articles to the perverse magazines (Edogawa 1952). Sightings of Mishima, who was already well known for his homosexual-themed novel *Kamen no kokuhaku* (*Confessions of a Mask,* 1950),[16] were often mentioned in the magazines' news sections.

The breadth of reference in these magazines, the association of sexual perversity with persons and periods of high cultural attainment and the fact that readers often wrote letters and contributed longer descriptive pieces about their own "perverse desires" meant that pathologizing medical, criminal and psychoanalytic theories did not establish such a firm hold on popular discourse about transgenderism and homosexuality in Japan as was the case in anglophone, particularly American, popular writings at this time. The voice of the experts was often muted, given that the magazines relied on contributions from readers for a substantial percentage of their copy and actively solicited confessional stories. Confessions had a well-established place in the history of sexuality; Krafft-Ebing himself had relied on them to provide many of the case studies for his *Psychopathia Sexualis,* first published in 1886. However, the facts that the perverse magazines were published on a monthly basis and featured letters columns and other features contributed by readers gave those who experienced queer desires the opportunity to engage with and sometimes contest the theories of the experts, thus permitting the circulation of previously "subjugated knowledges" (Foucault 2003: 7). To this extent, the postwar magazines were different from the erotic-grotesque publications of the late Taisho period. Angles notes how the prewar magazines were characterized by a "push-and-pull" dynamic that "appeal[ed] to the voyeuristic impulse to witness perverse forms of eroticism while at the same time allowing the reader to maintain the comfort of moral and ethical superiority" (2003: 195). Some contributions to the postwar magazines, however, transcended the paradigm of confession and expert advice, instead advocating the right of individuals to express sexual and gender diversity—a move quite as radical as anything taking place in the United States or Europe at this time. Indeed, the Japanese perverse press was much more radical in its portrayal of sexual and gender diversity and closer to present-day queer positions than to the assimilationist stance adopted by the U.S. groups of the '50s, to the extent that the emerging homophile movement in the United States tended to stress the "normality" of its members and actively recruited sympathetic "experts" to its cause (Stein 2000).

Another factor facilitating the discussion of sexual topics in postwar Japan was the fact that the coalition between religious fundamentalism and conservative politics that made open discussion of "sex variants" all but impossible in English-language cultures did not eventuate in Japan. Since Japan lacked the various sodomy laws that were used in most western societies to target homosexuals and cross-dressers, criminal discourse was also largely absent in these discussions. Consequently, there was no equivalent in Japan to the American discourse in the 1950s about the "homosexual menace" described by D'Emilio (1992), nor were there any antihomosexual purges, such as those staged by Senator McCarthy. Indeed, many writers asked for increased understanding and tolerance of a wide range of sexual behaviors, including male homosexuality (Ōta 1957: 420–1; Honshi 1954: 98; Ōgiya 1953: 160).

The range of topics covered by the perverse press, the diverse subject positions to which it gave voice and the indeterminate nature of the "experts" who wrote for a general audience of "cultured persons" constituted a very different rhetorical space for the discussion of sexual variety than existed in contemporary anglophone cultures. Regarding the latter, Eve Sedgwick comments,

> It is a rather amazing fact that, of the very many dimensions along which the genital activity of one person can be differentiated from that of another . . . precisely one, the gender of object choice, emerged from the turn of the [twentieth] century, and has remained as *the* dimension denoted by the now ubiquitous category of "sexual orientation." (1990: 8; emphasis in the original)

Sedgwick points out that given the vast proliferation of deviant sexualities circulating at the fin de siècle, it was by no means obvious that the category "the homosexual" would crystallize as the most prominent signifier of "sexual orientation" throughout anglophone societies during the twentieth century. To the extent that same-sex object choice was not the defining characteristic of queer desire in the perverse press, Japan's immediate postwar sexual culture was in some ways closer to the polymorphous perversity of Victorian London than to contemporary New York. Indeed, the topic of the mania magazines—*hentai seiyoku* (queer or perverse desire)—constituted a perverse paradigm that far exceeded homosexuality. No category as reductive as the English term "the homosexual," which in the anglophone context was increasingly understood as akin to an ethnic identity, was to emerge in Japan during this period. Postwar Japanese homosexual identities must accordingly be discussed in the plural.

MALE HOMOSEXUAL CATEGORIES

The perverse press offered thousands of articles, readers' letters and news items relating to homosexual practices, categories and identities in the immediate postwar period as well as a host of photographs and illustrations of a homoerotic nature. It is clear from these sources that at this time male homosexuality was not clearly differentiated from cross-dressing and transgenderism. Similar conflations were also apparent in anglophone discussions of "sexual inversion," early twentieth-century paradigms of homosexuality having been characterized by a "camp" culture that involved feminine performances known as "swish" and "drag" (Levine 1998: 22; Newton 1979). At this time effeminate homosexual men known as "faeries" sought out sex with straight-identified, masculine men referred to as "trade." However, the postwar emergence of the "gay man" in America was distinguished by a gradual movement away from the camp model toward the masculinization of both partners (Chauncey 1994: 358; Humphreys 1971), culminating in the gay-clone culture of the 1970s (Levine 1998). Several developments delayed this process of masculinization in Japan, the most important of them the long tradition and widespread popularity of transgender entertainers (and their associated trade of prostitution).

According to reports in the perverse press, the most visible homosexual category to appear immediately after the war was the *danshō,* or cross-dressing male prostitute, who adopted a style similar to the female-role performers of the kabuki, the *onnagata*. However, the most common term for such "passive" male homosexuals was *okama,* a slang term for the buttocks (and thereby an allusion to anal sex), which can be traced back to the Tokugawa period (Pflugfelder 1999: 323) and that is still used today to refer to homosexuals and other males who behave effeminately (McLelland 2000a: 8). Kabiya, for instance, notes, "When ordinary people speak about homosexuals in general, they refer to them as *okama*" (discussion cited in Ōta 1957: 421; see also S. Tanaka 1954: 19). In press reports, *okama* and *danshō* were often used interchangeably—*rubi* (superscripts used to aid pronunciation) being printed alongside the characters for *danshō* to indicate that the term is to be read *okama*.[17]

An incident that took place on the evening of 22 November 1947 resulted in the national exposure of the *danshō* subculture. That night a squad of policemen accompanied by journalists and photographers, sweeping through Tokyo's Ueno Park in an attempt to clear it of prostitutes and indigent youths, came upon a gathering of *danshō*. Angered by the intrusion and by a photographer's flashbulb, the *danshō* started a riot, which resulted in five arrests. The next morning's *Mainichi* newspaper featured headline coverage of the incident, complete with photographs, leading to a plethora of other articles.

A vivid account of this subculture is given in the novel *Danshō no mori* (Grove of male prostitutes), published in 1949 by Sumi Tatsuya. He describes a small scene for male sex workers who cross-dressed in traditional women's kimonos in Ueno Park. Ueno, like its close neighbor Asakusa, had long been a center for the sex trade, given its proximity to Yoshiwara, the traditional pleasure quarters of old Edo. Ueno was also the main rail terminal for trains serving the north of Japan, and immediately after the war it became a temporary home for people being repatriated from overseas to the provinces or returning to Tokyo from the countryside, where they had fled to avoid the air raids during the closing months of the war. While extreme poverty among this population no doubt drove many women and some men to prostitution in an effort to survive, it seems that Ueno had long been a site of male prostitution.

Sumi had himself conducted research among this underground population in preparation for his book, and its publication was received with interest by the mainstream press. For instance, the arts magazine *Bungei yomimono* (Arts reading matter) sent an investigative reporter and photographer to Ueno to document the lives of its *danshō;* it published a special report, complete with 15 photographs, in its February edition of 1949. However, general lawlessness and other problems caused by such a large concentration of indigent people resulted in heightened police surveillance of the area (Fushimi 2002: 208–9), and many *danshō* moved on to the red-light districts of Shimbashi and Shinjuku, as well as behind the kabuki theater in Ginza—another site with a long history of homosexual prostitution (Furukawa 1994: 106). Yet Ueno clearly remained an important area for *danshō;* Tomita (1958: 66) reports encountering there in the late 1950s male prostitutes who were still dressing in the traditional women's kimono, suggesting that police surveillance was intermittent.[18]

The magazines report several reasons for an apparent "boom" in male prostitution, the main one being that many men had been introduced to homosexual sex and developed a liking for it while serving in the army. It was also noted that some demobilized men, having lost contact with their families during the war and now living in a state of social confusion and poverty, were turning to prostitution to survive. Indeed, Sumi suggested that transgender prostitution was a characteristic of "defeated nations" (1949: 216).[19] Even after the occupation had ended and the economic situation had stabilized somewhat, media reports continued to associate male prostitution with low educational background and economic privation, with some men undertaking menial work (dressed as men) during the day and supplementing their income by working as *danshō* during the evening. In the early '50s there was apparently a "*danshō* school" in Ueno where experienced cross-dressers taught younger men how to dress, apply makeup and deport themselves like women (*Fūzoku kagaku* 1954a: 111).

However, men who prostituted themselves were considered not to do so out of poverty alone. Unlike the premodern paradigm of transvestite prostitution associated with the *onnagata* of the kabuki theater, contemporary *danshō* were thought to have a predilection for passive anal sex, a predilection that, although they may have been introduced to it while in the army, was part of their psychosocial makeup. Postwar writers largely followed paradigms established by the sexological writers of the Taisho period who had attempted to place the sexually perverse into distinct taxonomic categories based upon their supposed psychological or physiological constitutions. The category most commonly used to describe postwar *danshō* was "urning" *(ūruningu)*, a sexological term that had been devised by German sexologist and homosexual Karl Ulrichs (1825–1895) to designate a "female soul in a male body" and had achieved widespread currency in prewar sexological writings. Urning were considered to have womanlike bodies, small genitalia and an "innate" *(sententeki)* desire for passive anal sex that led them to turn to prostitution as a way of fulfilling their desires as well as earning a living.[20] They chose to practice as *transgendered* prostitutes because their constitution meant that they were already womanlike and they had a predisposition toward narcissism *(narushishizumu)* and took delight in dressing and making up like women. Urning were therefore quite distinct from the adult males who had taken on the "active" role in the previous *nanshoku* code. Their ideal sexual partners were not young *chigo* or slim, androgynous youths but "sportsmen, muscled laborers, soldiers and such like" (*Fūzoku zōshi* 1954: 103).

Since this system was based on a supposed heterosexual typology whereby opposites attract, the customers of the *danshō* were thought to be different sexual "types," referred to as *"pede"* or *"pederasuto"* (from pederast), terms that in the 1950s Japanese context signified men interested in transgendered as well as younger men. *Pede* were thought to have "acquired" *(kōtenteki)* homosexual interests, either during the war when the lack of female company resulted in older soldiers courting younger recruits or through disappointment in previous relations with biological women, and were considered to be the "active" partners in sex (Kabiya 1953a: 26–30; Shibukawa 1953: 71–7).[21] However, despite the strong association between male prostitution and effeminacy, there were male prostitutes who failed to conform to this system and dressed in "smart male clothes"; referred to as *dondengaeshi*, or "reversibles," they were considered able to go either way (Miyazono 1953: 79).

Ruth Benedict, in *The Chrysanthemum and the Sword*, her 1946 study of "Japanese patterns of culture" based on interviews with Japanese resident in America, offers one paragraph on Japanese attitudes toward homosexuality. Despite the many problems with this study (Benedict had never visited Japan and spoke no Japanese), her observations are intriguing. She comments that "the Japanese are especially shocked at adult passive homosexuals in the States," since "adult men in Japan . . . seek out boy partners" (1946: 188). Certainly, examples discussed in the previous chapter show that the dominant paradigm for sexual interaction between males in the first decades of the twentieth century was still strictly age related, with the older partner (if only by a few years) taking on the active role. "Boy love," or *shōnen'ai*, continued to be an important part of homosexual culture in Japan after the war, with a great many articles in the perverse press dedicated to the topic,[22] and boy love is still highlighted in Japanese gay magazines today to an extent unimaginable in anglophone gay cultures, which are keen to distance themselves from what could be perceived as pedophilia (McLelland 2000a: 138). However, numerous sources in the perverse magazines indicate that ideology aside, in actual practice there was no neat division between the "passive" prostitutes and their "active" clients. While freely acknowledging that some clients asked to be penetrated, this situation does seem to have been regarded as anomalous. Writers tried to maintain the integrity of the classificatory system by, for instance, suggesting that such clients suffered from "penis envy" *(fuarusu naido)*,[23] whereas the *danshō* who offered this service had both large penises and strong exhibitionist streaks (Honshi 1954: 95).

The frequent insistence on the *danshō*'s "passive" sexual nature was also confused by reports that some were heterosexually married, just as many kabuki *onnagata* had been (Honshi 1954: 93).[24] Indeed, one source (Kogure 1952: 30) refers to *okama* (in this article used interchangeably with *danshō*) who in their argot were termed *donten* (a contraction of *dondengaeshi*), who "become partners for both men and women." As Kabiya suggests, some *okama/danshō* were still available for assignations with women, just as their prewar counterparts the *onnagata* and *kagema* had been, although the number of women seeking their services was reportedly few (1954c: 143). One late 1940s account reputedly written by a *danshō* mentions that he was approached by a middle-aged female customer precisely because he resembled an *onnagata* with whom she had been infatuated in her youth. He reported that her lovemaking that night was "absolutely passionate" (Hirano 1947: 146). Other reports mention that Ishikawa Miyoshi, an *onnagata* who performed in a theater in Ueno, was a famous seducer of women, his lovers ranging from teenage girls to widows in their sixties (Misushu 1951). This suggests that popular sexological theories that constantly mixed up same-sex desire and transgenderism, diagnosing both as constitutional anomalies, were often undermined by actual practice, which could not be contained by neat systems.

In the United States at this time, there is evidence that an increasing number of gender-normative, masculine-identified men were entering into relationships with each other—relationships not structured according to the masculine and feminine gender roles that had been common earlier in the century. Chauncey notes how in the postwar period

> the transformation in gay culture suggested by the ascendancy of *gay* was closely tied to the masculinization of that culture. . . . Increasing numbers of conventionally masculine men identified themselves as gay, in part, because doing so no longer seemed to require the renunciation of their masculine identities. (1994: 358)

In Japan a similar process was taking place. Kabiya, for instance, notes how it was usually assumed that "sexual union" between homosexuals *(sodomia dōshi)* required that one partner take on the male role while the other took on the female. This had always been the pattern in Japan (at least in terms of representation), with adult males taking on the "active" role in relation to boy and transgender partners. As described in the previous chapter, liaisons between schoolboys in the prewar period also followed this pattern, with the older partner (if only by a few years) penetrating the younger. In the case of same-age cohorts, anal sex was avoided in favor of the more mutual practice of intercourse between the thighs. However, Kabiya notes that homosexual partners were increasingly swapping roles in the course of lovemaking—a point that he believes distinguishes homosexuality from heterosexuality *(hetero sekushuarite)*, since he assumed that men and women must maintain their "active" and "passive" roles until orgasm (1953b: 268). Other commentators too pointed to a change in the sexual practices between men in the postwar period, with anal sex gradually being replaced by fellatio and mutual masturbation. The master of Yakyoku, one of Tokyo's earliest gay bars, noted that "after the war kissing and fellatio have become extremely widespread" (*Fūzoku zōshi* 1953a: 170); sex critic Takahashi Tetsu (1954: 76) pointed out that "in this world, fellatio is said to be extremely popular." If true, this indicates a significant shift, given the almost total lack of reference to fellatio between men in Tokugawa literature (Leupp 1995: 191).

However, despite this growing awareness that male homosexuality was not necessarily role based as it had been in the traditional *nanshoku* system, there were cultural reasons why in the first postwar decades male homosexuality remained strongly associated with both transgenerational and transgender paradigms in the public imagination. One major reason is that the concept of *gei* (gay), although introduced into Japan during the occupation, developed along a quite different trajectory from its English homophone.

From the early 1950s, the perverse magazines began to interest themselves in a new form of homosexual expression—the *gei bōi* (gay boy)—whose place of work was not the streets but the bars. The early 1950s had seen the development of new American-style bars quite unlike those that had existed before the war. Although some of the cafés of the Taisho period had been staffed by waitresses who were available for assignations with the customers (Garon 1997: 107), prostitution had been restricted to officially licensed brothels, which provided girls and rented rooms. During the Edo period, such places had also existed for the hiring of male prostitutes; Furukawa suggests that these institutions continued into the Taisho period, albeit in a less overt fashion (1994: 107). However, in the run-up to the war, male prostitution had increasingly gone underground and tended to take place outdoors in designated cruising areas—such as Ueno Park, frequented by the *danshō*—or in certain cinemas, theaters and milk halls in the major cities (Fushimi 2002: 304; Fujii 1953).

At the beginning of the occupation, the old-style brothel system was reformed, but not in line with western notions of sexual propriety. Indeed, "Japanese political culture continued to tolerate extramarital liaisons with prostitutes, geisha, and mistresses at the highest levels of power" (Garon 1997: 199). Prostitution, which had been institutionalized in Japan for centuries, was allowed to continue, albeit in a less overt manner—brothels were renamed "special bars and restaurants," licensed quarters became "special zones regulated by the police" and prostitutes were termed "entertainers" (Garon 1997: 198). New kinds of establishment sprang up where "bar girls" entertained occupation troops in a variety of bars, cabarets and dance halls. As well as earning money by selling their services direct to the clients, bar girls could also receive commissions from the club owners by encouraging the customers to run up large tabs (de Vos 1973: 271).

Similar, though smaller, establishments serving a clientele of homosexual men also began to appear soon after the war's end. One of the earliest, Yakyoku (Nocturne), in Shinjuku, was reportedly opened as early as 1946 and was much frequented by foreigners (Kabiya 1962f: 102–3; Fujii 1953: 189; *Fūzoku zōshi* 1953a). Writing in *Fūzoku kitan*'s regular "Homo no mado" (Homos' window) column, Kabiya (1962a: 146) gives an account of the emergence of the terms *gei bōi* (gay boy) and *gei bā* (gay bar). Kabiya Kazuhiko had been a contributor to the prewar sexology magazines, specializing in male homosexuality, and he continued to publish numerous firsthand accounts about Tokyo's developing postwar homosexual scene in the perverse press. According to Kabiya, *gei bōi* was first used by homosexual *(danshoku aikōsha)* members of the occupation forces to refer to their young Japanese partners. In the immediate postwar period, the small bars where young Japanese men went to meet potential partners or clients had been referred to as *danshoku kissaten* (coffee shops) or *sakaba* (drinking spots), but in 1952 a staff member of a Shinjuku *danshoku* bar named Adonis who disliked these old-fashioned designations began to refer to his establishment as a *gei bā* (gay bar). The term quickly caught on and by the mid-1950s was widely used, even in the mainstream press. While the earliest bars seem to have been more informal, by the early 1950s the bars were staffed by between three and seven professional hosts, known as *gei bōi,* who served drinks and provided conversation for customers, often making themselves available for after-hours assignations (Ōta 1957: 306–10).

Like the *danshō, gei bōi* were effeminate in appearance, but they did not completely cross-dress, preferring to wear makeup and a few items of western women's clothing (Tomita 1958: 181–4). The majority of bar owners, on the other hand, who preferred to be called "mama" rather than the more conventional "master" (Ōta 1957: 307; Kabiya 1955), were liable to style themselves as *onnagata,* and some had performed as *onnagata* in their youth (XYZ 1955: 76). While the *mama-san* tended to be older men, the majority of *bōi* were in their late teens to mid-twenties. Ōta does mention that the *bōi* were occasionally boys in name only, that some bars located in Asakusa specialized in "old boys" whose age was around 40, but this was considered unusual, since *gei bōi* were thought to lose their attractiveness by age 25 or 26. Accordingly, some *mama-san* encouraged boys in their employ to invest their savings productively and study in their spare time so as to be able to support themselves after their looks had faded (Kabiya 1955).

The majority of *gei bōi* were, like the *danshō,* believed to be "urning" and thereby considered to have a "passive" predisposition toward feminine behavior that resulted in the desire both to cross-dress and to participate in sexual interaction with gender-normative men (Honshi 1954: 96–7). In the bar world these boys were referred to as *onēsan,* or "big sisters." However, it was also widely acknowledged that some "semiprofessional" *bōi* also worked in the bar world and were prepared to take either active or passive roles with male partners for money. This raises the question how the male partners of *danshō* and *gei bōi* were conceptualized. Since the *danshō* had been street prostitutes, offering quick sex in dark alleys, parks and temple and shrine precincts, it is likely that some of their clients had mistaken them for biological women. Indeed, discussing their experience in a magazine interview in 1949, three *danshō* explained that they always passed as real women and, as a result, never slept while with customers in hotel rooms lest their biological sex be inadvertently revealed (*OK erosu ando suriru* 1949). Somewhat later, Matsuba Yukari, writing of her experience as a part-time cross-dressing prostitute in the early 1960s, mentions that she was often unsure whether her clients understood that she was male; in order to avoid discovery, she preferred to take drunken clients, who were less likely to have their wits about them (Sugiura 2001: 31). This was a wise precaution; it was not unknown for *danshō* to be murdered by clients who had discovered their actual sex (Narumi 1951: 97). However, men who sought out sexual adventures in areas that, like Ueno Park, were well-known cruising sites for *danshō* were much more likely to be consciously on the lookout for a transgender partner. Also, the fact that *gei bōi* worked out of bars that capitalized on their effeminate mannerisms meant that there was little chance of their clients being unaware of their biological sex.

Since both *danshō* and *gei bōi* were viewed as occupational categories, their male partners were spoken of as "customers" *(kyaku)*. The assumption that the customers would be the "top" in any sexual interaction was signified by the use of the term *tachi* (literally a sword bearer but also used to refer to the leading male role in the kabuki theater). The *tachi* was the "masculine" partner in an essentially gendered relationship, where the *gei bōi* took on the role of a woman. However, a distinction was made between types of "top." Men who restricted their sexual activities to biological women were termed *jun tachi*, or "pure tops," signifying that men who sought out *gei bōi* as partners were to some degree less manly than men who sought out women. It was also acknowledged that there were many urning among the customers who sought attention from the *donten*, or "reversible" boys.

Much of the discussion about male homosexuality in the perverse press concerned conspicuous categories like *danshō* and *gei bōi*, which, because they operated in the commercial bar and entertainment world, are best understood as professional designations as much as sites of identity. As outlined above, the commercial scene had developed a vocabulary for describing the types of men who frequented the bars as well as of customers who purchased the services of professional homosexuals. However, how were men who avoided the bar scene, preferring to seek out homosexual interactions in other ways, described, and how did they conceive of themselves?

Contemporary texts provide evidence that opportunities for contracting informal homosexual liaisons were widespread in postwar Japan, not just in Tokyo but in other major cities such as Osaka and Kyoto as well (Fujii 1953). Although its origins are obscure, the still-current term *hattenba*, or "development spot," was already being used in postwar writing to describe places where homosexual activity took place. Certain bars, cinemas and theaters became known as places where homosexual interaction might "develop" (Ōta 1957: 418; Fujii 1953). These spots also included the parks mentioned above, as well as public conveniences, which were referred to in homosexual argot as *jimusho*, or "offices." Mishima Yukio, in his novel *Kinjiki* (Forbidden colors), serialized in the early '50s, about the postwar homosexual subculture, describes one such meeting place:

> He entered the dim, clammy lamplight of the rest room, and saw what is called an "office" among the fellowship. (There are four or five such important places in Tokyo.) It was an office where the tacit procedure is based on winks instead of documents, tiny gestures instead of print, code communication in place of a telephone. (1968: 55)

The perverse magazines facilitated interaction between men with homosexual interests by describing these places and even providing maps to find them, as well as offering advice on how to understand the codes of behavior that applied there (see for example Kabiya 1955; 1954a; 1954b). This advice was often couched in terms of empirical observation, describing how men with the "same intent" *(dōshi)*—or perhaps better, "kindred souls"—made themselves recognizable to each other.[25] These descriptions were obviously useful to men hoping to seek out homosexual interactions, and they anticipated the *hattenba* guides that were to become a staple of Japan's commercial gay press in the 1970s.

A variety of designations were used by men who wrote in the perverse press about their own same-sex experiences. These include the neologism *danshokuKA,* which conjoins an alternative reading of the traditional characters *nanshoku* (male-male eroticism) and the nominalizing suffix *ka* or "ist"—hence *danshoku*-ist, or "practitioner of *danshoku*." This term was widely used; it was the designation preferred by Mishima in *Kinjiki*. Mishima, reputed to be a habitué of the postwar gay bars, was later to write appreciatively of Japan's lost tradition of *nanshoku* (Mishima 1977); he was perhaps hoping, by retaining this term, to establish a link with previous sensibilities. Certainly, his depiction of the modern, foreign "gay" subculture of the U.S. occupation is extremely unattractive.

Danshoku was also variously neologized as *danshokuSHA,* or *danshoku*-person, and less frequently, as *danshokuTŌ*, or "*danshoku*-clique," both of which might suggest that those involved in *danshoku*, whatever their level or mode of participation, were seen as distinct types of persons. However, the fact that some writers also spoke of *danshoku aikōsha* ("lovers," or "admirers," of *danshoku*) harks back to the Edo-period term *nanshoku-zuki,* or "lover of *nanshoku*," *zuki* being an alternative reading of the character *kō* (meaning to like or love), an echo in turn from a previous era.

Another, more colorful, term widely used in the immediate postwar years was *sodomia,* from the English "sodomite" (or perhaps "sodomy"), which derived from the Old Testament story of the destruction of the cities of Sodom and Gomorrah, supposedly on account of the poor sexual etiquette of their populations. Ōta (1957: 26) explains that although in English and French sodomy was used to refer to male homosexuals, in German, the language most prevalent in Japanese prewar discussion, it was used more specifically to relate to anal sex (with either gender), which explains the term's relative lack of currency in the prewar period.

In the postwar magazines, *sodomia* did not refer to anal sex but described male homosexuality in general and could also be used as a designation for individual homosexuals. Hence "*Sodomia wa anata no tonari ni iru*," the title of an article in the March 1954 edition of *Fūzoku kagaku* (Furuta 1954: 160–5), could be translated as either "Homosexuality is next to you" or "Homosexuals are next to you." That the term was sometimes used as a self-designation is illustrated by a letter writer in the February

1954 issue who introduces himself as a 35-year-old "homosexual" *(sodomiya)*—though his spelling of the term as *sodomiYA* is nonstandard. However, other writers do not use the term as a noun but as an adjective, speaking of their *sodomia* "interests" *(shumi)* or their *sodomii* "relations" *(kankei)*.[26] *Sodomia* was also used as a group designation or form of address, as in *"sodomia no minna san,"* or "all you homosexuals," and it could also be conceived of as a state into which one could enter, as in *"sodomia ni naru"* ("become sodomitical").

Sodomia was the term chosen by *Fūzoku zōshi* as the title of its regular correspondence column, *Sodomia tsūshin,* which featured letters from homosexual men. *Sodomia* was also commonly used when a comparison or contrast with female homosexuality was being made, the latter being referred to as *resubosu* (or Lesbos), from the Greek island associated with Sappho, the ancient Greek poet, whose surviving verse contains many stanzas celebrating the beauty of girls. *Fūzoku zōshi* also ran a correspondence column for women entitled *Resubosu tsūshin,* both columns being described as "salon for persons who love the same sex *(dōsei wo ai suru kata)* or persons interested in same-sex love *(dōseiai)*." The fact that *sodomia* was paired with *resubosu* in this way suggests that it would be wrong to translate the term as "sodomite," which was at this time still a criminal category in most legal codes deriving from English law. In the Japanese case, both *sodomia* and *resubosu* were seen rather as colorful classical allusions and consequently did not carry the weight of centuries of legal and religious stigmatization that clung to the English terms.

The English term "homosexual" was also widely used in transliterated form as *homosekusharu,* often abbreviated *homo.* The Japanese translation of homosexual into kanji, *dōseiai* (literally "same-sex love"), also appears in the postwar publications, often conjoined with the suffix *-sha,* or "person." However, *dōseiai* frequently appears with the superscript *homo.* Since the term *gei bōi* had strong transgender connotations, *homo,* used as an alternative reading for the characters *dōseiai,* or written separately in the katakana script for foreign loanwords, came to be the most common designation for all men engaged in same-sex sexual activity, and it was until about 1955 sometimes used to describe homosexual women, as in the term *josei no homo,* or "female homos."

Kabiya, writing in Ōta (1957: 311), points out that while *homo* was widespread in the 1950s it was not much used by the clientele of the *gei bā,* who tended to refer to each other in terms of sexual "type." In the argot of the period these types included *tachi,* or "tops"; *onē* (from *onēsan,* or big sister) for effeminate men; *donten,* or the "reversible" boys, who serviced both men and women; *chigoka,*[27] or older men interested in youths; *jibika,*[28] who preferred older partners; and *ritsu,*[29] or "gold diggers," who were in search of sponsors. However, *homo* did become much more widespread as a designation, especially from the early 1960s, when media interest in the *gei bōi* phenomenon resulted in a diversification in the clientele for *gei bā*. From this time onward, *homo bā* was used to designate bars that catered exclusively to homosexual men, and *homo* came to designate men with homosexual tastes but who were otherwise gender-normative.

In the immediate postwar period it is impossible to discern a pattern in the usage of these terms, since they are often used interchangeably in the same discussion. For instance, the January 1954 edition of *Fūzoku zōshi* contains an article by Kabiya (1954a) entitled *"Danshoku kissaten,"* or *danshoku* "coffee shops," which introduces some of the "brand-new homosexual *(sodomia)* meeting places" where both "homo" *(homo)* and "non-homo" *(homo denai)* customers can be found (usually gathering in different parts of the same establishment). Kabiya frequently switches between terms, speaking of "bars for homosexuals," where the designation is *sodomia;* mentioning also *danshokusha,* in which the suffix *-sha,* or "person," is conjoined with *danshoku,* hence "male-male eroticism persons"; and elsewhere using *homo.*

As mentioned, the ability of the Japanese written language to use characters signifying a certain meaning alongside a superscript designating a nonstandard pronunciation is a cause of confusion. While "traditional" terms such as *danshoku* lived on well into the postwar period, by that time the meaning of these terms had obviously shifted. The nontraditional use of nominalizing suffixes such as *-ka* (-ist) or *-sha* (-person), now used to designate specific types of sexual being, were employed alongside *rubi* to suggest new readings of old terms. In the August 1953 edition of *Fūzoku kagaku,* for instance, *danshoku* appears with the reading *sodomia* printed alongside.[30] What nuance this linguistic play added to these terms, or if such nuances were understood in the same way by all readers, is very difficult to discern.

Indeed, the instability of the categories makes it impossible to talk about a singular emerging "homosexual identity" in postwar Japan, especially since there was such a strong division between commercial identities represented by the *danshō* and *gei bōi* and the wider world of *homo* or *sodomia*—that is, men who participated in Japan's rapidly expanding homosexual scene as customers, or who avoided the scene altogether, preferring to make assignations with other gender-normative men. This is perhaps why, when *Fūzoku kagaku* established a social club for men interested in homosexuality in 1954,[31] it avoided nominalization altogether, instead advertising for "men with absolutely no feelings for women." Men who wrote letters to the magazines also often avoided the use of these categories, instead choosing to define themselves in terms of their lack of interest in women. One man seeking a partner writes to the September issue of *Fūzoku zōshi,* "Although I'm a 27-year-old man, I have no interest whatsoever in the opposite sex." These strategies echo the designation *onnagirai*, or "woman hater," a term from the older *nanshoku* code, which grouped same-sex-desiring men together not because of their love for boys but because of their antipathy toward women.

FEMALE HOMOSEXUAL CATEGORIES

While the main focus of the perverse press was upon the male subject and his desires, whether heterosexually oriented (as in discussions of sadomasochism, fetishism, masturbation and sex techniques) or homosexually oriented (as in the many articles on transgender prostitution and meeting places for homosexual men), women's sexuality was not overlooked entirely. Indeed, compared with prewar writing, which tended to deny women's sexual agency, the postwar press recognized that women were as liable to sexual perversity as were men, although the framework within which women's same-sex love was discussed was unrelentingly "masculinist." That is, it was dependent upon categories derived from male-male paradigms by a professional body of male experts (Blackwood and Wieringa 1999: 44–5).

Yet despite the fact that there were fewer articles discussing female same-sex sexuality, "Lesbos love" *(resubosu ai)* was a subgenre of considerable extent, created by writers using both male and female pen names. Some of these writers, at least, attempted to approach the subject of women's same-sex love seriously, albeit within the masculinist parameters available at the time, whereas others produced works of fiction quite as prurient as those seen in the U.S. genre of lesbian pulp, which also sprang up after the war (Zimet 1999). In these graphically illustrated stories, the "sadistic" lesbian was a figure that evoked fascination in both men and women alike. Under titles such as "Under my elder sister's whip" (Narushima 1954) and "Torture delicate skin" (Kita 1953), the purportedly female writers described sadomasochistic scenarios with relish.

Despite the existence of these documents, searching for actual women's experience in the postwar period is rendered problematic by the fact that many heterosexual men were interested in fantasizing about lesbianism; it is difficult to distinguish between fantasy writing in which lesbian desire was scripted (either by male or female writers) so as to appeal to a heterosexual male readership and that which was written by women themselves who experienced same-sex desire and wrote to the magazines in the hope of making contact with other women. Certainly, by the mid-1950s *Kitan kurabu* was regularly featuring stories about lesbian love that were scripted in terms of male fantasy, as is suggested by the illustrations of high-school girls dressed in their sailor-suit blouses (Hanamura 1954)

Figure 2.4 Illustration for Kita's story "Torture delicate skin." ***Fūzoku zōshi*** **(Sex-customs storybook), August 1953**

and the "perverse" nature of some of the articles, such as "Lesbos and enemas" (Hamura 1955). Indeed, by the late 1950s lesbianism had become a central fantasy trope in male pornography and was closely associated with sadomasochism, an association that has been maintained till the present day (see figure 2.4).

However, in the early postwar years there does appear to have been some attempt to include women's same-sex experiences and perspectives in the perverse press. In the early 1950s, when men's homosexual desire was spoken of as *"sodomia"* (Sodom), mention was often made of the female equivalent, referred to as *"resubosu"* (Lesbos). Yet although men who engaged in the world of Sodom were described by a variety of labels—such as *danshō, okama, gei, onē, donten* or *tachi,* depending upon their sexual roles—women were defined by a narrower range of concepts, sometimes being referred to solely as "female homos" *(josei no homo).* This is not surprising given the extremely restricted paradigms within which women's sexuality had been discussed in prewar literature. As outlined in chapter 1, elite women had been considered equipped with maternal instincts, and it was both their duty and their destiny to give birth to new citizens of the empire; if from poor backgrounds or subject nations, women were conceived as instruments through which men could evacuate their excess and potentially troublesome desires. The notion that women had autonomous sexual desires or that they might prefer to express themselves "carnally" with other women was not widely discussed.

The perverse press, however, entertained both these possibilities. An unsigned article in the December 1953 issue of *Fūzoku zōshi* entitled "Various phases of Lesbos love," for instance, mentioned that *resubosu* ranged from such "insignificant" things as exchanges of love letters between schoolgirls to more serious matters "which would make men blush," going on to describe the various ways in which women had historically pleasured themselves and each other, deriving examples from ancient Greece, Muromachi-period Japan and Africa (*Fūzoku zōshi* 1953b: 299).

As well as providing examples of Lesbos love, analysts were also keen to offer explanations of its genesis. Some writers followed sexologists like Krafft-Ebing, who argued that "masculinized" women with small breasts, little subcutaneous fat and narrow pelvises and who spoke with "sonorous voices" were likely candidates for same-sex love (QR 1954). However, in line with prewar discussion of young women's sentimental same-sex relationships (Wu 2002), homosexual feelings were more often understood to be situational, likely to occur in all-female environments, such as girls' schools and dormitories for nurses and female factory workers (Ōta 1957: 398; QR 1954). These desires were not considered permanent but something that would be outgrown once the women married.

The conflation of these two lines of thought about the origin of "Lesbos love" is put to considerable (but probably unintended) comic effect in an unsigned article in the September 1954 edition of *Fūzoku kagaku*, purporting to be a conversation between an 18-year-old high-school girl and her home tutor (*Fūzoku kagaku* 1954b). The young woman confesses that the reason she has been spending so much time away from home is, as her tutor suspects, because she has taken a lover. Her tutor asks what kind of man he is, to which she replies "A man? What are you talking about?" The conversation continues:

> Tutor: I'm shocked. Do you mean to say the partner you are hot for is of the same sex? In other words are you saying it's a matter of lesbianism *(resubosu)?*
>
> Girl: That's right, so you needn't worry.
>
> Tutor: Not at all. Hearing that it is lesbianism makes me worry all the more. . . . Getting involved in homosexuality *(dōseiai)* is unnatural and abnormal.
>
> Girl: You say it's abnormal?
>
> Tutor: . . . Yes, don't you know the cause of lesbianism? It became popular in the shogun's harem. It was a sexual outlet for women in a place where

there was only one sex. . . . Nowadays it happens in factory dormitories and women's prisons.

Girl: Oh, how unpleasant!

The conversation proceeds with the young woman telling her tutor more about her lover, a 27-year-old schoolteacher. The teacher had run away from her husband on her wedding night and was now living in a nearby boarding house so that the two could spend more time together. The tutor asks, "Is this teacher by any chance on the tall side, muscular, with small breasts and hips and does she speak in a sonorous voice?" To which the girl replies "Yes, that's absolutely right, it sounds as if you've met her!" The tutor then goes on to explain that the girl's teacher is clearly a member of the "intermediate sex" *(chūsei)* but that the girl herself is simply going through a phase of "spiritual" *(seishinteki)* love directed toward the more masculine elements of an older woman, a phase that she will outgrow. His concluding words are, "Once your passion for this teacher has cooled, you ought next to exert yourself wholeheartedly and discover the good things about men."

This article suggests that there are two modes of female same-sex love, one innate and the other acquired. In the case of the masculine teacher, identified as a member of the "intermediate sex," homosexual attraction seems to be an inborn state, whereas her young, feminine lover is understood as responding to the charms of a masculine-acting woman. In the girl's case it is the man she discerns in the woman that is the real object of her affection; her feelings represent a preliminary kind of love, one that will soon be replaced by a more mature attraction to men. The conceptual framework offered for understanding female same-sex love is consequently both minoritizing (for masculine women) and universalizing (for their feminine partners). While only a small percentage of women, those described as of the "intermediate sex," were considered to be innately perverse, any feminine young woman, given the right circumstances, was thought liable to fall for a masculine-acting female partner. This tidy conceptual division of same-sex-desiring women into masculine and feminine, of course, mirrors similar divisions made between types of homosexual men, yet, as with love between men, in other contexts the distinction proves difficult to maintain.

While the articles described above were most likely written by men or women who aimed at attracting an audience primarily of men, some discussions of Lesbos love do claim to be based on the experience of actual women. For instance, from its April issue of 1953, *Fūzoku zōshi* began an intermittent column entitled "Lesbos Communication" *(Resubosu tsūshin)*, which was described as "A secret love salon for women only." While the column was headed by a person using the name Sonomura Keiko, a woman's name, the actual gender of the writer is probably in question, since Keiko's eager rhapsodizing about the beauty of women's bodies seems suspiciously close to male fantasies of lesbian desire. For instance, she describes herself as a "man hater" *(otokogirai)* because of the manner in which "bestial" men "take beautiful young women by force" and, unlike Keiko herself, pay no heed to the natural delicacy of "young virgins." Keiko is adamant that her caresses are different from those of men and that only under her ministrations can tender maidens reach satisfaction (Sonomura 1953a).

There are also other problems with Keiko's personality as it is expressed in her column, particularly her use of language that is rather chatty in tone and employs a substantial number of feminine markers, such as the sentence finals *"wa," "no"* and *"kashira."* This gives the impression that the writer is self-consciously attempting to create the persona of a woman rather than expressing the sensibility of an actual woman. In several instances Keiko's tone is distinctly coquettish, but while not wanting to deny that communication between lesbians, like that of gay men, can be camp and playful, she seems to be playing to male and not female fantasies. For instance, in her September 1953 column Keiko responds to various queries supposedly sent in by readers (although the letters themselves are not reproduced). Her response to "A-*sama*" seems sexually provocative and tailored to stimulate the prurient interest of men:

> Asking me such a question is in really bad taste. It's embarrassing. I don't know what to say. I've never seen that kind of thing. I don't use them. They're scary. You've destroyed my peace of mind. If I were to explain that kind of thing to a young girl, then afterwards I'd reproach myself. Why is it that men have interest in such things I wonder? (Sonomura 1953b: 123)

Quite what Keiko's interlocutor had in mind is left up to the imagination of the reader.

It is also not possible to identify the persona of Keiko as that of "a lesbian," since neither the term *resubian* nor the more common *rezubian* appears in her column and both were, in fact, rarely used in the perverse press until the early 1960s. Rather, Keiko speaks of her interest in "Lesbos love" and of her "Lesbos experiences," suggesting, it could be supposed, that she may later be redeemed for heterosexual love in a manner that would prove impossible for the "innately perverse" male homosexual. Indeed, it seems to have been widely held at this time that female homosexuality *(joshi dōseiai)* was easier to cure than the male variety, being a more "spiritual" *(seishinteki)* than "carnal" *(nikutaiteki)* desire. For instance, an advice columnist writing in *Amatoria* in 1953 advises a husband afraid that his wife may be having an affair with another woman that she can easily be "cured" if he will create a more romantic atmosphere in the home, take her on hiking trips and, most importantly, pay more attention to foreplay (Nishijima 1953).

Suspicions about the real audience for Keiko's column are also raised by an advertisement calling for correspondents. Although initially asking for letters from "women only" concerning the "delicate" feelings that women share, as well as "deeper" questions concerning physical relationships, letters are also welcomed from "men who have an interest in the love of Lesbos," letters that Keiko offers to answer. In the magazine's August 1953 column, Keiko answers one such letter. In response to an inquiry about what exactly she finds most attractive about the same sex, Keiko finds it difficult to come up with an explanation other than that "while riding in the train, when I see the nape of the neck of a young female student, I'm overcome with the desire to kiss her." The fact that in the next month's column (September 1953) Keiko elects to answer a letter from a 17-year-old high-school girl, enabling her to adopt the role of "big sister" (which in this context has erotic overtones) further fuels the suspicion that "Lesbos Communication," in this magazine at least, is being carried out between men. This impression is further heightened by an essay on "Lesbos techniques" contributed by Keiko to the Autumn 1953 special edition of *Fūzoku zōshi*, where she again chooses schoolgirls to illustrate the delights of Lesbos love. She writes, "Embracing [her partner] while sitting on her lap, red lips touch red lips; the lips of young girls exude the odor of milk." This description is immediately followed by a section on "finger play" (Sonomura 1953c: 215).

The fact that descriptions of Lesbos love in the pages of the perverse press were more than likely tailored for a male readership does not, however, mean that they were never read or enjoyed by women. Given the paucity of other contexts in which women's same-sex desire was discussed in the 1950s, many American lesbians, for instance, purchased lesbian-themed pulp novels aimed at men but "had to read between the lines and ignore the homophobic or moralistic storylines" (Zimet 1999: 21; see also Weismann and Fernie 1992).[32] However, without corroborating evidence from women who read and responded to these magazines, it is extremely difficult to know to what extent, if at all, the perverse press impacted on the lives of same-sex-desiring women in Japan.

While numerous letters from homosexual men were printed in these magazines testifying to the value of the information offered, there were far fewer letters from women reflecting on their own feelings about "Lesbos love," and what letters were published tended to be from women asking the magazine to put them in contact with like-minded women. For instance, a letter in the December 1954 edition of *Fūzoku kagaku* was published under the heading "I want female homosexuality" *(josei dōseiai hoshii)*.[33] The author, who signed herself Azamiko, asked that the magazine pay greater attention to the needs of "female homos" by including more discussion of their concerns as well as sponsoring an organization for women similar to one it had set up for male homosexuals. Some of the lesbian-themed fiction too was followed by a few brief comments purportedly from women readers. Almost without exception, these readers mention how much they enjoyed the articles and ask the magazine editors to include more. In the April 1954 edition of *Fūzoku kagaku*,[34] one woman, signing herself as Homoko (*ko* being a common character used in women's names), complains that "since you mainly print articles about perverse love among men, it seems that you think that perverse love between women is extremely rare but in fact I think that it is very common. . . . Please will the editors include many more articles about female homosexuals [*josei no homo*]." Another woman, signing herself as Hyacinth, writes in to the same edition, "I'm a 27-year-old office worker and since my girlhood have never had any interest in men . . . it seems from reading your magazine that there are a large number of articles for men with no interest in women but please consider that there are many other women like me. How about including . . . many more articles that would satisfy women like me?" In both cases responses from the editors promise to include more discussion of women's love.

There is some reason to consider such comments as genuine. The February 1955 edition of the magazine, for instance, printed another letter (Yume 1955) asking the editors to establish an "association for female homos" *(josei homo no kai)*. This does suggest there was a female readership for the magazine and that the editors made a genuine effort to respond to it by printing such letters. The (apparently female) letter writer, who signed herself Yume Miruko (Ms. Dreamer), pointed out that while numerous coffee shops and bars exist where "male homos" can meet, no such venues existed for women. Since it was difficult for women to socialize with like-minded peers, she asked the magazine to organize occasional meetings, such as trips to the "cinema, jazz clubs and hiking," that would be suitable for women in search of female partners. Unfortunately, the magazine folded soon after this letter was printed, and it is unknown whether such meetings ever eventuated.

Another article that suggests a genuine attempt on the part of the magazine's editors to engage women readers was printed in the March 1955 edition of *Fūzoku kagaku*, under the title "Female homos here we go" (Saijō 1955). The discussion was organized as a roundtable, or *zadankai*, a common academic mode of discourse in Japan, the results of which are often transcribed and published. It is considered to be a useful, relatively nonhierarchical way of approaching a topic, allowing a variety of opinions, and was to become a staple form of communication in lesbian and gay organizations of the future. The participants are identified as a male writer who is a "researcher of male homosexuality," a male chairperson representing the magazine, and three women, one identified as the madam of a bar and two as office workers.

The discussion opens with the chairperson explaining that there has been a long tradition of research into "male homos" in Japan but that the homosexual experience of women has largely been overlooked. He mentions that many women readers of the magazine had written to ask the editors to include discussion of women's homosexual experience and that other letters asking the magazine to set up a social club for female homosexuals, similar to one it had sponsored for men, had also been received. After a discussion of the contents of some of these letters, the chair moves on to discuss whether female homosexuality, like male, can be understood in terms of the "innate" and "acquired" typology discussed earlier. The chair asks the women, "Is it the case that you innately hate men?"

This rather reductive inquiry proves problematic in this instance, since the bar madam (who identifies herself as much older than the two office workers) mentions that she was brought up in a family consisting mainly of men and had at one time been married; she did not think men had any particular charm, but neither did she dislike them. However, all three women were unanimous that this "constituent" *(yōso)* of their personalities had been present in their childhood and that they did not welcome advances from men. They pointed out that women's romantic feelings for each other were not particularly unusual and that such relationships were common among all-female theater groups, students at girls' schools and among female factory workers who lived in on-site dormitories, as well as among women working in the entertainment trade. The chair agreed that "as you'd expect, female homos are by no means uncommon," citing an incident he had witnessed late at night, on his way home from a year-end party, of two women kissing in a bar.

As mentioned earlier, the terms of the discussion are unrelentingly "masculinist," since they are largely determined by the chairman, who relies upon notions framing male homosexual experience when posing his questions. However, the female discussants are not passive in this exchange and seem uninterested in pursuing comparisons with male homosexuals. Although the bar madam agrees that among "female homos" there are many who adopt "male" *(dansei gata)* and "female" *(josei gata)* roles, she insists that there are also many women who do not, including those present at the discussion. The female participants also point out that contrary to male homosexuals, women are more liable to "fall head over heels in love" *(chi michi wo agete shimau)* with actresses and female singers in an "entirely spiritual" *(zenzen seishinteki)* manner—

recalling the prewar notion that women were more predisposed to "psychological love," a capacity that men were supposed to lack (Fruhstuck 2003: 126). Yet the participants acknowledge that while some women may be satisfied with this kind of relationship, it does not satisfy all.

The women are also asked if they experience "vagina envy" *(yoni naido)* similar to the "penis envy" *(fuarusu naido)* supposedly common among male homosexuals—a question that they initially fail to understand, since they do not recognize the terms "yoni" (a Sanskrit term) or "phallus"—one woman exclaiming, "Speak Japanese!" This leads to a discussion of whether or not the size and shape of the vagina is of erotic interest for women—it being decided that women's breasts and skin are, for most women, more important sites of attraction. It is also pointed out that another important difference between male and female homosexuals is that the "professional" and "semiprofessional" categories of sex worker common among male homosexuals are not part of the women's scene. The discussion then intriguingly moves on to the topic of famous female homosexuals, it being pointed out that many women in the entertainment world, including a novelist and several screen and stage stars, were rumored to live with female companions (unfortunately, their names have been edited out of the text).

It is difficult to know how to read these lesbian-themed articles in *Fūzoku kagaku*. On the surface there does seem to be a genuine attempt to engage with actual women's experience, and yet despite the stress on the more "spiritual" side of women's same-sex love, the roundtable discussion was illustrated with two suggestively posed bikini-clad western women—a gesture to the prominence of western notions of female beauty, which became widespread in Japan under the occupation. Under the caption "women's heaven," one of the models says, "I'm calling you," and the illustration can probably be regarded as an address to the magazine's male readership as much as to a potentially lesbian audience. Yet such tactics should not necessarily be read as alienating a female readership. Bannon, for instance, points out how same-sex-desiring American women reclaimed the raunchy covers of lesbian-themed pulp fiction of the 1950s by reading them "iconically" (1999: 12). The existence of male-oriented lesbian pulp fiction notwithstanding (Zimet 1999), it should also be remembered that the publication of such an uninhibited portrayal of lesbianism would have been quite impossible in an English commercial magazine at a time when the very mention of the word "lesbian" could be considered obscene.[35]

Both *Fūzoku kagaku* and *Fūzoku zōshi*, the two perverse magazines that seemed most genuinely to attempt to engage women readers, folded in 1955. Ironically, discussion of "Lesbos love" actually increased in succeeding ventures, such as *Fūzoku kitan*, *Ura mado* and the many SM magazines that appeared in the late 1960s and early '70s, reversing the balance of the earlier magazines, where male homosexuality had been of most interest. Yet a male voice and audience is clearly discernible behind these later publications, and "Lesbos love" is reduced to a male fantasy trope. For instance, the men's pornographic magazine *SM Fan* ran its own "Lesbos Communication" *(Resubosu tsūshin)* column from February to June 1973. Intriguingly, this column was attributed to a person writing under the female name of Sonoyama Keiko, which differs by only one character from Sonomura Keiko, the author of the original 1953 column. This is surely no coincidence, yet whether the later author was writing in tribute to the earlier, or was even the same person, remains unknown, as does his or her actual gender.[36] Given that during the 1960s the image of the lesbian became and thereafter remained a common staple in male pornographic magazines, it is unlikely that female names relate to actual women writers or that these writings express female subjectivities.[37]

During the 1960s "Lesbos love" was gradually replaced by the term *rezubian*,[38] and by the end of the decade this had been further reduced to *rezu*[39]—both terms strongly associated with sadomasochism and male pornography. A look at the authors of these many articles shows that the vast majority are writing under male names, with only a handful using female designations. Given the difficulty of establishing whether or not in the context of these magazines female names represent actual women, it is probably safe to assume that despite early efforts, "Lesbos love," in the perverse press at least, was primarily a conversation carried on between men.[40] If and how lesbian women made use of these narratives remains unclear. Accounts of lesbian history written by Japanese (*Aniisu* 2001; Izumo et al. 1997) and western writers alike (Chalmers 2002)[41] tend to take the birth of women's liberation in Japan in the early 1970s as the starting point for the development of a modern lesbian consciousness. This is partly because earlier transgender paradigms developed in the bar world, in which one partner adopted a "male role" *(otokoyaku)*, were difficult to reconcile with newly invigorated feminist critiques of the patriarchal sex and gender system. Attempts such as those made recently by individuals from Japan's gay male community to reclaim the perverse press as part of postwar gay history (see Fushimi 2002) have so far not been made in the context of lesbian history writing—although there is clearly much more that could be done with this material.

CONCLUSION

As will be discussed in chapter 5, the relatively late development in Japan of western-style gay and lesbian activist organizations is often understood to imply that Japan is somehow "behind" the west in terms of the development of sexual minority identity and community formation. However, to focus on the emergence of gay activism as a defining event anticipates a specifically western construction of what, exactly, constitutes a gay history. The widespread discussion of "perverse sexuality" in Japan's postwar press must necessarily make us rethink what we know about the rapid emergence of lesbian and gay identities in the west in the postwar period and their supposedly more gradual development in other societies in recent decades.

In the immediate postwar period Japan saw an explosion of queer discussion and representation in the popular press which is not paralleled by media in any anglophone society until the early 1970s. Japan's first homophile publication, *Adonis,* predates the founding of America's *ONE* and was longer-lived and able to be more graphic in its support for a homosexual subjectivity than its U.S. counterpart. More significantly, in the postwar period homosexuality was not notably segregated from other forms of "perverse" sexual expression in Japanese discourse. Both male and female homosexuality were seen as part of a wider family of perversions, including sadomasochism and cross-dressing, which, due to the wide historical and geographical range of the articles in the perverse press, were understood to be part of the general human condition, not simply in present-day Japan but in other historical eras and cultures as well. Hence, the manner in which homosexuality was isolated as a distinct and particularly dangerous pathology in English-language sources of the 1950s was unparalleled in Japan at this time.

Perhaps one of the difficulties contemporary Japanese gay rights' activists have faced in reclaiming this history is its very diversity and the fact that the sexual categories of Japan's postwar perverse press do not map very convincingly onto today's "ethnic model" of lesbian or gay identities. In the mid-1980s, when western rights-based gay and lesbian modes of organization began to impact on Japanese sexual minorities, the labels "lesbian" and "gay" were, in fact, *reimported* into Japan and then had to compete with the already indigenized meanings of the terms *rezu* and *gei,* which had been in circulation in Japanese popular media for far longer than they had in the United States. *Gei,* as we have seen, was already a widespread term for effeminate young men who worked in the entertainment industry by the mid-1950s, and *rezu* had become a category of heterosexual male pornography by the middle 1960s.

Hence, while it is clear that Japan's encounter with the Allied forces during the occupation resulted very quickly in the generation of new types of sexual discourse and the proliferation of new modes of homosexual practice and identity, these Japanese subcultures were very different from the developing "gay" subcultures in the United States at this time, not least in terms of their apparent openness and the freedom with which they were discussed in the press. While *gei* is certainly related to, and most probably derives from, the use of "gay" in English, this latter term had *itself* only won out as a preferred term for self-designation within U.S. homosexual communities during the war, and *gei* became widespread in the Japanese media some 20 years before "gay" came to be so widely used in English. The convenient homophony of *gei* as "gay" and *gei* as "artistic accomplishment" only serves to reinforce the hybridized manner in which this term came to be used in Japanese to signify a new kind of sexual being—the *gei bōi*. However, the *gei bōi* was as different from the American gay man as he was different from the *danshō* or male prostitute who had preceded him. Indeed, as will be argued further in the next chapter, the *gei bōi* can be seen as a specifically homosexual response to new sexual spaces opened up by Japan's postwar modernity in much the same way that the *abekku* rapidly emerged as a new kind of heterosexual couple.

In order to understand the changes that took place in Japan's sexual topography that will be discussed in ensuing chapters, it is particularly important to understand the already hybridized nature of Japan's postwar sexual culture. Commentators, Japanese and western alike (Summerhawk 1998; Itō and Yanase 2000), who see the emergence of "lesbian" and "gay" identities as a kind of advancement over native Japanese categories usually fail to discuss the complex and hybrid nature of Japanese sexological discourse in the postwar period, which makes it impossible to plot the trajectory of a unitary model of homosexual identity. While Japan's sexual culture clearly changed in relation to the U.S. occupation, to see this as a process of cultural encroachment or "advancement" or as a displacement of "native" ideologies by "western" forces is to fail to recognize the already hybridized nature of Japan's sexual culture—evidenced by the fact that German sexological terms such as "urning" lived on in Japanese postwar discourse alongside native Japanese terms (themselves written in Chinese characters).[42] Indeed the very "hybrid" nature of the Japanese writing system itself, which allowed new, unofficial readings of "traditional" concepts to be written alongside Chinese characters, shows that there was more taking place than a "simple" process of translation. This "borrowing" from the west is then best understood in terms of Japan's long tradition of "editing" aspects of other cultures to suit Japanese conditions (Iwabuchi 2002: 13–4).

In the case of Japan, this process of hybridization is apparent from the time of the Meiji Restoration (1867), which took place at *precisely* the same time that European sexual categories were themselves being redefined in terms of the newly emerging "science" of German sexology. As Martin argues, it is unhelpful to view sexualities as "inert, autochthonous forces planted in the soil of a given location"; rather, a more productive manner of reading would see them as "densely overwritten and hyper-dynamic texts caught in a continual process of transformation that occurs with the ongoing accretion of fresh discursive traces" (2003: 251). This is, of course, as true of western models of sexual identity, which are themselves hardly static.

Rather than being replaced by western ones or gradually evolving toward western models, Japanese understandings of sexuality were developing in tandem with and in relation to western understandings—a process that began not with the occupation but with Japan's encounter with the west in the Meiji period. Yet it is important to remember that although many Japanese borrowings of certain terms, originally from German and later from English, result in homophones, these are not synonyms. This is very much apparent in the development of the figure of the *gei bōi*. Rather than representing a convergence between Japanese and developing U.S. notions of "gay" identity in the postwar period, the Japanese *gei bōi* follows a very specific trajectory, engaging with characteristically modern notions of gender and sexuality but with quite different results, as is described in the next chapter.

NOTES

1. For a philosophical reflection on postwar decadence, see Sakaguchi (1986), originally published in the monthly magazine *Shinchō* in 1946.

2. *Kasutori* is literally a poor-quality wine distilled from sake lees. Drinkers were supposed to collapse after only three glasses—just as these magazines tended to fold after their third issue (Matsuzawa 1997: 59).

3. Novelist Nosaka Akiyuki, who was a teenager during the occupation, describes in his novella *Amerikan hijiki* (1967) an incident where the Japanese narrator takes an American guest who had served in the occupation to a sex show featuring the man with the biggest penis in Japan. However, the performer's penis remains shriveled, a symptom that the narrator puts down to the presence of the American and the memories he invokes of the routine humiliations Japanese men experienced when faced with the "huge build" of American GIs during the occupation.

4. Nealon points out that although there was also an explosion in pulp literature in postwar America, its treatment of homosexuality was unremittingly negative, since "the prevailing language for homosexuality in the 1950s was a toxic mix of the psychopathological and the criminal." Homosexuality appealed to the publishers of pulp literature, which focused on the "dark side of American life" (2001: 148–9).

5. In Japan, however, homosexuality was associated with the right, not left, of the political spectrum, as exemplified in the life and work of Mishima Yukio.

6. Witch hunts increased in the UK after the 1951 defection to Russia of homo-

sexual spy Guy Burgess. The level of prosecutions for "homosexual offences" greatly increased during the 1950s and involved such high-profile figures as Lord Montagu and Sir John Gielgud. Although the Wolfenden Report of 1957 recommended that male homosexuality under certain strict circumstances be decriminalized, due to public sentiment this was not acted on by government until 1966. Similarly, Australia saw a rapid increase in the prosecution of homosexual offenses at this time (Wotherspoon 1991: 109–38).

7. The two biggest changes for women in the postwar period were effected by the Allied powers. These were the granting of suffrage and of the right to participate in politics at all levels and the abolition of the feudal family system, which had subordinated women's rights of choice of partner, inheritance, access to divorce, etc., to those of men. However, Tanaka (2002) points out Japanese women were also sexually exploited by the occupying forces—although his equation of this exploitation with that of the imperial army's "comfort women" system is hardly convincing.

8. Compared with the immediate prewar period, sexual minority subcultures were able to develop rapidly, apparently unhindered by police investigation or harassment.

9. Many of these boys offered themselves for a price and preferred foreigners, since they could be charged more. Apparently, the price for an all-night stay with a male prostitute ran from 3,000 to 10,000 yen, whereas the most that a Japanese client could be expected to pay was 8,000 yen (*Fūzoku kagaku* 1954: 111).

10. One such account is by Kenneth Marlowe, whose 1964 book *Mr. Madam* describes his career as a female impersonator and later as a boss of a call-boy outfit. Marlowe is completely unrepentant about his activities and actually gives a very upbeat account of gay life. However, the book is introduced by a medical expert, Dr. Leonard A. Lowag, who justifies the book's publication on the grounds that it will assist "experts" in helping and advising sufferers from homosexuality, whose lives he describes as "pathetic."

11. Designating the exact dates at which these magazines began and ceased publication is difficult. These approximate dates are based on the collection held by Tokyo's Fūzoku Shiryōkan and my own search of online databases posted by secondhand booksellers.

12. *Fūzoku kitan* changed its name in November 1974 to *SM Fantajia* (SM fantasia), the last issue of which was published in September 1975.

13. Literally "one who came before" but often used to refer to teachers or other acknowledged experts in a given field.

14. During the Meiji period, *fūzoku*, or "customs," was used in magazine titles to refer to contemporary customs or popular trends, but before the war it began to be used as a circumlocution for sexual customs, as a means of avoiding the censor's gaze (Matsuzawa: 1997: 61–2).

15. The Genroku period (1688–1704) is considered to be the first great flourishing of townspeople culture under Tokugawa rule. At this time such popular arts as kabuki, woodblock prints and fiction saw some of their greatest exponents, the latter exemplified by Ihara Saikaku, whose work contains many descriptions of *nanshoku*, or male-male eroticism.

16. The sadomasochistic preoccupations of the novel's narrator have much in common with themes prevalent in the perverse press, yet the literature on Mishima is largely silent on this cultural context.

17. For examples, see Kogure (1952); Sumi (1949: 215).

18. Cross-dressed male prostitutes can still be seen today in Ueno Park after dusk—although they now seem to prefer western women's clothing.

19. The supposed upsurge in the visibility of male homosexuality in the early postwar years was sometimes put down to the psychology of defeat. A brief, unsigned article on page 83 of the November 1952 edition of *Amatoria,* for instance, points out that the incidence of homosexuality rose in Germany after its defeat at the end of the First World War and that a similar increase was to be found in Japan, where bars catering to foreign soldiers were frequented by Japanese *okama.*

20. Sumi (1949: 216), however, notes that although some *danshō* believed they had small genitalia, this "inferiority complex" was often delusional. Also, the practice of "sodomy" *(keikan)* among *danshō* was not as prevalent as many believed, since some used a special "technique" with their customers (probably interfemoral intercourse). Sex researcher Takahashi Tetsu tells of how he went to a public bath known to be frequented by *okama* in the afternoons in order to get a glimpse of their penises. He says, "So I thought I'd get a look at their penises. I saw just one. But I didn't get to see any others at all no matter how hard I tried" (Takahashi and Lane 1952: 46). The size of the penis observed was not recorded.

21. See also the regular advice columns "Sodomia tsūshin" in *Fūzoku zōshi* and "Homo no peiji" in *Fūzoku kagaku* for discussion of various homosexual and transgender types.

22. See for example the series "Shōnen'ai no keifu" (A genealogy of boy love) published in *Fūzoku kitan* from July 1970 to May 1971.

23. The Japanese term *naido* seems to be a borrowing from the German *Neid,* meaning "envy," as in *Fallus Neid.* I am grateful to Wim Lunsing for pointing this out.

24. This seems to be the case even today. The writer Donald Richie, who has lived by Ueno Park for over 40 years, often encounters cross-dressed male prostitutes during his evening strolls. When he inquired of one if he had a wife, Richie received the reply, "Of course, whose clothes do you think I'm wearing?" (Personal communication).

25. *Dōshi* in fact became an argot term designating homosexual men. Intriguingly, this term also came to be used in Chinese from the 1990s as a general signifier for lesbian, gay and other queer identities (*tongzhi* in Chinese), although this derivation seems to have come from its use in the Republican era, when it designated "comrade."

26. *Sodomiya* occurs on page 103 of the February 1954 edition of *Fūzoku kagaku,* whereas *sodomia shumi* occurs in a letter reproduced on page 168 of the November 1953 issue. The term is also occasionally spelled as *sodomii* as on page 89 of the October 1953 issue, which speaks of *sodomii kankei,* and on page 102 of the September 1954 edition of *Fūzoku zōshi.* The rendering *sodomisuto* also occurs, although rarely; for example, see the reader's letter on page 60 of the August 1953 edition of *Fūzoku zōshi.*

27. *Chigo* is a term deriving from the older *nanshoku* code. It originally designated a young temple acolyte but came to refer to the younger partner in a transgenerational homosexual relationship. *Ka* here is a suffix meaning "-ist."

28. *Jibika* here is made up of the characters for ear and nose, as in the medical "ear, nose and throat specialist." Kabiya suggests that its use derives from the fact that older men were hard of hearing. He also mentions *fukesen* or "specialists in older men."

29. *Ritsu* means a rate or percentage.

30. *"Sodomia wa ryūkō suru,"* p. 40.

31. *Fūzoku kagaku*, September 1954, p. 83.

32. One example of Japanese lesbians reading against the grain occurs in the context of 1970s "boy love" comics, such as *June* and *Allan*; numerous lesbian biographies offer accounts of how women readers identified with these androgynous same-sex couples. See the discussion in chapter 5.

33. Page 37.

34. Page 159.

35. As Zimet points out, it was an important convention of the lesbian-pulp genre that "the lesbian go crazy in the end—otherwise the post office might seize the books as obscene" (1999: 20). Even pulp novels written by lesbians themselves were constrained by regulations requiring an unhappy ending, since lesbianism was not to be "promoted as something to be admired or desired."

36. Leonie Strickland has pointed out to me that this is probably a pen name. If the interchangeable characters *mura/yama* are deleted, the name reads Sono Keiko, a near homophone for *sono keikō,* which means "that tendency"—a reference to homosexual desires.

37. Furuda (1995: 96) notes that the editor of *Fūzoku kitan* was approached about starting a magazine solely for homosexual men in 1970 but refused, because he did not think there was a sufficient market. Although *Fūzoku kitan* continued to print a few articles about male homosexuality, its two staples were lesbianism and SM—both clearly directed at a heterosexual male market.

38. "Lesbiasm" [*sic*] in roman followed by the katakana *resubiazumu* occurs in an article on page 74 of the March 1951 edition of *Amatoria*. The first instance of the use of *resubian* (with an *s*) I have found in the title of an article is in the August 1960 special "Resubian no seitai" (Lesbian way of life) edition of *Fūzoku kitan*. *Rezubian* (with a *z*) appears in the title of an article in the January 1961 edition of the same magazine.

39. The first instance of the use of *rezu* in the title of an article I have come across is in the April 1969 edition of *Kitan kurabu,* after which it becomes extremely popular, outstripping both *"resubosu ai"* and *rezubian.*

40. Writing on lesbianism was not the only context in the postwar period in which women's experience was appropriated by male writers. Molasky (2001: 123) analyzes several pulp novels published in the 1950s that purport to expose the sexual exploitation of Japanese women by foreign men. While the authors' names and the narrative voices in these texts were female, the works later turned out to have been written by men. These texts' eroticization of rape is similar to the manner in which lesbian sex was eroticized so as to appeal to a male readership.

41. Chalmers does attempt to find traces of lesbian history in the 1960s, but all she finds is, intriguingly, an informant who had discovered American lesbian pulp fiction.

42. As late as 1960, German terminology was still being offered alongside Japanese concepts. See for example Kabiya Kazuhiko's article "Shōnen'ai no hitobito" (Boy lovers) in the November 1960 edition of *Fūzoku kitan* (pp. 130–5), where the Sino-Japanese term *shōnen'ai* (boy love) is accompanied by *rubi,* designating the reading *kunāben riibu* (i.e., *Knabenliebe,* the German term for pedophilia).

3

Gay Boys, Blue Boys and Brother Girls

The previous chapter looked at the widespread proliferation of a "perverse paradigm" throughout Japanese media of the postwar period that grouped together a wide range of identities and practices on the basis that they fell outside of "normal" sexual interests. This chapter looks at how one identity, the *gei bōi*, came to prominence in the late 1950s and captured the imagination of the general public to such an extent that the *gei bōi* became *the* public face of male homosexuality for the next 20 years, until a variety of factors led to a reconfiguration of the term *gei* and a gradual dissociation of homosexuality from transgender identity and performance. Despite the homophony of *gei* and "gay," this discussion will reveal that the Japanese *gei bōi* was quite distinct from the emerging American gay man.

As outlined in the previous chapter, although *gei* was borrowed from the English "gay" in the immediate postwar period and its use expanded and developed in Japanese popular culture throughout precisely the same period that "gay" was emerging as the most common referent for homosexual men in the United States, these terms are not the same. In this chapter I use the romanized form of the Japanese word to emphasize that *gei* in Japan and "gay" in the United States not only had very different nuances but also circulated in very different contexts. The category "gay" in the anglophone world developed in relation to two specific movements. First was the rejection by emerging gay communities of models of sin, pathology and crime with which homosexual behavior had long been associated in religious, medical and criminal discourse in English, in favor of a quasi-ethnic understanding of "gay identity" based on citizenship and rights (Epstein 1998; Plummer 1995: 90). This was accompanied by a parallel movement away from transgender paradigms of homosexual identity and an adoption of a more masculine, or at times hypermasculine, mode of self-presentation (Levine 1998). In the earlier paradigm, effeminate "faeries," considered to be the real homosexuals, had sought out sexual interaction with straight-identified "trade" (Chauncey 1994: 358). However, it became increasingly common in the postwar period for masculine gay men to seek out sex with other masculine-identified gays and establish what Greenberg (1988) has termed "egalitarian" homosexual relationships. Cory, writing in 1951, captures this parallel development when he describes the need for a term like "gay":

> Needed for years was an ordinary, everyday, matter-of-fact word that could express the concept of homosexuality without glorification or condemnation. It must have no odium of the effeminate stereotype about it. Such a word has long been in existence and, in recent years, has grown in popularity. The word is "gay." (1951: 107)

Before the war it would have been considered strange by many homosexuals for two adult masculine men from the same class to have had sexual interactions with each other. However, the Second World War seems to have brought about a drastic change to these two systems (Berube 1990; Chauncey 1984), and homosexual interaction, as it took place within the developing "gay" subculture, increasingly occurred between men who were equally masculine. Chauncey points to the "new virile look" common among younger homosexuals at the war's end, a look that became normative as "growing numbers adopted a self-consciously masculine style" (1994: 358). This trend was reflected in the burgeoning trade in "physique" magazines throughout the 1950s and was to reach its peak in the machismo gay-clone culture of the 1970s (Levine 1998). Ostensibly directed at the body-building market, physique magazines were read primarily by gay men (Hooven 1995), some of whom would congregate at places like California's "Muscle Beach" and other bathing places in London and elsewhere (Westwood 1960: 89). This turn toward masculinity also affected how nascent gay-rights groups reacted toward more effeminate homosexuals, often excluding them from membership (Kaiser 1997: 131).

In the Japanese case, however, from the mid-1950s, *gei* emerged as a transgender category strongly associated with the entertainment world and was not available as a designation for more gender-normative, masculine homosexual men. Furthermore, while the term "gay" in the United States was used to refer to both men and women and a commonality between these two groups could be expressed in phrases such as "gay boys," "gay girls" or, collectively, "gay people" (Stein 2000: 365; Newton

1979: 26), no such commonality was expressed by the Japanese term that was reserved (and remains so today) specifically for men. As outlined below, *gei* culture did have an effect upon women's homosexual subcultures, but this was largely due to the adoption by women's bars of the successful commercial patterns that had been developed in the *gei* subculture; it had little to do with mixing between the two worlds. Although homosexual women, particularly those who tended toward transgender behavior, did achieve some visibility during this period, the 1960s in particular were dominated by the figure of the *gei bōi*.

The difference in the rhetorical space in which discussion of male homosexuality circulated in Japan and the United States is clear when it is considered that, as Charles Kaiser notes, "almost every New York City newspaper reference to lesbians and gay men in the fifties was connected to a crime" (1997: 82). In the Japanese case, however, it would not be an exaggeration to say that from about 1958 almost every newspaper and magazine reference to *gei bōi* was connected to the entertainment world, a world that has continued to prove hospitable to sexually ambivalent performers, both male and female.

THE RISE OF THE *GEI BŌI*

The adoption of the English term "gay" into the Japanese homosexual subculture is an interesting example of cultural "glocalization." One of the first references to *gei* in print occurs in Mishima Yukio's early '50s novel *Kinjiki* (*Forbidden colors*), where he glosses it as "American slang for *danshokuka*" (1973: 200). As explained in chapter 2, the latter term was a neologism made up of the traditional term for male-male love *nan/danshoku* and the nominalizing suffix "*-ka*," or "ist,"[1] which was commonly used in the perverse press. However, the fact that Mishima had to gloss the term suggests that it was not widely understood outside of what he refers to as "*gei no shakai*" (gay society) at this time. Indeed, "gay," as a signifier for homosexual men and women, was not widely understood even in the United States in the 1950s. The term established itself as a common referent among homosexual subcultures in the United States only as a result of the mass mobilization during the war, which brought a diverse number of homosexual men and women together from all parts of the country and helped to standardize gay slang (Faderman 1992: 163; Berube 1990: 117; Cory 1951: 107–8). Yet, as Cory points out, even in the early 1950s "gay" was "practically unknown outside of homosexual circles, except for police officers, theatrical groups and a few others" (1951: 108). The fact that Cory first mentions the currency of the term among the police force is an indication of the extent to which the homosexual community was under surveillance at this time in the United States.

Compared with the slow dissemination of the word "gay" throughout anglophone societies, where it was to take another 25 years before becoming general currency, the rise of *gei* in Japanese was meteoric. Gay *(gei)* entered Japanese immediately after the war via gay men in the occupation forces, who referred to their Japanese partners as *gei bōi* or "gay boys" (Kabiya 1962a: 146). By the mid-1950s *gei*, especially as part of the compound *gei bōi*, was being used in the Japanese media to describe effeminate homosexual men. The sudden popularity of the term was largely due to the fact that *gei* (written in the katakana syllables used to transcribe foreign loanwords) is a homophone of *gei* (written with the character for "artistic accomplishment"—as in "geisha"). Gay boys were sometimes spoken of as *gei wo uri*—that is, "selling *gei*"—and it was easy to make a semantic slip between *geinōjin* (an entertainer, where *gei* is written with the character for artistic accomplishment) and *gei bōi* (where *gei* is a transliteration of "gay"). *Gei bōi* therefore came to be understood, at least in part, as an occupational category.

The widespread use of the term *gei* in the Japanese media clearly predates the use of "gay" in English, which did not become a common referent for homosexuals outside of specific subcultures in the United States until the early 1970s. In Australia, for example, "gay" was not much used in the homosexual subculture until the mid-1970s, homosexual men and women instead referring to each other as "camp" (Dow 2001: 91–2; Wotherspoon 1991: 192), whereas in the UK in the '50s and '60s the preferred term was "queer" (Westwood 1960: 207). Indeed, Tomita suggests that the use of "gay" to refer to homosexuals was "absolutely a Japanese interpretation" of the word and that similar use in English was the result of "re-exportation" *(gyaku yushutsu)* from the Japanese (1958: 188). The work of historians such as Berube (1990) shows this not to have been the case, inasmuch as "gay" was already in use in some homosexual subcultures in the United States from at least the 1920s (Cory 1951: 107), but Tomita's assertion is evidence of the speed with which *gei* became an indigenized Japanese category and its foreign antecedents forgotten.[2]

In 1958 Tomita Eizō[3] used *gei* as the title of a book in which he described *gei bōi* as "more feminine than today's boyish young women" (1958: 181). Tomita's use of *gei*, which was also widely used in the popular press at this time, had a more limited semantic range than the English term. The Japanese category *gei* was never applied to women or to gender-normative homosexual men (who by the late 1950s were widely referred to as *homo*) but only to those men who displayed transgender characteristics and worked in the entertainment world.

Gei bōi was not, however, the only term used by the media to describe effeminate entertainers. In the late 1950s there were numerous soft and refined male singers, such as Miwa Akihiro;[4] after the success of the 1956 Hollywood movie *Tea and Sympathy* (released in Japan as *Ocha to dōjō*) they became known as *shisutā bōi*, or "sister boys." In the movie, John Kerr played a prep-school student who prefers the arts to sports and is accordingly dubbed a "sister boy" by his more macho peers, although his sensitivity endears him to his housemaster's wife, with whom he has an affair. His sensitivity and refinement notwithstanding, Kerr's character is actually heterosexual, and the Japanized term originally referred to effeminate male youths who were kept by wealthy middle-aged women as "pets" (*Hyakuman nin no yoru* 1963c: 153; see also Tomita 1958: 190). However, the mass media tended to conflate *shisutā bōi* and *gei bōi*, using both interchangeably, until *shisutā bōi* was eclipsed by the latter term by the beginning of the 1960s.

The celebration of effeminate men in Japan's entertainment world was, of course, nothing new. Roden, for instance, describes the craze for what he terms "the effeminate male star" (1990: 48) in the movies of the '20s and '30s. Known as *nimaime*, a term deriving from kabuki and signifying a second or subsidiary star, these male actors appeared rather soft and flimsy when paired with the newly emergent woman actors on screen. Some, like Hasegawa Kazuo (1908–1984), had received their early training as kabuki female-role performers, or *onnagata*. Hasegawa played the role of an *onnagata* in the extremely popular movie *Yukinojo henge* (An actor's revenge), which was originally filmed in 1935 and remade in 1962, with Hasegawa playing the lead in both versions. The story basically concerns Hasegawa's attempt to exact revenge on a theater owner and his cronies, who had defrauded his father and caused his suicide. He does this through seducing and then betraying one of the shogun's concubines (an ardent theatergoer), which he does *while dressed as and presenting himself as a woman*. The plot is plausible only to the extent the audience understands that transgender performance is not *in itself* incompatible with heterosexual interests and moreover, that a transgendered man could be considered a suitable love interest for women.

In 1957 Ōta Tenrei published an edited volume, entitled *Dai san no sei* (The third sex), that was probably the first book about homosexual men in Japanese to be written with the cooperation of homosexual men themselves. The discussion in the book drew upon survey data that had been collected from 100 men who were all members of the FKK club, an organization for homosexual men founded by the magazine *Fūzoku kagaku* in 1954. Ōta also conducted research himself into the *gei bā* that currently existed in Tokyo, pointing out that such bars had not existed before the war. Ōta discovered nine *gei bā* in Asakusa, seven in Shinjuku and one each in Ginza, Shimbashi, Ikebukuro, Shibuya and Kanda, a total of 21 in all (Ōta 1957: 306). Even compared with major cities in the United States at this time, this was a fairly large number and considerably more than the four bars that Miwa Akihiro claims existed in Tokyo at the beginning of the decade (Itō 2001: 2). However, according to Ōta's account, most of the bars were modest watering holes with only basic amenities, since earlier attempts to provide more high-class surroundings had failed. This was all to change very suddenly in the next few years as Japan saw a "boom" in *gei* life resulting in a proliferation of bars as well as a significant shift in the kind of clientele they attracted.

JAPAN'S ORIGINAL "GAY BOOM"

In the early 1990s Japanese media were swept by a "gay boom" *(gei būmu),* which saw a rapid escalation in the amount of attention given to minority sexuality issues in the press, on television and in movies. Although this development has been widely discussed in English (see for example, Hall 2000: 37–43; Lunsing 1997) and Japanese (Yajima 1997; Fushimi 2002), no commentators have observed that Japan's first gay boom, using precisely this term, had actually taken place 35 years previously, in 1958. While in the early 1990s the concept *gei* was beginning to be articulated in a more political sense, often in the context of discussion of a *gei* and *rezubian* "movement" *(undō),* the late 1950s use of this term was quite different and is a clear illustration of how the meanings of terms can shift radically over even short periods of time.

The most significant event that enabled the rapid expansion of the *gei* subculture took place in 1956, when, after years of campaigning, women's groups forced the government to pass an anti-prostitution bill. The criminalization of prostitution (or rather brothel keeping, pimping and soliciting) was to have a major impact on *gei bā.* As many businesses that had relied on heterosexual prostitution closed down or restructured their activities, space was opened up in former red-light areas for new sex-related businesses, including those catering to homosexual men and cross-dressers. Since the law was targeted at the open and conspicuous world of mainstream heterosexual prostitution, its impact upon more covert homosexual practice was less severe and to an extent allowed homosexual operations to move into these former heterosexual red-light areas. As mentioned, neither homosexuality nor cross-dressing was illegal in Japan, and homosexual meeting places were not raided by the police, as was routine in anglophone societies. While in the United States at this time "a person who want[ed] to wear drag must [have been] able to pass for a woman on the street or else risk arrest" (Newton 1979: 36), Japanese transgenders were able to go about their business in these districts without fear of police harassment. The only restriction on *gei bā* intermittently enforced by the police was the 1948 Entertainment and Amusement Trade Law, which ostensibly forbade trading between midnight and sunrise. Consequently, Shinjuku Ni-chōme (Shinjuku's second ward), which had been a heterosexual red-light district, was gradually taken over by *gei* businesses from this time; it now houses the largest collection of bars catering to a homosexual clientele in Japan (Ōtsuka 1995: 14–9; Fushimi 2002: 247–58).

Although in 1957 there had only been 20 or so *gei bā* in Tokyo, catering primarily to a clientele of homosexual men, in 1958 the mainstream press began talking about a "gay boom" *(gei būmu)* that had seen the number of *gei bā* shoot up to nearly 60, largely due to the crossover appeal of these establishments to a clientele outside the homosexual world (*Shūkan taishū* 1958: 24). *Gei bōi* were no longer catering to an exclusively male (or homosexual) clientele but also provided companionship for women. Ōta points out that while a large majority of the *gei bōi* working in the bars were by temperament "urning," there were also boys who were not homosexual *(homo de nai)*, including students and other "semi professionals" who simply worked for a time in the bars in order to earn money (1957: 308–9) and were happy to entertain both male and female clients. Indeed, by the early '60s, evening editions of the tabloid papers regularly featured over 20 advertisements recruiting "boys" or "beautiful boys" to work as hosts in private clubs for "gentlemen." Known as "assisted boys" *(enjo sareru shōnen)* (Satō 1960), these youths anticipated the "compensated dating" *(enjo kōsai)* schemes later devised by Japanese high-school girls by some quarter of a century.

The growing popularity of the *gei bā* among a more mainstream clientele makes it difficult to equate these institutions with the developing gay bar subculture in the United States or other western countries. As Nancy Achilles points out, widespread sodomy laws and restrictions on indecent behavior (such as members of the same-sex dancing together) made it difficult for gay bars to advertise their presence in the 1950s and early 1960s in the United States; news of their opening tended to be passed on via word of mouth (1967: 232–3). Esther Newton (1979), in *Mother Camp*, an investigation of 1960s drag shows in the United States, does draw a distinction between "gay bars," where homosexuals met, and the more upmarket "tourist clubs," which put on drag shows for a predominantly heterosexual clientele, but the latter were comparatively few and remained largely subcultural with little impact on mainstream culture. In Japan, however, the early '60s witnessed widespread media interest in the *gei bōi* phenomenon.

For instance, an unsigned article in the April 1963 edition of the magazine *Ura mado* refers to the "touristization" *(kankōka)* that was sweeping through Japan's *gei bā* scene wherein "homosexuals" *(homo)* were being displaced by "ordinary customers" *(futsū no kyaku),* including many women.[5] An article in *Fūzoku kitan,* also published in April 1963, warns homosexual men who visit "gay bars" in the expectation of making assignations with the boys working there that some boys also "service" women.[6] The author suggests that when referring to such boys, *panpan bōi* (after the *panpan* girls who catered to GIs during the occupation), would be a better designation—although he does point out that rather than "servicing" female clients "as a man," the boys "receive caresses like pets," rather like the sister boys of the 1950s. Although Miwa Akihiro reported that at the beginning of the 1950s *gei bā* were rather furtive establishments where customers could be seen passing to and fro waiting for a quiet moment to slip inside (Itō 2001: 2), by the end of the decade such bars had become avant-garde places of entertainment for a more mainstream clientele.

Media interest in *gei bōi* spread far beyond the perverse magazines. Although overlooked by the respectable press, the tabloids were fascinated by the subculture and made *gei bōi* like Miwa Akihiro household names. The interest that mainstream media showed in the *gei bōi* phenomenon resulted in information about the *gei* subculture being disseminated even to the farthest corners of Japan. Carrousel Maki, for instance, who was to become Japan's most high-profile sex-change entertainer, grew up in the remote town of Kushiro in Hokkaido. She recalls the impact that reading about Miwa had upon her during her teens; clutching articles about Miwa cut from the weekly tabloids, she left home at the age of 15 to start life as a *gei bā* entertainer in Sapporo (Maruo 1966: 64).

In 1958, the popular magazine *Shūkan taishū* (Weekly popular culture) wrote about Japan's "gay boom" *(gei būmu),* describing it as "the best in the world." Unlike the previous category of *danshō,* who were street prostitutes working by night, *gei bōi* were considered to have "evolved" a new kind of "gay style" *(gei sutairu)*—one that could "parade itself in an imposing manner even in daylight." Communities of *gei bōi* were developing around *gei bā* all over Japan, estimates running to 2,500 in Tokyo, 1,000 in Osaka, 500 each in Kyoto and Kobe and another 1,000 or so spread throughout the rest of Japan (*Shūkan taishū* 1958: 25). These reports encouraged the conception that *gei* was very much a commercial category, with there being "in excess of 5000 persons to whom the name gay *(gei)* is applied professionally."

While the "feminine" style preferred by *danshō* had been a retrospective one, consisting of women's kimono and wigs in which long hair was tied up in a chignon reminiscent of geisha, the *gei bōi* were more modern, even pioneering, in their self-presentation. They had little interest in passing as women and did not see themselves as female impersonators, considering their androgynous *(chūsei)*, boyish style to be "a new disposition" *(atarashii keikō)*, more in keeping with the modern world (Satō 1960: 60). *Gei bōi* were mostly in their late teens and early twenties, and although born during the war would have remembered little from this period. They had no nostalgia for Japan's imperial past but looked abroad instead for inspiration when fashioning their self-identities. In the late 1950s, *gei bōi* were sporting the short-style "Cécile cut"[7] popularized by actress Jean Seberg, the androgynous star of *Saint Joan* (1957), *Bonjour Tristesse* (1958) and *À bout de souffle* (1959). They wore light makeup and dressed in newly fashionable slacks, under which they wore women's pantyhose. They also had a preference for perfume, especially Chanel No. 5. Jean Seberg represented a new, more androgynous model for women than had previously been popular, and the *gei bōi* saw themselves as "cultural women" *(bunka josei)*—that is, they had acquired their femininity by incorporating particular sartorial codes and modes of behavior associated with cultural constructions of the feminine. *Gei bōi* pointed out that while the basic categories of "man" and "woman" had not changed since the time of Adam and Eve, they represented a new "sexual idea" *(sei kannen)*—the cultural woman who constituted a third sex *(dai san no sei)*.[8]

Although the *gei bōi* were clearly keen to differentiate themselves from the *danshō*, both identities illustrate how the feminine was not reducible to the female body but could be seen as a set of practices able to be expressed by either male- or female-bodied individuals. The femininity of the *gei bōi* was, however, by definition modern and both forward and outward looking. The *danshō*, in continuing to dress and wear their hair like "traditional" Japanese women, had carried over prewar modes of transgender identity and performance, but when it came to the performance of femininity, *gei bōi* presented themselves as quintessentially modern. Matsumoto Toshio's 1969 movie *Bara no sōretsu* (Funeral parade of roses), the vehicle that launched *gei bōi* "Peter" on his career, features a fight scene between Peter and his *gei bōi* companions and a gang of real girls, whom they dismiss as *tada no onna*—"mere women"—in a move recalling earlier paradigms that regarded kabuki *onnagata* as more accomplished performers of femininity than female actresses.[9] Following Judith Butler, we may ask whether this is "a colonizing 'appropriation' of the feminine"—a question that has moral force only in a belief system that "assumes that the feminine belongs to women" (1990: 122). Historically, this has not been the case in Japan, where sexual tension had long been generated by the "dissonant juxtaposition" of feminine gender performance played out with male bodies. *Bara no sōretsu* itself plays with this dissonance in a scene where Peter (or Eddie, as he is named in the movie) and his *gei bōi* companions enter a male toilet and stand together at the urinals—much to the consternation of the other male users.[10] As Newton points out, "drag questions the 'naturalness' of the sex-role system *in toto;* if sex-role behavior can be achieved by the 'wrong' sex, it logically follows that it is in reality also achieved, not inherited by the 'right' sex" (1979: 103). What Peter and the "real" girls are fighting over is not therefore some residual or authentic expression of an inner femininity but rather the right to enact femininity as a style, or even a "way" of being in the world, a project to which biology has little to contribute.

Although *gei bōi* stressed their modernity, they had much in common with their prewar counterparts, and their popularity was enabled by enduring assumptions about gender, particularly as it was played out in the entertainment world, assumptions that survived into the postwar period. Drawing upon previous paradigms of transgender performance, there was a tendency to view *gei* not so much as a sexual orientation but more as a kind of artistic skill. The fact that, unlike *danshō, gei bōi* were not primarily prostitutes but worked in the bars taking care of and providing entertainment for guests—similar to female hostesses in regular bars—enabled them to develop skills as performers. One aspect of this performance was heightened transgendered behavior, a trend that accelerated in the next decade. In 1961, for instance, *Fūzoku kitan* (1961a: 63) described the "flourishing" business for "geisha boys" at high-class restaurants in Tokyo who, dressing as *onnagata,* performed for an elite clientele. Also in the early 1960s, nightclubs such as Tokyo's Golden Akasaka were frequently staging "imitation girl contests," which gave contestants drawn from the country's *gei bā* opportunities to compete with each other for prizes (*Hyakuman nin no yoru* 1963b). In both cases *gei bōi* (homosexual) elides into *geisha bōi* (entertainer), such that the stress is not on sexual orientation so much as artistic performance. Hence, at a time when homophile organizations in the United States were "earnestly seeking respectability" (Stein 2000: 200), Japanese *gei bōi* actually embraced paradigms that emphasized their difference. Nineteenth-century German notions positing male homosexuals as a separate "third sex" and contemporary European codes of androgynous beauty were fused with traditional Japanese understandings of transgender performance to create the figure of the *gei bōi*. While sociologists Simon and Gagnon described the homosexual community in the United States as "an impoverished cultural unit" (1967), Japan's *gei bōi* were clearly cultural innovators and, via their role as entertainers, were able to have an impact on society far wider than the confines of *kono sekai*.

The fact that the *gei bōi* was able to emerge so rapidly as a "new sexual idea" in the postwar period was in large part due to the fact that prewar nationalist notions of embodiment had collapsed along with the government's rigid regulatory regime at the war's end. The ideology of the prewar regime was so discredited that space was opened up in the ruins of

Japan's cities for the celebration of "the raw, erotic energy of Japanese bodies" (Igarashi 2000: 48), enabling the development of new forms of hetero- and homosexual play, practice and identity. The *gei bōi* rejected the aggressive masculine gender performance and the procreative imperative of the prewar regime, but instead of aligning himself with discredited modes of "traditional" femininity, he sought to embody the new androgynous ideal of beauty emerging in Europe that was to dominate the cultural scene of the late '60s. The hybridized gender performance of Japan's *gei bōi*, then, which drew upon earlier paradigms of the transgender entertainer coupled with new western ideals of androgyny, is an instance of what Iwabuchi terms "transformative local practices," which result in "the formation of non-Western indigenized modernity" (2002: 40). The *gei bōi*, like the American gay man, can therefore be seen as a mode of subjectivity enabled by changes taking place in postwar modernity, but *gei bōi* is a Japanese category that arose in relation to local Japanese conditions, not some copy of a western original.

Despite the visibility that *gei bōi* had achieved in mainstream Japanese media by the early 1960s, the term itself was to be challenged for a while by another innovation from overseas—the "blue boys," or transsexual performers associated with Le Carrousel de Paris, Europe's most famous transsexual cabaret. Although *gei bōi* were often beautiful, theirs was the androgynous beauty associated with the *bishōnen*, or "beautiful youth"; many did not attempt to pass as women but understood themselves in terms of a third sex. The blue boys, however, went one stage further and sought to change their bodies through a variety of medical procedures so as to become women.

THE BLUE-BOY BOOM

In the early 1960s there was great excitement generated in the Japanese media by a touring cabaret of French transsexual and transgender performers known as Le Carrousel de Paris. Japanese audiences had first been introduced to Le Carrousel through the movie *Europa di notte* (dir. Alessandro Blasetti, 1959), which was released in Japan as *Yōroppa no yoru* (European night) in 1961. The movie, shot in documentary style, describes the nightlife of several European capitals and, in the Paris section, features the singer Coccinelle, Le Carrousel's most famous transsexual performer. Coccinelle's performance sparked interest in both the perverse press and mainstream media,[11] and members of the cabaret were subsequently invited to perform in Japan.

Le Carrousel first performed in Tokyo in 1963 at the Golden Akasaka nightclub, and such was the troupe's critical success that it was invited back in 1964 and 1965. (See figure 3.1.) The most famous members had undergone sex-change surgery in Casablanca, and much was made of them in the Japanese media. In 1964, for instance, the scandal magazine *Hyakuman nin no yoru* ran an article entitled "The man-made beauties from Paris," which led to a spate of articles about sex-change operations. The term most widely used to refer to the transgender performers from Le Carrousel was "blue boy" *(burū bōi),* the origin of which is obscure but is probably a famous Gainsborough portrait of that name depicting an effeminate youth. The new term did not displace *gei bōi* but was used alongside it, especially to refer to those performers who had undergone surgical procedures. The media were obviously interested in the sexual preferences of the visiting performers, it being noted that while Cappucine was living in a "husband and wife relationship" *(fūfu kankei)* with a partner named Michael, and consequently did not have affairs, the others "set off nightly on a hunt for Japanese men" (*Asahi geinō* 1964).

Figure 3.1 Promotional flier for Le Carrousel performance at Tokyo's Golden Akasaka nightclub, 1963

The discussion surrounding Le Carrousel was not the first time that Japanese media had shown interest in the phenomenon of "sex change" *(seitenkan);* several high-profile performers had already undergone sex reassignment surgery in Japan. Japan's first male-to-female operation, on cabaret singer Nagai Akiko, is reported to have occurred in 1951, one year *before* the case of Christine Jorgensen brought international attention to the procedure. The first female-to-male sex change to be widely reported was that of athletics star Tsutsumi Taeko, who, after transitioning, reentered society as a salaryman named Kiyotaka (*Kingu gurafu* 1954). Reports of Nagai's sex change and the success of her subsequent entertainment career proved an inspiration for other transgenders, who followed suit (Saitō 1959: 151), although not all went so far as the complete operation. Later, in 1962, Ginza Rose, who had begun her career as a show dancer for the occupation forces, received a sex-change operation so that she could get married (albeit her husband was officially entered into her family register as her adopted younger brother). She was followed in 1964 by the singer Carrousel Maki, who had her testicles removed (Maruo 1966: 63) as the first stage in her transition to womanhood, which was finally completed in Morocco in 1973.

For Japan's *gei* world, surprise at the phenomenal success of the Carrousel performers has been likened to a similar sense of shock experienced after the arrival of the black ships[12] a century earlier (Mitsuhashi 2001). Some *gei bōi,* who were already conspicuous for their effeminate mannerisms, were encouraged to go further in developing a transgendered appearance, paralleling a situation also taking place in the United States at this time. As Newton points out, the world of female impersonators in the United States saw a steady increase in the number of "hormone queens" who were using hormones, implants and surgical procedures to enhance their feminine appeal (1979: 102). *Hyakuman nin no yoru* (1963b) points to 1963 as the year in which "it became extremely popular in the gay world [*gei kai*] to come close to being perfect women"—the first stage of which was to undergo both silicone and hormone injections to develop breasts that were "indistinguishable from the real thing." While sex-change operations were not without precedent in the 1950s, many transgenders in the immediate postwar period remained identified with the kabuki *onnagata* model, where "even though they maintained a male body, [*onnagata*] took particular pride in the fact that they were able to appear more feminine than women" (Saitō 1959: 152). The 1960s, however, saw a movement away from this traditional mode of feminine performance toward the surgical creation of a womanlike body.[13]

Whether these procedures were undertaken for purely personal or for economic reasons is difficult to ascertain. Mitsuhashi suggests that many *gei bōi* were encouraged to transgender themselves further, even to the extent of undergoing surgical procedures, for primarily economic reasons. As she comments, "For the purposes of entertainment, the value of male nudity was basically nil. Accordingly, if men changed sex to female, their value would be raised," all the more so since such performers were relatively scarce (2001: 7). "Formerly male female performers" became an item in many cabarets and traveling revues, engaging in exotic dancing and stripping as well as singing chansons in their husky voices.

A fascinating glimpse of the impact the Carrousel troupe had upon transgender culture of the time is given by Taiwanese author Wu Jiwen, whose chapter "Rose is the past tense of rise," from the novel *Galaxies in Ecstasies* (trans. Martin 2003), describes the (formerly male) character Seikei, who was working as a "sister boy" in an Osaka bar at the time of Le Carrousel's first tour. In Wu's story, the Chinese Seikei is not a particularly successful cross-dresser until she sees the Carrousel show and later visits one of the transsexual members of the troupe in her hotel room. At this meeting she is given the card of a surgeon in Morocco who performs sex-change operations; she decides to commit herself to a path of gender transformation. The story describes Seikei's move to an elite transgender club in Tokyo's Kabuki-chō area in Shinjuku, where the proprietor gives her an advance to begin hormone treatment. The transformation in her appearance produced by the hormones vastly increases her earning capacity, enabling her some years later to travel to Morocco for the surgery—a path also taken by Japan's most famous transsexual entertainer, Carrousel Maki.

Partly due to the influence of Le Carrousel, the 1960s saw a proliferation in the number of establishments, known as "show bars" *(shō bā),* offering floor shows that featured *gei bōi* who performed for audiences of heterosexual tourists.[14] One such boy was "Peter" (b. 1952; named after his resemblance to Peter Pan), who had left home at age 15 and was dancing in a Roppongi show bar when he was spotted by a talent scout and cast in Matsumoto Toshio's 1969 movie *Bara no sōretsu* (Funeral parade of roses). (See figure 3.2.) Peter is a well-known face on Japanese television, being one of a number of transgendered "talents" who frequently appear on variety shows. International audiences may also be familiar with him from Kurosawa Akira's film *Ran* (loosely based on *King Lear*), in which he played the fool.

Shot in a semidocumentary style, *Bara no sōretsu* provides a glimpse into the late-1960s avant-garde world of a *gei bā* named Genet. Eddie (played by Peter) is a beautiful *gei bōi* who works as a hostess in the bar, eventually stealing away the sponsor (and lover) of the bar's mama. Eddie is an orphan who was deserted by his father at an early age and had killed his own mother in a domestic dispute. As the plot unfolds, Eddie comes

Figure 3.2 Promotional flier for Peter in *Funeral Parade of Roses,* 1969

to realize that his new lover is none other than his own father, whom he no longer recognized. Shocked at the discovery, Eddie blinds himself, in a take on the Oedipus myth. Of more interest than the main plot, however, are the fascinating scenes inside the bar where the boys are interviewed about their lives, the director asking them how they came to choose "this path" *(kono michi)*. The gender differentiation in the bar is very clear: the staff is made up of cross-dressing effeminate youths, whereas the customers are older, masculine men, including foreigners.

Other than their impact upon transgender identity and performance, Le Carrousel had another lasting impact, this time upon Japanese medical practice. As mentioned earlier, during the 1950s and early 1960s a number of castration and sex-change operations had been performed on male entertainers. However, in 1965, in what became known as the "Blue Boy Trial" *(burū bōi saiban)*, a doctor was investigated for removing the male sex organs of three men who were later arrested on prostitution charges. In 1969, a ruling was passed down that since he had interfered with otherwise healthy sex organs, he was in violation of Clause 28 of the Eugenic Protection Law, which forbade any unnecessary procedure resulting in sterilization (Miyano 1978: 76–7). From this time on sex-change operations were deemed illegal in Japan, until in 1998 strict new ethical guidelines for the procedure were enacted (Ishida 2002). Meanwhile, the category of "blue boy" faded from public consciousness, leaving *gei bōi* as the primary term for describing transgender/homosexual men who worked in the entertainment world.

FEMALE TRANSGENDER IDENTITIES

In Japanese queer subcultures, as in the United States at this time, "the males considered as a group, [had] a much more elaborate subculture and contribute[d] disproportionately to distinctively homosexual concepts, styles and terminology" (Newton 1979: 27). Indeed, as pointed out in chapter 2, discussion of female same-sex sexuality in the Japanese media was largely a process of back-formation, in which female terms were devised in relation to preexisting male categories, identities and institutions. However, the United States differed from Japan in that there was considerable interaction in the former between male and female homosexual worlds. In Japan, there was comparatively little interaction between queer men and women, since few social spaces existed in which they could rub shoulders. This meant there was little scope for the development of a shared agenda.

Esther Newton points out how in the U.S. "gay bars" of the 1960s the term "gay" was often used to emphasize solidarity between male and female homosexuals, as in the phrase "gay people" (1979: 26). In Japan, however, *gei* was used exclusively for effeminate males in the entertainment industry; there was no designation other than the clinical *dōseiaisha,* the Chinese-character translation of the English "homosexual," used by medical experts but not individuals themselves, that could express a sense of commonality between men and women, who occupied largely separate corners of *kono sekai*. However, despite the fact that men and women with homosexual interests were less likely to share the same spaces in Japan than in the United States or other anglophone cultures, the developing *gei* world did have an impact upon female same-sex practice and community formation, with "brother girls," female equivalents of the *gei bōi,* finding their own niche in the bar and entertainment trade.

However, before outlining this development, it will be helpful to take a brief look at the history of female transgender practice in Japan. Although in the modern period female cross-dressing has been most often associated with the Takarazuka and other all-girl theater troupes (Robertson

1998), women dressing as men were not without precedent in premodern Japan. From the twelfth to the fourteenth centuries, female entertainers dressed in male attire when performing "male dancing" at the Kyoto court (Leupp 1998: 31). In the early Edo period (1600–1867) Okuni, the leader of "women's kabuki," and her dancers played both male and female roles on stage. However, official disapproval of women taking male roles as well as anxieties about the actresses engaging in unlicensed prostitution led to women being banned from the stage and to the establishment of the tradition of male actors playing both male and female roles in kabuki.

Later in the period, legal records indicate a cross-dressing woman known as Takejirō (a man's name) was arrested on several occasions for petty theft and, after repeatedly being told not to wear men's clothes, was banished from Edo (Seki 1980). Other records suggest that some women travelers, whose freedom of movement was more circumscribed than that of men,[15] dressed as men while on the road so as to avoid trouble with the authorities (and, one presumes, fellow travelers) (Vaporis 1994: 155–9; 183). When discovered, these women, rather than being punished, seem simply to have been turned back, suggesting that cross-dressing in this context was not considered a very serious infringement of the rules.

Women dressing as men in order to take advantage of men's greater freedom of movement seems to have carried on in the early Meiji period. According to newspaper reports, the relaxation of dress and hairstyle codes (women had previously been required to wear their hair long) had apparently led to a spate of women dressing as men so as to move more freely about town (Shimokawa 1995a: 56–7). Robertson also mentions the famous male-dresser Kawashima Yoshiko (1906–1948), "who had donned a military uniform and passed as a man during the early stages of Japanese imperialism in China and Manchuria" (1992: 429). No doubt there were many other passing women in other contexts who did not come to the authorities' attention.

"Situational" accounts of cross-dressing also exist in the postwar literature. Immediately after the war there was a large imbalance between the female and male population of Japan's cities, since so many Japanese soldiers had died in the war and others were still stranded overseas in internment camps waiting to be repatriated—for many, a process that extended over the better part of a decade. Dower notes that the result was "a large cohort of women, most of them born between 1916 and 1926, confronted [by] the prospect not merely of coping with postwar hardships without a marriage partner, but of never marrying at all" (2000: 107). An unsigned article entitled "Male-dressing mania" in the June 1954 issue of *Fūzoku kagaku*[16] suggests that some women adopted an innovative strategy in the face of this absence of men. The author notes that because of the lack of eligible bachelors, some women were forming same-sex relationships, wherein one partner took on a male identity and worked as a man "for material reasons" without others being aware of her biological sex.[17] Unfortunately, unlike the cross-dressing male prostitutes, whose activities were well documented by the perverse press, women who passed as men on an ad hoc basis out of economic necessity left few records of their experiences and it is difficult to know whether their cross-dressing was partly the result of same-sex desire. However, from the late 1950s, an increasing number of articles relating to female cross-dressers *(dansō)* began to appear in both the perverse and the tabloid press, suggesting that the popularity of female-to-male transgender entertainers was now widespread. This impacted upon women with same-sex and transgender interests, creating increased space within the entertainment and bar world for female-to-male transgender performance—albeit this subculture was far less extensive than that available to men.

The existence of bars catering to women-loving women is less well documented than that of those frequented by men. The earliest reference to such a bar I have come across occurs in Sonomura Keiko's "Lesbos communication" column of August 1954 (Sonomura 1954).[18] However, as described in the previous chapter, it is difficult to take her observations at face value, since doubt exists as to the reliability of her observations about women's same-sex love. In the column, Keiko claims to have been taken by a friend to a members-only all-woman coffee shop *(kissaten)* named Narushisu (perhaps Narcissus?), in San-chōme (probably Shinjuku). The coffee shop (or rather bar, since alcohol was served) was situated on the second floor of a building above a beauty parlor and consisted of one small room with a bar counter and about five box seats. The madam was a woman named Mayumi, who dressed in men's suits; the female waiters, or "boys" *(bōi),* also dressed in slim-cut men's slacks.

Keiko was served by a "boy" named Lily, about 17 years of age, who had short hair and was dressed in gray slacks and a black sweater. After serving the drinks, Lily stayed on in the box to chat with Keiko and her friend, much like a hostess in a regular bar. Keiko noted that all the other customers were women and that there was consternation in the box seat near the window, where a young woman was crying. Sonomura Keiko goes on to describe the argument taking place between a young girl and a married woman in the prurient manner characteristic of her column, again raising questions about her reliability as a witness. However, Keiko's description of the bar, particularly the manner in which the "boys" cross-dressed and acted toward the female customers as men—taking the lead, for instance, when dancing to records—does anticipate more reliable accounts of such bars dating from the 1960s.

In the early '60s, cross-dressed female bar workers were known as *dansō no reijin*, or "male-dressing beauties," a term that had been used to describe the male-role players *(otoko yaku)* in the all-women Takarazuka revue from the mid-1930s (Robertson 1992: 429; Curran and Welker in press). Other terms employed included *burazā gāruzu*, or "brother girls," the female equivalent of the male "sister boys" (Toyama 1999: 214–5) who worked in similar establishments for men. The cross-dressed employees were also described as *bōisshu*, or "boyish," especially in the Kansai region (Toyama 1999: 217). An article in *Fūzoku kitan* describes the five brother girls who worked as bartenders in "Bar T," an establishment owned by a former woman professional wrestler. The author says the women gave the impression of being "fine fellows," with their hair cut short like GIs, dressed in black trousers, white shirt and black tie, and sporting accessories like men's shoes and watches. Their behavior too was masculine—he notes how they laughed "open mouthed" with their shoulders shaking—but the impression was a pleasing one, since they seemed to the author like "beautiful boys" *(bishōnen)* (Nakamura 1960: 103).

These bars, although few compared to those staffed by male cross-dressers, provided some women with opportunities to live and work outside the heterosexual economy and the constraining gender roles that more typical employment allowed. Eru (b. 1958), who worked in one such club in the 1970s, comments that she found ordinary daytime work as a woman in a patriarchal society to be "feudal" but that in her night job as a cross-dressed bartender "I felt released from men's flirting. . . . I felt at home" (Toyama 1999: 164).

One of the earliest clubs to feature cross-dressed female staff, the existence of which is well documented, was Yume no Shiro (Dream Castle), which opened in the early '60s. The club, described in the media as a *dansō no reijin no mise* (bar of male-dressing beauties), featured female bar tenders who cross-dressed in suit and tie, as well as female hostesses who wore conventional feminine attire (Toyama 1999: 215). This bar, like the "gay bars," did not cater to a transgendered clientele but appealed to regular customers who were looking for something different.[19] Mizuno (b. 1942), one of the bartenders who worked at the Yume no Shiro at this time, described the clientele as approximately 80 percent men who were interested in the female hostesses and 20 percent women with an interest in the cross-dressed bartenders. She also points out that it was common for the bartenders to date and have sex with the hostesses who worked in the club (Toyama 1999: 216–7).

The middle '60s saw a boom in interest in female cross-dressers that, although smaller in scope, paralleled the similar media interest in male cross-dressers. Several bars featuring cross-dressed hosts sprang up in entertainment districts in Tokyo as well as in Osaka, Kyoto and Nagoya

(Shiba 1997: 111). Indeed, such was the demand for hosts that bars began to advertise in the women's press for "male dressing beauties" (Toyama 1999: 65). In 1965 Mizuno started work at a new kind of club, called Meme, where all staff members were cross-dressed women. The Meme featured three bartenders and eight floor staff dressed either in tuxedos or in suits. This was still a time before unisex fashions were common, and a woman in an expensively tailored man's suit was eye-catching. Unlike earlier clubs, the clientele of these new establishments was mainly women who were attracted to the atmosphere created by the cross-dressed staff; the customers included professional female hostesses, geisha, models, female pro wrestlers, Takarazuka actresses and rich housewives (Toyama 1999: 218; Shiba 1997: 110–1). In the new-style bars, the hosts were expected to be able to sing and to dance with the customers as well as mix drinks and provide stimulating conversation.

Bars that catered exclusively to women seeking relationships with other women were rarer. Mei (b. 1925) mentions a small bar called Gorō, operating in Asakusa, Tokyo, in the early '60s, where hostesses in conventional women's clothes, as well as women customers, were drinking partners for cross-dressed women (Toyama 1999: 64). At this time, a common paradigm for woman-woman liaisons that used the same terminology as was applied to homosexual men was *tachi* (literally a sword bearer—referring to the active role) and *neko* (a cat, perhaps because of the mewling sound made during lovemaking). Women who dressed in male clothes and presented themselves through characteristically male behavior would date and have sex with women who maintained a conventional feminine appearance and demeanor. This division paralleled the butch/femme relationships common among working-class lesbians in the United States during the 1950s and '60s (Faderman 1992: 167–74), but in Japan it was not a class-based phenomenon; given the high cost of drinking at such bars and the large clientele they drew from the entertainment world, it was purchasing power rather than class background that gave women access to this scene.

Another club often mentioned in transgendered women's accounts was Kikōshi (Young Noble), opened in Roppongi, Tokyo, in 1973; there the hosts cross-dressed in very expensive suits tailored to fit the contours of a woman's body. The clientele of this bar included many women attracted to other women, although the high cost of spending an evening at the bar placed it out of the reach of most (Toyama 1999: 165). Although *okama* or *gei* bars that provided floor shows for a general audience remained consistently popular, cross-dressing women's bars oriented specifically toward women faced severe financial constraints and largely disappeared after the boom period in the late '60s and early '70s (Shiba 1997). Among the problems faced by women's bars was the fact that women had less disposable income than men; also, while men would spend time and money in the bars whether or not they were in a relationship, women tended to use the bars to meet partners and then drop out of the scene while the relationships lasted (Shiba 1997). It was not until 1985 that a new kind of "lesbian" bar that largely dispensed with the *tachi/neko* division appeared—the Mars Bar, which opened in Shinjuku, Tokyo (Kuiia sutadiizu henshū iinkai 1997: 32).[20]

One other context in which lesbian love was sometimes discussed was women's professional wrestling *(joshi puroresu)*. American-style (male) professional wrestling had been introduced to Japan in the early 1950s through the efforts of Rikidōzan (1924–1963), whose syncretistic fighting style and overt showmanship endeared him to fans. Women's wrestling too broke into the mainstream in 1954 after a successful Japan tour by American world champion Mildred Burke (1915–1989). While women's wrestling was officially performed as a sport, bouts also took place in strip clubs, vaudeville theaters and among traveling theater companies—many of which were set up to entertain the U.S. forces during the occupation and the Korean War. This underworld was a rich source of material for writers of lesbian pulp fiction who imagined various amorous and sadomasochistic scenarios taking place between these "tempestuous" and "barbarous" women, scenarios that were no doubt enjoyed by male and female readers alike (see for example Kyōgaku 1959).

The boom in women's wrestling drew attention in the perverse press, with numerous articles philosophizing on the reasons for the sport's attraction to a mainly male audience. Since the venues for many wrestling bouts were strip clubs, it was not the prospect of seeing (nearly) naked women that enticed audiences. Rather, some commentators regarded the shows as sadomasochistic performances, since they offered viewers the opportunity to experience vicariously women's more "barbarous" sadistic side (Oniyama 1955). However, pro wrestling was also of interest to many women, since it offered the unusual spectacle of women engaging in the previously masculine-gendered performance of public violence. Also, the short hairstyles, the muscled, athletic bodies and the masculinized speech of the female wrestlers made this scene attractive to some women who preferred to express themselves through male-gendered behavior.

There was also some crossover between the wrestling and bar worlds. Successful women wrestlers could often earn a large amount of money, enabling them to retire and open their own bars, which they staffed with fellow ex-wrestlers and other "brother girls" (Shiba 1997: 110; Nakamura 1960: 106). Meke (b. 1937), for instance, speaks of performing as a pro wrestler for a few years in her late teens before an injury to her knee led to her retirement. Afterward, she performed comic pro wrestling as part of a touring theater troupe that also included cross-dressed female singers and comics. Meke found a further application for her wrestling skills while working as a host in the Yume no Shiro, when she threw an unruly male customer into a fishpond that stood in the middle of the room (Toyama 1999: 100–2).

Just as the terms relating to male transgenders have changed over time, terminology describing female transgenders has also shifted. From the early 1970s the word *onabe* began to replace the terms "brother girl," *dansōsha* (male-dresser) and *dansō no reijin* (male-dressing beauty). *Onabe* means "pan" and is patterned on the traditional term *okama,* or "pot," also a slang term for the buttocks that in the Taisho period (1912–1925) came to designate a passive male homosexual. For a period from the late '80s through the '90s, the term "Miss Dandy" was widely used in the media and was also in vogue in certain clubs and such host bars as Club Marilyn, described by Robertson (1998: 144). The term also featured as the title of Toyama Hitomi's (1999) collection of life stories of "women living as men."

However, *onabe* has become, and remains, the most visible and widely understood female transgender category in Japan and is now quite distinct from *rezu* (from the English "lesbian"), which is generally understood to refer to women engaged in same-sex play for a male audience. To avoid this association, many same-sex-desiring women in Japan use the full English loanword *rezubian,* or, dropping the offensive "*rezu*" part, refer to themselves simply as *bian*. Others use another English loanword, *daiku* (dyke), which in Japanese means "carpenter" (Izumo et al. 1997), thus making it a useful argot term for discussing lesbian issues in situations where the conversation may be overheard. Although comparatively few, lesbian bars do exist in Tokyo and have appeared sporadically in other major cities but *onabe bā* (*onabe* bars) have been more successful. *Onabe bā,* like their more numerous *gei* counterparts, cater to a broad clientele, both women with an interest in transgender women and regular customers looking for something different (Maree 2003; Longinetto 1996), testifying once again to the enduring popularity of transgender performance in the entertainment world.

THE DECLINE OF THE *GEI BŌI*

Despite the brief efflorescence of the blue boys and limited media interest in "cross-dressing beauties" and brother girls, *gei bōi* remained the most conspicuous homosexual category in Japanese popular culture until the early 1980s. During this time *gei bā* (distinct from *homo bā,* where homosexual men would meet) developed in major cities all over Japan, offering entertainment to a largely straight clientele, often comprising local office workers and tourists from the countryside. These bars, which offered cabaret-style performances, were often discussed in the press; *gei bōi* were featured in photo essays as well as in photography collections. Famous media *tarento* (personalities) who had begun their careers as *gei bōi*, such as Miwa Akihiro, Carrousel Maki and Peter, continued to appear on television, and new *gei bōi* performers continued to make the transition from the subculture to the mainstream.

Ironically, the success of one such *gei bōi* was to result in the demise of the category itself. In 1982, Betty, the mama-san of Betty's Mayonnaise, an Osaka *gei bā*, introduced a new term, *nyūhāfu* (new half), as a designation for transgender performers. "Half," or *hāfu* in Japanese, is used to signify individuals of mixed race, usually Japanese and Caucasian; Betty said of herself, "I'm half man and half woman, therefore I'm a *new half*." Like *gei bōi*, *nyūhāfu* was a trendy fusion of two English words, but with a very specific Japanese meaning; it soon caught on in the press and began to be adopted as a self-designation by many transgender performers (McLelland 2004).

Significantly, the rise of the category *nyūhāfu* occurred just prior to the founding of a branch of the International Lesbian and Gay Association (ILGA) in Osaka in 1984, which led to an increased use of *gei*, as part of the phrase *rezubian to gei* (lesbian and gay) in the Japanese press, and enabled a more political conceptualization of homosexuality as a sexual minority category, akin to other minority populations in Japan. The result was that by the time of Japan's second "gay boom" in the early 1990s (McLelland 2000a: 32–6), the terms *rezubian* and *gei* were being used in a manner very similar to their English homophones. These factors, along with the widespread adoption of *gei* as a self-referent by homosexual men on the Japanese Internet (McLelland 2000b: 153), mean that the term *gei bōi* now has an old-fashioned, provincial connotation and is seldom used except by older people.

CONCLUSION

As outlined above, from the late 1950s Japan underwent a "gay boom" that saw an explosion of homosexual discussion and representation in the popular media unparalleled by developments in any anglophone society until the early 1970s. *Gei* had already been established as a term for effeminate young men who worked in the entertainment industry by the middle 1950s—some 20 years prior to the adoption of the term "gay" in English-language media. Although *gei* is certainly related to "gay" in English, this latter term had *itself* only won out as a preferred term for self-designation within U.S. homosexual communities during the war and was not picked up by mainstream media until the early 1970s. Hence, while it is clear that Japan's encounter with the Allied forces during the occupation resulted very quickly in the generation of new types of sexual discourse and the proliferation of new modes of homosexual play, practice and identity, these Japanese subcultures were very different from the developing gay subcultures in the United States at this time, not least in terms of their apparent openness and the freedom with which they were discussed in the press.

While in the postwar period in the United States "gay" was associated with the development of essentialist, masculine homosexual identities, in Japan the development of *gei* as primarily a *transgender* and later a *commercial* category encouraged a movement in the opposite direction. The convenient homophony of *gei* as "gay" and *gei* as "artistic accomplishment" only served to reinforce the hybridized manner in which this term came to be used in Japanese to signify a new kind of sexual being—the *gei bōi,* who was defined more in terms of his role as entertainer than in terms of his choice of sexual partner. Consequently, the Japanese *gei bōi* was as different from the American gay man as he was different from the *danshō* or male prostitute who had preceded him. Rather than being viewed as a cultural imposition from "the west," the *gei bōi* should be seen as a specifically Japanese response to the new opportunities for gendered embodiment opened up by Japan's postwar modernity.

Although *gei* in Japanese was not used in the more general English sense (and is still not used in this sense today) to refer to "gay people" of both sexes, *gei* culture did have an important impact on the development of subcultures of same-sex-desiring women; sister girls gave rise to brother girls, *okama* (pots) to *onabe* (pans) and *gei bā* to bars for cross-dressing beauties. Like *gei bōi,* who were conspicuous for dressing, speaking and acting in a manner normally reserved for women, the gender performance of female transgenders was similarly "inverted" through their adoption of male dress codes and speaking patterns and, most conspicuously, in the public display of violence. However, men's and women's homosexual cultures remained largely separate, and there was little concept of a common cause or identity shared between male and female occupants of *kono sekai.* This changed little during the next decade, when yet another queer category emerged into the media spotlight. The next chapter discusses how, during the 1970s, the image of the *homo,* or masculine-identified homosexual man, rose to challenge the transgender model of homosexual identity and behavior personified by the *gei bōi.*

NOTES

1. The term "homosexualist" was occasionally used in the reports of regulatory agents such as police, doctors and private investigators in the United States prior to World War II (Chauncey 1994: 15).

2. An article in *Hyakuman nin no yoru* (1963c: 153) also mentions the reexportation theory of "gay," but this probably derives from Tomita's book.

3. Tomita Eizō was a manga artist and an example of the kind of public "intellectual" *(interi)* who interested himself in Japan's world of sex customs. After the publication of his book *Gei* he became something of a spokesman for transgender issues. See, for instance, his comments in *Shūkan gendai* 1965.

4. Miwa's later role as the stunning femme fatale in Fukusawa Kinji's 1968 movie *Kuro Tokage* (Black lizard) established him as Japan's leading transgender artist; the popular magazine *Bungei shunjū* declared that "a man more woman-like than women is born" *(onna yori onnarashii otoko ga tanjō suru).*

5. Pages 138–9.

6. Page 125.

7. Cécile was the name of Seberg's character sporting this hairstyle in *Bonjour Tristesse.*

8. The term "third sex" was a common designation for homosexual men in the postwar period, and like most of the other terms imported into Japanese at this time, such as *homo, gei* and *sodomia,* it referred only to men. There were some attempts to refer to female homosexuals as a "fourth sex," but this never caught on (Ōta 1957: 26).

9. Since there was no indigenous tradition of women actors, women's roles in many of Japan's early films, from 1909 to 1919, were played by male actors trained as *onnagata* (Mitsuhashi, 2001: 5), which led to lively debates in the media about the relative abilities of male and female actors to perform as "women."

10. *Tachiben,* or "standing to pee," is a key signifier of masculine identity that some male-to-female transgenders in Toyama's (1999) collection *Miss Dandy* express regret they are unable to do.

11. See for example *Fūzoku kitan* (1961b) and *Shūkan bunshun* (1961).

12. "Black ships" refers to the American ships that visited Japan heralding the end of Tokugawa rule in 1853. The image of the ships, when used as a metaphor, expresses the sense of disorientation generated by exposure to a totally new, alien culture.

13. The use of female hormones by men who cross-dressed professionally was, of course, not without precedent in the 1950s. The earliest account of hormone use I have come across is a passing mention in an article on cross-dressing in the August 1956 edition of the magazine *Kappa;* see Shiga (1956).

14. An article in the April 1963 (pp. 138–9) edition of the magazine *Ura Mado* (Rear window) refers to the "touristization" *(kankōka)* that was sweeping through Japan's gay bars at this time, wherein "homosexuals" *(homo)* were being displaced by "ordinary customers" *(futsū no kyaku),* including many women.

15. This was partly due to the *sankin kōtai,* or "alternate attendance," system maintained by the shogunate, which required *daimyō* or regional lords to maintain residences in Edo, where their wives, concubines and children served as virtual hostages, thus ensuring their continued loyalty. Samurai women were not allowed to travel between Edo and their home provinces without special passports. Numerous checkpoints were set up along the main roadway linking Edo with provinces to the south.

16. "Dansō maniya," pp. 148–9.

17. Tanaka (2002: 113) mentions that some local authorities urged parents to

disguise their female children as boys during the early days of the occupation, fearing that they would otherwise become the objects of sexual predation by the Allied troops.

18. There is actually a very brief mention of an exclusive coffee shop in Shimbashi where "women go to buy women" in an article in the March 1954 *Fūzoku kurabu,* but it is added as an afterthought, and as the anonymous author points out, it is based on hearsay (K 1954).

19. Faderman (1992: 127) mentions that bars catering to gay men and lesbians as well as heterosexual tourists "who came to gawk" proliferated in the United States during the war years; an example was New York's 181 Club, which featured butch lesbians in tuxedos and female impersonators.

20. Lesbian parties had, however, been held at the gay bar Matsuri in Shinjuku since 1982.

4

The Development of a *Homo* Subculture

The discussion of postwar perverse culture in preceding chapters has shown how Japanese media pioneered in the openness with which they represented a wide range of nonmainstream sexual and gender practices and identities. As early as 1954, magazines such as *Fūzoku kitan, Fūzoku kagaku* and *Fūzoku zōshi* not only published upbeat and informative articles about both male and female homosexuality in their roundtable discussion format but also made efforts toward establishing social clubs for their same-sex-desiring readers. Since membership in the clubs was often tied in with the purchase of subscriptions to the magazines, this was an early acknowledgment of the existence of a homosexual *market*.

Although *Fūzoku kagaku* and *Fūzoku zōshi,* the two commercial magazines that did the most to support and foster the notion of a homosexual identity, did not survive past the middle 1950s, articles reflecting the experience of male sexual nonconformists, whether cross-dressers or homosexuals or both, continued to be printed in longer-lasting perverse magazines, such as *Fūzoku kitan* and *Kitan kurabu,* until the 1970s. Articles about lesbianism also commonly appeared in their pages, but unlike the early 1950s discussion of "Lesbos love," which seemed to genuinely engage with women's experience, these later articles presented the figure of the *rezubian* as an object of male desire, and their accounts were almost invariably authored by or directed at men.

During the 1960s there was a distinct change in the nature of the perverse press. The 1960s was a decade of increasing consumer choice in Japan; for most people the privations of the war years had been left behind, and there was a trend toward more personal, lifestyle-oriented consumption. Throughout the decade, there was also an accompanying trend toward specialization in the perverse press. The polymorphous perverse collections of the 1950s, in which articles on male and female homosexuality, a variety of fetishes, cross-dressing, personal confessions, letters seeking advice on sexual issues and advertisements for a range of sex-related products and publications could all appear between the covers of the same magazines, gradually gave way to a more male-oriented heterosexual focus as other niche publications arose to cater to nonheterosexual minorities.

By the mid-1970s what Shimokawa refers to as "perverse general department-store magazines" (1995b) had all but given way to more niche-oriented publications. *Fūzoku kitan*, the last surviving perverse magazine of the postwar period, was eventually remodeled and reissued under the new name *SM Fantajia* (SM fantasia) in 1975; the trend was definitely toward greater specialization.[1] By this time the world of *sodomia*, populated by *homo*, or more masculine-identified homosexual men, was largely divorced from the world occupied by *josōsha*, or cross-dressers, as well from as the commercial world of the *gei bōi*, as acknowledged by the development of niche magazines oriented toward a *homo* readership. At the same time, different social spaces were developing that served the different groups within *kono sekai*.

This chapter looks at the development of niche media and social organizations catering to *homo*—that is, masculine-identified homosexual men—who increasingly rejected both the transgender and intergenerational paradigms of homosexual identity and practice that had previously structured sexual interaction between men, instead moving toward more egalitarian relationships characteristic of how modern gay identity has come to be understood.

EARLY HOMOSEXUAL NETWORKING

The perverse magazines of the 1950s had given their readers a new vocabulary through which to conceptualize their desires and, importantly, gave ample testimony to the fact that no matter how seemingly perverse or abnormal an individual's fantasies might be, there were others, indeed many others, who shared them. In a group-oriented society like Japan where the pressure on the individual to conform to "commonsense" notions of propriety can be strong (Tōgō 2002; Lunsing 2001), the perverse magazines gave diverse individuals a means to imagine themselves part of a wider community, and a sense of belonging to "this world," or *kono sekai*. Many were able to take comfort in the fact that they were not alone in treading "this path" *(kono michi)*, a path toward purely private fantasy and fulfillment divorced from the official roles they might otherwise play as fathers, mothers, workers or productive citizens of a rapidly rebuilding Japan. One reader, for instance, describes how his discovery of magazines like *Fūzoku kurabu* and *Fūzoku kitan* released him from the daily grind as a salaryman by opening up a new world of sexual experience. Through reading the stories in the magazines, he was able to nurture fantasies that had previously been buried at the back of his mind, and through the magazines' personals columns and advertisements he was able to find his entrée into the world of cross-dressing and sadomasochism (Yajima 2000: 67).

Readers seem to have responded to the perverse press in numerous ways. While some letter writers expressed a more academic interest in *nanshoku* (the use of the traditional term here suggests a certain historical distance from the topic) disavowing any "sodomite tastes" *(sodomii shumi)* themselves (see for example Shinagawa 1953), the homoeroticism expressed in many other letters is remarkable, especially if the constraints on such expression in the anglophone world are borne in mind. One man comments that "even if I see a woman and think she's beautiful I absolutely don't feel any attraction in my heart but when I see a handsome man in the street I feel pangs in my chest" (Fukui 1953). It is clear from such readers' contributions to the perverse press that there was a developing audience of men who recognized themselves in the magazines' pages.

Hence, these early magazines were important not simply because they described, in nonpejorative terms, a range of sexual practices outside of state-sanctioned reproductive heterosexuality but also because they offered a means for people to find each other and thereby imagine and experience community. In December 1953, for instance, *Fūzoku zōshi* published a discussion between participants in a "Sodom Symposium" that took place in Yakyoku, Tokyo's oldest gay bar, about issues associated with homosexuality. It was noted by the speakers that many (mainly rural) readers of the magazine had been sending in letters asking that the magazine set up an introduction and discussion service. They also noted that for inhabitants of the cities, opportunities for homosexual liaisons had increased rapidly after the war; numerous coffee shops, bars and movie theaters catered to homosexual clientele, and there was a thriving male-prostitution industry as well.[2]

The transformation of the first postwar *danshoku kisssaten* (homosexual coffee shops) into the *gei bā* (gay bars) of the early 1950s was outlined in chapter 2. One of the best-known of these bars was named the Brunswick, in Ginza. Mishima Yukio was a frequent visitor and used it as a model for Rudon's, the bar in his early '50s novel *Kinjiki (Forbidden Colors)* (Mishima 1968: 85; Kabiya 1955: 41). Writing in the July 1955 edition of *Amatoria,* Kabiya Kazuhiko has left an account of a visit to the Brunswick along with several other *gei bā,* including the Silver Dragon in Kanda and Bobby's Club in Shimbashi. Upon entering the Brunswick Kabiya notes that although the customer was greeted by a "door boy" of ambiguous gender, the ground floor was actually a café popular with mixed couples and young women. It featured six or seven tables, a long bar area and a fish tank along one wall. It was the second floor, reached by a staircase near the entrance, that contained a bar catering to men who walked "that path." Compared with other *gei* venues of the early '50s, the Brunswick was a large, classy venue, with its long bar, seven or eight box seats and a small dance area that could accommodate three or four couples at a time.

The Brunswick's master was, unlike the *mama-san* of many other *gei* meeting places, a professional café owner who had managed other venues before the war and whose wife ran a nearby dumpling restaurant. Kabiya describes him as a *shudō aikōsha*—that is, a "lover of the way of boys," or in more modern parlance, a *pede,* or pederast; he staffed both the café and the bar exclusively with beautiful young men. These included Miwa Akihiro, later to become Japan's most popular transgender artist, who started work there in 1951 at the tender age of 16 (Itō 2001: 3). It had not, apparently, been the owner's intention to open a gay bar, but the beauty of the boys on the staff soon attracted a following among homosexual men. Since the bar was staffed by beautiful boys, the customers tended to be other *pede,* who were interested in establishing after-hours liaisons with the waiters. Indeed, this seems to have been a common pattern at the time, gay bars being more akin to host bars, where the customer hoped to come to some arrangement with the staff for extra service rather than to network or develop relationships with other customers.

The bars were not, of course, the only homosexual venues where sexual assignations could be arranged. Chapter 2 detailed the rapid emergence of a variety of *hattenba,* or "development spots," including parks, temple grounds and public conveniences, where homosexual men would gather after hours. These *yagaikei,* or "outdoor" venues, were complemented by numerous indoor meeting places. Kabiya mentions the existence of an elite "homo club" in Tokyo that met once a month in rented premises, where members engaged in chat, dancing and flirtation; Mishima Yukio was rumored to be among the regular attendees (1962c: 92–3). There were also privately sponsored "gay parties" *(gei pāti)* originally organized to cater to ranking occupation officers. Mishima describes one such event in *Kinjiki* where transportation was provided to a remote country house for both Allied servicemen and Japanese youths, who engaged in an all-night sex party (1968: 145). The perverse press also included rumors of a members-only homosexual club and a Chinese restaurant in Tokyo that became a homosexual meeting place after hours. According to Kabiya, the lights in the restaurant would be switched off for five minutes at a time, giving the customers the opportunity to discreetly grope each other but not to indulge in more-overt sexual acts (1962d: 92). Osaka, about which less is recorded, was, apart from the usual bars, also known to support several homosexual "orgy inns" *(inran ryokan),* with communal rooms in which much futon hopping took place. One such establishment, Takenoya (Bamboo house), first opened in 1955, still exists today and is run by the niece of the original owner (Fushimi 2002: 235).

EARLY HOMOSEXUAL ORGANIZATIONS

Although commercial operations such as bars, clubs and inns were largely organized around sexual escapades, several homosexual organizations were founded in the early postwar years through the auspices of the perverse press. In the September 1954 edition of *Fūzoku kagaku,* for instance, there appeared an advertisement for a club named the Fūzoku Kagaku Kenkyūkai (FKK)[3] stating, "The purpose of our organization is to bring together men who have absolutely no interest in women, to offer mutual encouragement and consolation, and so gain confidence in life and strive to live on in a cheerful manner." That the club was intended for a homosexual membership is clear from the club's motto: "Homosexuals [*sodomia*] have confidence! You are not perverts!"[4] This was a remarkable statement given the time and place, and it parallels similar sentiments that were being expressed in the U.S. homophile press of the time.

One person closely associated with the FKK club was Ōgiya Afu, author of numerous homosexual-themed articles and of the 1958 book *Sodomia banka* (Elegy to homosexuality), and the person in charge of answering letters sent to *Fūzoku kagaku* on the topic of "*sodomia.*" Although Ōgiya was not "out" in a contemporary sense about his homosexual preference, many of Ōgiya's writings come very close to advocacy of what could be described as the "homosexual cause"—especially in his stress on the equivalence of love between men with that between men and women. His letters column, in particular, gave him the opportunity to voice a variety of views about homosexuality—some of them very contemporary in tone. For instance, he reproduces a remarkable letter in his column "*F.K.K. dayori*" (News about FKK) in the September 1954 issue of *Fūzoku kagaku,* where the letter writer asks him to write a "homosexual constitution" *(sodomia kenpō),* asserting that male-male love is as valid as that between men and women and that it is no business of the law to "regulate" love between men as happens in Europe and America (Ōgiya 1954: 84). Such letters show that in the early 1950s in Japan, a time when there was much discussion of democratization and constitutional matters in the wake of the end of the occupation, some homosexually inclined men were beginning to consider the political ramifications of their desires, much as was happening at the same time in the United States and Europe.

Fūzoku kagaku's official sponsorship of an organization for homosexual men is indicative of the positive attitude the editors took toward sexual practices widely considered perverse, but perhaps more realistically it is also an indication of the editors' awareness that there existed a nascent homosexual market. This is made clear in numerous readers' letters asking that the editors consider publishing more articles on homosexuality[5] or even a separate *sodomia* magazine; one man commented that such a venture would "undoubtedly sell out"—especially if it were well illustrated with photographs of well-muscled young men in wet swimming pants (Tomita 1953). There appears to have been an attempt to create such a specialist magazine. An advertisement appeared in the August 1954 edition of *Fūzoku kagaku* for a monthly publication entitled *MAN,* which was to be dedicated to "homo literature and research," contributed to by members of the club and available only by subscription. This publication was not sponsored by the FKK club but by another organization named Ryūyō, a word made up of the Chinese characters for "dragon" and "yang" (as in yin and yang), or the male principle. The advertisement was placed by Kabiya Kazuhiko, another prolific writer on homosexuality whose interest in the topic was surely more than academic.

Whether *MAN* ever saw the light of day remains unknown, but *Fūzoku kagaku,* like its direct competitor *Fūzoku zōshi,* frequently included articles of a practical nature for its homosexual readership—including discussions of bars and other meeting places. This service was much appreciated by some readers, particularly those who lived in rural areas, who wrote in to mention their "delight" at discovering the magazine and to ask for help in contacting other "like-minded" *(dōkō)* men (Fukui 1953) or in finding out information about homosexual meeting places in their local area. *Fūzoku kagaku*'s sponsorship of an organization for homosexual men can therefore be seen as a further attempt to appeal to this market, especially as membership was dependent upon purchasing at least a four-month advance subscription to the magazine. Unfortunately, this ploy appears to have failed; both magazines went out of business in 1955. It is therefore unclear how successful the FKK club was or how long it survived the demise of its sponsor. However, one of the club's legacies was survey data collected from 100 members, which found its way into Ōta Tenrei's[6] edited collection *Dai san no sei* (The third sex). Published in 1957, this is probably the first book written in Japanese to be based on actual engagement with members of Japan's homosexual world.

The FKK club was not, however, Japan's first homosexual association. The Adonis Kai, or Adonis Organization, had been founded as early as 1952 and published an in-house magazine for its members, entitled

Adonis. This modest magazine, usually running to a little over 40 pages, was published from 1952 until 1962, totaling 63 issues in all. *Adonis* was contemporaneous with *ONE*, America's first homophile magazine, which had a print run of 3,000 (Ramakers 2000: 79). Unlike the perverse magazines, but like its U.S. counterpart, *Adonis* was not available from booksellers (although some copies later ended up in secondhand stores) and could be subscribed to only by joining the organization. This meant that it had an extremely limited circulation, never exceeding 300 (Furuda 1995: 97).[7] However, it was to prove an influential publication, since some contributors were later to get involved as writers and illustrators for the first commercial homosexual magazines of the early 1970s.

The noncommercial nature and restricted circulation of *Adonis* allowed it to focus entirely on articles of interest to its target audience of homosexual men, and it was free to print stories and photos of a blatantly erotic nature. Although photographs and illustrations of naked men had occasionally appeared in the perverse press, these were often taken from European artworks or the "physique" magazines popular in America after the war; they featured either rear views or models dressed in swimwear or posing pouches (see figure 4.1).[8] Photographs of naked Japanese men also occurred, but these figures were usually posed in sadomasochistic situations, where full-frontal exposure was avoided (see figure 4.2).[9] The photos published in *Adonis*, however, often featured naked Japanese men, at times with a full-frontal view of erect penises (see figure 4.3). Pictures of foreign men were also used, but these were never full frontal, since such pictures were extremely hard to come by in the early 1950s. As mentioned in chapter 2, the American homophile publication *ONE* had been seized by the U.S. Post Office in 1953 for publishing a picture of a model provocatively clad in pajamas. It is therefore without irony that a "Bob Smith," the only *Adonis* reader I have come across to have submitted a letter in English, could write, "As a foreigner in Japan, I have found 'Adonis' a very enlightening magazine. Although not versed in the Japanese language, I have found the pictures to be most stimulating."[10]

Had Bob been able to read Japanese, he would also have been stimulated by and no doubt surprised at the graphic nature of the sex described in some *Adonis* articles—both fiction and nonfiction. Again, there was at this time no parallel in English to this kind of pornographic representation. *ONE* magazine, constantly mindful of the censors, was always careful to avoid any hint of "obscenity"; the European publication *Der Kreis* (The circle), published in Zurich, containing articles in German and French (and from 1952 in English), was equally discreet in both its photographs and its fiction. Yet even this publication was not safe in the United States, since approximately every fourth issue was confiscated by Customs on the grounds that it was obscene (Steward 1981: 108–9). It was not

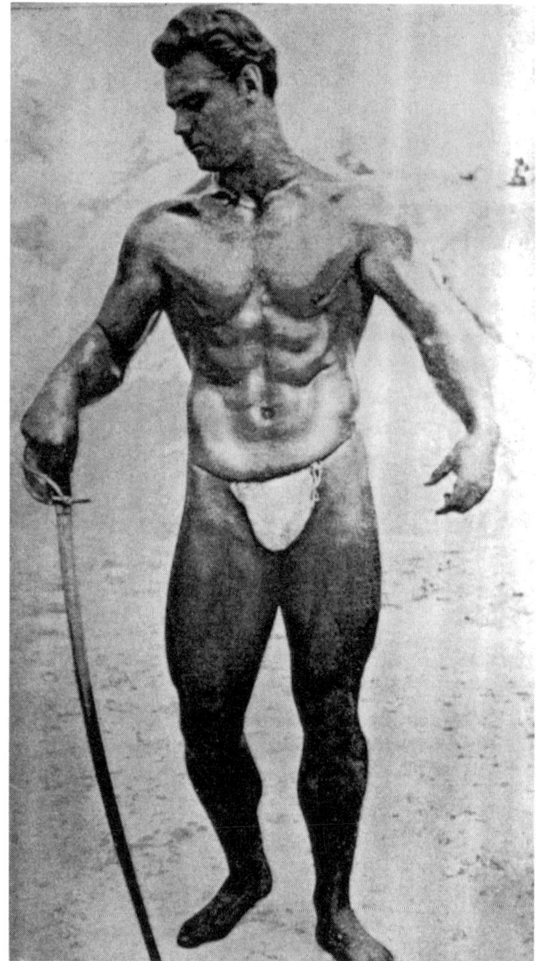

Figure 4.1 Western male model in posing pouch.
***Fūzoku kagaku* (Sex-customs science), August 1954**

until the mid-1960s in the United States that the *Roth* decision, restricting the definition of obscenity to material "utterly without any redeeming social value," opened the way for more frank representations of homosexuality, including those of a pornographic nature. The first full-frontal male nude did not appear in an American gay magazine until 1965, when *Drum* published a drawing of a male nude with genitalia clearly visible (Ramakers 2000: 5).

Because perverse sexuality was thought to be a topic of particular inter-

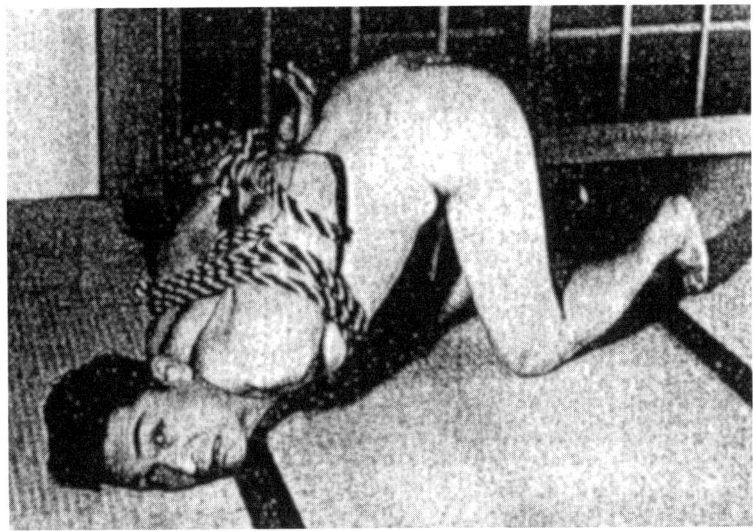

Figure 4.2 Naked-Japanese male model in masochistic pose. *Fūzoku zōshi* (Sex-customs storybook), December 1953

est to intellectuals, the readership of *Adonis* included many novelists, poets and academics (Akitomo 2002: 5). Mishima Yukio was rumored to be among the magazine's subscribers, and it has been suggested that he even authored some of its erotic fiction (Furuda 1995: 97; Akitomo 2002: 6). Artist Mishima Gō (who adopted this pen name in homage to his mentor, Mishima Yukio) contributed erotic line drawings; his hairy, muscled, well-endowed figures pioneered a new, hard-core, sexualized representation of Japanese masculinity. Such images were completely distinct from the "beautiful boys" of the *nanshoku* tradition and the feminized *gei bōi* depicted in mainstream media. Although Japan has had a long tradition of male erotic art, stretching back to the fourteenth-century "Acolyte Scroll" and including more recent shunga or erotic prints from the Edo period (Watanabe and Iwata 1989: 41–3, 137–45), the emphasis had always been upon the feminine beauty of the younger lover. This trend continued into the Taisho and early Showa periods, when Takabatake Kashō drew many homoerotic pictures of beautiful boys for the covers of such boys' magazines as *Nippon shōnen* and *Shōnen kurabu* (Bessatsu Taiyō 1995). Many of Takabatake's pictures included boys engaged in sports like swimming or boxing so as to show off their lithe bodies, but despite these masculine environments the figures had a fresh, youthful beauty and used the same coloring as his pictures of young girls. Although many of Takabatake's cover illustrations were of modern boys participating in

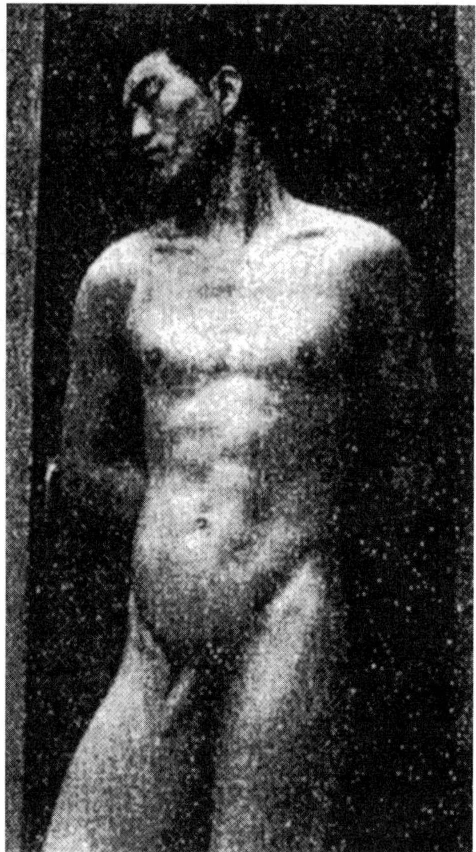

Figure 4.3 Full-frontal naked Japanese model. *Adonis*, June 1954

the same kinds of games and sports that could be found on the covers of English magazines, he also contributed a large number of illustrations for stories from Japan's martial past. These included many tales in which beautiful samurai youth fought and died together. The connection between Japan's traditional warrior arts, or *bushidō*, and homoeroticism has been discussed widely in Japanese (Ujiie 1995; Mishima 1977 [1968]). The figure of the samurai,[11] as well as his modern descendant, the yakuza, was to feature as a central fantasy trope in the emerging homosexual art of the 1950s and '60s. However, whereas Takabatake's art was part of the old tradition of *nanshoku*, which celebrated "boy love" *(shōnen'ai)*, postwar artists such as Mishima drew adult, fully "masculine" male figures. Tagame asserts that "Mishima was the first artist to present the image of gay Japanese macho" (2003: 170); his work pioneered images of the mature adult male that were offered for the erotic appreciation of other adult males.

The illustrations in *Adonis* are evidence that the process of masculinization that was transforming the gay world of the United States and other anglophone societies was taking place in Japan also, albeit within a restricted range. For the first time, images of masculine adult men were understood to be of erotic interest to other masculine-identified adult men. *Adonis* was therefore important in helping further differentiate *homo*, or masculine homosexual men, from the commercial world of the *gei bōi*. Although the circulation of *Adonis* was small, the impact that the magazine had upon the development of a new kind of homosexual style should not be underestimated, especially as the magazine served as a catalyst for several special editions dedicated to homosexual fiction and photographs. Mishima Gō went on to create drawings for some of the first commercial homosexual magazines of the early 1970s (Tagame 2003: 169), particularly *Sabu* (first published in 1974), which developed a reputation for its "hard" illustrations depicting muscled men in loincloths, often featuring tattoos.

The strong association of the category *gei bōi* with the commercial entertainment world and the fact that it was largely understood as a transgender category meant that *gei* was not used as a self-designation for masculine homosexual men, among whom the term *homo* had by this time emerged as the most common self-referent. This does not mean, however, that the two terms were clearly differentiated by everyone. For instance, a young man wrote in to an advice column published in *Fūzoku kitan* in 1965 to complain about the effeminate dress and mannerisms of many of the *homo* he encountered in cinemas, parks and other cruise spots. The columnist's response is to advise the man not to confuse the category *homo* with that of *gei bōi*. He points out that the feminine behavior of the latter is a business requirement *(gyōmu)*, not a defining characteristic of male homosexuality, and further that *homo* are men who like other men, not women, and are therefore unlikely to want to be or act like women. In so doing, he is reiterating arguments previously developed in *Adonis* that similarly disavowed effeminacy among men who embarked on "this path" because of their dislike of feminine things (see for example S. Tanaka 1954: 19). Stating that "if you are a real homo, you don't dress in red shirts, have fashionable hair almost as long as a woman's or speak like a woman," the columnist goes on to suggest that if readers wish to attract more masculine partners, the secret is to dress and act in a more masculine manner themselves (Ijyūin 1965: 141). One of the legacies of *Adonis* was therefore to assist in the development of a more masculine-identified *homo* culture that was to emerge fully into public view in the early 1970s.

Adonis was also groundbreaking in its regular ''members' introduction'' column, which enabled men who were interested in meeting up with like-minded partners to publish their photographs, along with personal details such as their age, home city, hobbies and desired qualities in a partner. This column is further evidence of the shift that had begun in the *sodomia* and *lesbos* letters sections of the perverse magazines—a shift away from the perverse paradigm that had bundled together a wide range of nonnormative sexual *acts* toward an understanding of homosexual desire as a kind of inner state or *identity* shared by a particular group of people. Looking back, Japanese gay men today recognize some continuity between their own lives and the experience of these earlier writers. Fushimi, for instance, comments:

> The feeling of the language may be a bit antiquated but the nuance is hardly different from today. In the last 50 years how many gays *(gei tachi)* have got together and parted through using this space? [This column] offers us the history of an unimaginable human drama. (2002: 279)

Adonis ceased publication in 1962. There are conflicting reports as to the reason for its demise. Fushimi mentions both trouble from the police, who considered some of the contents to be obscene, and rivalry from another underground homosexual publication (2002: 279–80). Another privately circulated homosexual publication entitled *Dōkō* (Same preference) had been founded in the Osaka region (*Adonis* was based in Tokyo) in 1959. An editorial in the magazine's second anniversary edition claimed that the number of subscribers had exceeded 1,000, which, if true, would have far exceeded the circulation of *Adonis*. I have not been able to consult any copies of *Dōkō,* but Fushimi reports that the photographs and fiction were even more explicit than those of *Adonis* and that the magazine also included advertisements for bars, making it a more commercial venture than its Tokyo rival (2002: 283).

After the demise of *Adonis* in 1962, magazines in the ''perverse'' genre like *Ura mado* and *Fūzoku kitan* continued to include the occasional article of interest to homosexual men. Although by this time the topic of lesbianism in these magazines had been co-opted as a fantasy genre for heterosexual men, male homosexuality was still being written about sympathetically, and some of the writers, such as Kabiya Kazuhiko, who had made his name as an expert on the male homosexual subculture in the early postwar magazines, continued to write for the more heterosexually oriented publications of the '60s.

Of the surviving perverse magazines, *Fūzoku kitan* seems to have been the most active in canvassing a male homosexual readership. In the early 1960s, the magazine featured several regular columns clearly directed at a constituency of homosexual men who were not part of the *gei bōi* world. These were, in succession, *"Homo no mado"* (Homos' window), *"Zenkoku no homo hattenba"* (Nationwide homo cruising spots) and *"Homo no hondana"* (Homos' bookshelf). Kabiya Kazuhiko was behind these ventures, and his regular column *"Homo no mado,"* published in *Fūzoku kitan* throughout 1961 and 1962, served as a valuable source of information about cultural and other events occurring on Tokyo's homosexual scene. He mentions, for instance, a *dōjinshi*, or privately circulated magazine, called *Seto naikai* (Inland Sea), that featured fiction on homosexual themes written by young writers (1962b: 146). From 1962 to 1965 *Fūzoku kitan* featured an average of three clearly homoerotic illustrations on its covers each year. These illustrations drew upon the fantasy types—sailors, bikers, cowboys, lumberjacks—developed in the art of George Quaintance and Tom of Finland, whose illustrations had been popular since the late 1950s in U.S. proto-gay publications, such as *Physique Pictorial.*[12] Tom of Finland's work is illustrative of the changes that were taking place in American and European gay subcultures at this time in which the previous emphasis on youth as an object of desire was being displaced by representations of heightened masculinity (Ramakers 2000: 57). *Fūzoku kitan*'s choice of a very "masculine" style of homosexual imagery is further evidence of the growing distinction between transgender and more masculine modes of homosexual identity and experience that were also developing in Japan during this period.

Why the magazine ceased to use homoerotic imagery on its covers in the middle '60s, even at a time when there were no commercial magazines targeting an exclusively homosexual readership, is difficult to know. One possibility is that the strategy proved counterproductive in that it scared off a primarily heterosexual readership that, by the mid-1960s, increasingly saw male homosexuality as a minority interest. It is also possible that this western-style imagery proved alienating to a Japanese homosexual audience. As described below, the development of an indigenous homosexual aesthetic in the late '60s and early '70s was based upon the sadomasochistic legacy of Japan's own perverse press far more than it was on the emerging muscle-queen culture of the United States. From 1965, although *Fūzoku kitan* continued to publish articles about male homosexuality, regular columns aimed at giving practical advice to homosexual men disappeared from its pages, and in 1975 the magazine was relaunched as *SM fantajia* (SM fantasia). From this time on, male homosexuality (unlike lesbianism) was no longer a regular topic for discussion.

It was through readers' requests to *Fūzoku kitan* that a second attempt was made to establish a privately circulated magazine focusing exclusively on the interests of homosexual men. In 1963 a simple paper-bound magazine running from 42 to 58 pages and entitled *Bara* (Rose) appeared. Like *Adonis,* it was available by subscription only—in order to receive copies, subscribers had to send a fee of 150 yen directly to the publisher by the fifteenth of each month. *Bara*'s contents were largely similar to those of *Adonis,* including discussion articles, erotic stories and photographs and illustrations by Mishima Gō, although the full-frontal nudity of the earlier publication was not repeated. (See figure 4.4.)

Like *Adonis, Bara* also offered its readers the chance to engage in communication with each other. In sections such as "Let's all think" *(Minna de kangaeyō)* subscribers were encouraged to submit their thoughts on a

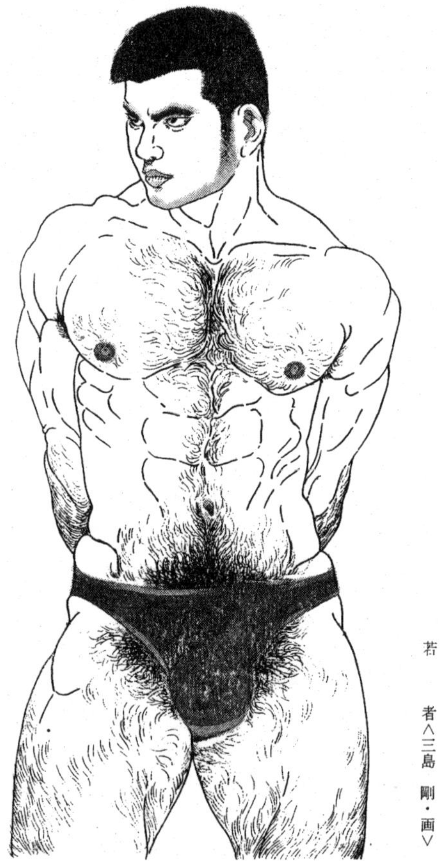

Figure 4.4 Line drawing by Mishima Gō. *Bara*, July 1965

number of topics of interest to homosexual men. The section "My say" *(Boku no kotoba)* accepted brief comments or reflections (often on the contents or comments published in previous issues), and, of course, there was a personals column. When writing in, the contributors would sign themselves by district and membership number—for example, "Tokyo 173"—thus enabling readers to gain a sense of the kind of homosexual men residing in their own locality. *Bara* did not, however, represent a total break with the more sexological focus of the earlier perverse magazines and continued to promulgate modes of sexological knowledge. This was achieved through regular columns such as *"Homo kankei yōgo no kaisetsu"* (An explanation of terminology relating to homos), which still largely relied upon German vocabulary for describing a range of paraphilia such as scatology and gerontophilia. Some of the writers for *Bara* were also familiar names from the earlier publications, the most conspicuous being Kabiya Kazuhiko, the most prolific popular writer on homosexuality in the postwar period.

Bara seems to have been more than just a publication, also arranging social functions for its readers. For instance, issue 24 (June 1966) advertises the fifth members' party, to be held on the night of August 13 at a cost of 2,000 yen. Readers are asked to write in and recommend suitable venues. Unfortunately, it is difficult to know when *Bara* went out of circulation, since copies are much harder to trace than those of *Adonis*. The number of subscribers also remains a mystery, although the copies that I have consulted have all been stamped with individual "member's numbers" ranging from 11 to 684; if the members' numbers relate to the order of subscription, it is possible that the magazine had a circulation of at least the latter figure.

Male groups such as the homophile Adonis Kai were able to intermittently publish newsletters for their members, and although membership was never high, they did offer the opportunity for members to meet and discuss issues relating to sexually nonconformist practices and identities outside of the more restricted paradigms offered by the mainstream press in which transgender images predominated. Same-sex-desiring women, however, due to a range of factors, including their more precarious social and economic position and the lack of subcultural institutions, such as bars, catering to their needs, were not able to achieve the critical mass necessary for the production of these kinds of publications until the effects of second-wave feminism were felt in Japan in the early 1970s.

BARAZOKU—JAPAN'S FIRST COMMERCIAL *HOMO* MAGAZINE

While *Fūzoku kagaku* and *Fūzoku zōshi*, both published in the early 1950s, represent the first commercial attempts to produce a magazine catering in large part to a homosexual audience, it is significant that both these ventures went out of print in 1955 while the more generally (and heterosexually) perverse *Kitan kurabu* lived on into the 1970s. No further attempts were made to produce a commercial magazine aimed specifically at homosexual men until the early 1970s, when the heterosexual publisher Itō Bungaku discerned a market that more conventional sex-related publishing houses had overlooked.

Itō originally approached the editor of *Fūzoku kitan,* the longest-lived of the postwar perverse magazines, with the idea of a joint venture targeting male homosexuals. *Fūzoku kitan* did occasionally feature articles about male homosexuality, but its main emphasis was on SM and "lesbianism" directed at a primarily male heterosexual audience. Its editor felt that a magazine focusing solely on male homosexual concerns would not have the crossover appeal necessary to achieve financial success. Itō disagreed, and in 1971 he launched *Barazoku,* or "Rose tribe," Japan's first commercial *homo* magazine.

Although it is conventional to refer to *Barazoku* as Japan's first commercial "gay" magazine, the term *gei* was avoided in its pages, because of the strong transgender and commercial association of this term. *Gei* (or more often "gay," written in roman type) does appear in some articles and editorials about U.S. gay life (see for example Ōno 1972), but, regarding Japan, *homo* was by far the most common referent for male homosexuality not just in *Barazoku* but also in other 1970s *homo* magazines like *Sabu* and *Adon.*[13] A flurry of articles about these new publications in mainstream magazines such as *Asahi geinō* and *Shūkan josei* further ensured that *homo* would enter the vernacular and become a common referent for non-transgender homosexual men. Despite the fact that in contemporary Japanese usage *homo* is considered by many to have harsh overtones and to be discriminatory, it was actually widely used in the 1960s and '70s by homosexual men themselves as a self-designation. *Fūzoku kitan,* for instance, used the term in its regular *"Homo sōdan zatsuwa"* (Homo advice) column, and it was also used in personal ads in the same magazine. Indeed, as late as the early 1980s, in a survey by gay magazine *Badi,* Fushimi relates that many "gay bar" owners rejected this appellation, insisting, "We're not a gay bar, we're a homo bar!" (Fushimi et al. 2002: 9). Hence, in this chapter I refer to *Barazoku* as a *homo* magazine so as to underline the fact that it was the product of a homosexual culture quite distinct from the commercial *gei* world, which was still primarily associated with transgender performance.

Itō's motivation in launching *Barazoku* was not entirely philanthropic, although he is generally recognized as a sincere and well-meaning figure by Japan's contemporary gay scene. Rather, Itō's previous publications experience had led him to believe that a magazine aimed at homosexual men could be a financial success as well as serve an important social function. Back in 1965 Itō had received a manuscript on masturbation practices by a male writer on sexual customs, Akiyama Masami. Thinking back to his youth, when masturbation was still spoken of as harmful, he thought that a book showing that masturbation on the contrary was healthy and to be enjoyed would come as a relief (Saotome 1998). He clearly discerned a market for the book, even in the more liberal climate of the 1960s, and released it in 1966 under the title *Hitori bottchi no sei seikatsu* (A solitary sex life).

The book was an immediate success and continued to sell well over the next decade. Itō received numerous letters relating to the book, including letters from men who confessed that they found the illustrations of naked men sexually arousing, and he began to wonder if there was a market for a book concerning male homosexuality. However, he decided that as a first venture it would be better to publish a book on lesbianism, since this would appeal to a crossover market of heterosexual men as well as women with an interest in other women. Accordingly, he commissioned Akiyama to write a book entitled *Resubian tekunikku* (Lesbian technique), with the enticing subtitle "Women-women's sex life." Contrary to appearance, the book actually offered a literary, social and historical survey of lesbianism that explained same-sex desire as a preliminary stage on the road to heterosexuality and was therefore unlikely to be welcomed by women themselves. Nevertheless, it proved popular.

Heartened by the success of *Lesbian Technique,* Itō thought the time was right for a book on male homosexuality, also written by Akiyama, which he released in 1968 under the title *Homo Technique*. He was fortunate in that he was able, through his connections in the publishing industry, to obtain as illustrations for the book a series of male nude photographs that had been commissioned by the women's magazine *Josei sebun*. The photos proved a strong selling point, particularly in the bookshops in the Shinjuku area, which housed the largest conglomeration of *homo* bars. The book became a hit on the homosexual circuit, with men passing around copies and recommending it to their friends. Ironically, although the pictures were no doubt stimulating, the text itself followed the same line as in the previous lesbian publication, arguing that homosexuality was essentially a provisional and ultimately immature mode of sexual experience. This is not surprising, since Akiyama was himself heterosexual and the prolific author of a number of provocatively titled sex manuals, including *Advice on Petting* (1967) and *Mischief in Bed* (1970).

Since the book was difficult to obtain other than in bookstores in the commercial *homo* bar areas, Itō was approached directly by many homosexual men seeking to buy copies. As a consequence, for the first time in his life Itō came face to face with real homosexuals and developed a more realistic understanding of their lives and their needs. He was particularly struck by the problems faced by homosexuals from areas without bars that could serve as venues for socializing with other like-minded men. Realizing that homosexuality was a national phenomenon and that a homosexual magazine would likely be of interest to (and more importantly be subscribed to by) men all over Japan, Itō decided on a trial run for a publication aimed specifically at homosexual men.

The publication of a homosexual magazine was, however, by no means straightforward. Firstly, as a heterosexual man with very limited experience of Japan's homosexual world, he did not really know what kind of magazine would best appeal to homosexual men's interests and consequently needed to assemble an editorial team made up of men from the subculture. Also, although many photographers produced pictures of naked women for Japan's sprawling male pornography industry, he knew of no photographers who were experienced in photographing the male body or who would be interested in doing so. The recruitment of male models was also problematic (Saotome 1998). Indeed, it was by no means obvious what kind of male bodies would most appeal to a homosexual readership at this time. As *Adonis* shows, there was a growing constituency in Japan of masculine-identified homosexual men who sought out relationships with other masculine adults, but there were also many adult men whose desire only flowed vertically toward younger "beautiful boys," as well as many masculine-identified men who enjoyed the sexual services of transgender men. However, Itō's growing contacts with Japan's homosexual scene proved fruitful, and he was able to assemble a small staff that helped get the publication off the ground and establish its style.

Itō also had to battle the still ingrained assumption among publishers that material aimed exclusively at homosexual men would not sell; also, because of the magazine's sexual content, he worried that distributors would not agree to handle the publication and that it would not make it into the bookstores. Nonetheless, through his connections in the publishing world Itō was able to persuade Japan's largest distributor, Toppan, to take copies, and with other, smaller distributors on board as well he was able to ship the magazine to stores nationwide. Hence, just as the Japanese press had pioneered the open discussion of minority sexuality issues in the immediate postwar period through numerous perverse magazines, Japan was also to launch one of the first commercial magazines aimed exclusively at a male homosexual audience.

Early editions of the magazine, which for its first few years was published bimonthly, ran to around 70 pages and included a variety of content, including film and book reviews, erotic stories, brief articles, readers' letters, a personals column and some erotic photos—mainly of male figures posed in loincloths, swimwear or briefs. *Barazoku*'s personals column was particularly important in establishing what Aoki identifies as *rentaikan*, or a "sense of solidarity" (2004: 49) between *homo* on a national level. Although the perverse press of the preceding decades had provided a limited opportunity for men with *homo* interests to contact each other, *Barazoku* was the first nationally available magazine aimed exclusively at a *homo* audience to enable like-minded men to seek partners in all of Japan's prefectures. Aoki notes that Itō himself saw the personals service (which was provided for free—Mrs. Itō sorted the replies on her kitchen table) as essential to developing this sense of solidarity. The service was enthusiastically embraced from its inception; the 57 ads placed in the magazine's second edition received over 700 replies (Aoki 2004: 53).

Barazoku was similar in many ways to nascent gay magazines that began to proliferate in the anglophone west in the early '70s. One major difference in content between *Barazoku* and equivalent English publications of the period was, however, the space given to *shōnen'ai*, or "boy love," in the Japanese press. As outlined in chapter 1, intergenerational homosexual interaction had been one of two paradigms (the other being a transgender model) that had typified "traditional" Japanese homosexuality for centuries, and it was never eradicated by more modern conventions. *Barazoku*, like subsequent *homo* magazines, represented a break with the perverse press by excluding transgender homosexuality from its pages but continued to present stories and illustrations dedicated to the love of boys. The August edition of 1972, for instance, featured a series of readers' letters concerning "low-teen love" in which the beauty of young boys' thighs was much discussed (Kamiizumi 1972). A decade later, in 1982, *Barazoku* brought out a special boy-love photo collection and round-table discussion, where it was mooted that boys of 16 or 17 were already considered "old codgers" *(ossan)* by most boy watchers (Shōnen hantā 1982: 17). While they do not contain posed child pornography, *Barazoku* and other *homo* magazines have always featured photographs and illustrations of boys as objects for erotic appreciation and have published stories that detail sexual interaction between adult men and boys as young as 12 (see for example Shiroyama 1994).

Despite the fact that the western artistic canon, drawing upon both classical and biblical themes, has long appreciated the erotic attraction of boys, as Germaine Greer points out, late-twentieth-century fears about pedophilia resulted in a "criminalization of awareness of the desires and charms of boys," the result being that "they are now considered attractive only to a perverted taste" (2003: 10). In anglophone societies where, until recently, all sexual interaction between men was illegal, the transgression of generational lines was considered particularly heinous, and some jurisdictions still maintain higher age-of-consent laws for male-male sex than for heterosexual contact. Indeed, Greer notes that "it is more likely than ever before in our history that intimacy between individuals of disparate ages will be stigmatized as perverted" (2003: 29). Boy love is, in the English-speaking world at least, considered highly pathological and deliberately excluded from gay publications for fear of fueling public anxieties about pedophilia. However, as Aoyama (in press) points out, Greer's concerns would be considered "completely unnecessary in Japan, where men and women . . . did and still do admire the beauty of androgynous boys and girls in the visual, performing, and literary arts."

While Greer suggests that in English the notion of male beauty is "oxymoronic, even perverse" (2003: 7), the Sino-Japanese character *bi,* meaning "beauty," is often conjoined with other characters to signify a range of beautiful male figures—*bishōnen,* or beautiful boys; *biseinen,* or beautiful youths; and *binan,* or beautiful men. Since beauty in Japan was never assumed to be, de facto, a feminine attribute (Miller 2003: 52), as early as the Meiji period there was a line of cosmetics aimed at men. Indeed, the category "cosmetics" *(keishōhin)* "was never strictly gendered as it is in the US," and there is a booming industry today of male cosmetics (Miller 2003: 44). Male beauty in Japan does not necessarily connote effeminacy, as is clear from Takabatake Kashō's illustrations of beautiful boys engaged in a range of male-gendered activities, such as boxing, riding and fencing. Thus, while effeminate *gei bōi* were often spoken of as *bishōnen,* or "beautiful boys," it was also possible for the beauty of male youth to be appreciated in the more masculine-identified *homo* culture.

While boys have been and remain a subject frequently depicted in Japanese art, boy love has also been taken seriously as a moral, psychological and philosophical issue. For instance, Inagaki Taruho, a poet and fiction writer, published an influential essay entitled *"A kankaku to V kankaku"* (The A sensibility and the V sensibility), in the well-known literary magazine *Gunzō* in 1954, where he developed the idea that the "anal sensibility," which he associated with pederasty, was superior to the "vaginal sensibility," or heterosexuality, in relation to the creative imagination—a theme that was often taken up in the perverse press, which associated homosexuality with artistic genius. Inagaki was to return to this theme when in 1969 he published the book-length study *Shōnen'ai no bigaku* (The aesthetics of boy love), which won a literary prize sponsored by the Shinchōsha publishing house, leading to a boom in interest in the topic of boy love.

Due to this cultural background, the aesthetic attraction of children of both sexes is unselfconsciously represented in a wide range of Japanese media, particularly manga (McLelland 2001), to an extent unimaginable in anglophone culture. Yet whether this results in a higher incidence of intergenerational sex between adults and children is difficult to ascertain. Japan is a signatory to international conventions protecting the rights of children and in 1999 enacted the Criminal Code for Child Prostitution and Child Pornography (Jidō baishun poruno kinshi hō), which forbids soliciting children (under the age of 18) of either sex. However, since male-male sex is not mentioned in Japan's legal code, technically there is no age of consent for boys (McLelland 2000a: 38), although some prefectures have recently enacted local legislation that covers both boys and girls. The age of consent for girls is generally 13 (although some prefectures have set the age at 16). Given Japan's very different aesthetic and legal traditions relating to appreciation of the beauty of boys, it has been possible for boy-love stories to remain a central homosexual fantasy, and such stories continue to appeal to a wide audience, including homosexual men and heterosexual women.

Indeed, "boy-love" *(shōnen'ai)* manga for women emerged as a genre at approximately the same time as magazines aimed specifically at homosexual men (McLelland 2001; 2000a: 61–87).[14] These girls' magazines, more than those directed at *homo,* inherited the long tradition of the aesthetics of boy love; these female-authored stories and illustrations associated male homosexuality with decadence and high culture. *Allan,* a popular boy-love magazine published in the early 1980s, for example, described itself on the cover as an "aesthetes' *(tanbiha)* magazine for girls" and contained reportage about Japan's *homo* bar scene as well as stories and pictures depicting "beautiful boys" (see figure 4.5). Indeed, *Allan*'s August 1983 edition contained a report on Shinjuku ni-chōme, describing it (somewhat fancifully) as "full of *bishōnen* like those in the world of girls' comics" (cited in Welker in press). Although these magazines were created by and for young women, their influence on social perceptions of male homosexuality was to have important consequences for how male homosexuality was more broadly understood. Activist Ōtsuka Takashi, for instance, mentions that up to 80 percent of the mail he received while hosting the gay spot on the *Snake Man Show* in the late 1970s was from young women who thought that "gays are lovely," based on the impressions of male-male relationships they had received from girls' manga (personal communication).

In fact, women's interest in male homosexuality was such that *Barazoku* seems to have developed a small female readership early in its history. In 1976 an editorial in *Barazoku* mentioned that the number of letters the magazine was receiving from women was increasing, and the magazine created a special section entitled *Yurizoku* in which to publish some of them. Patterned on *Barazoku,* or "rose tribe," *Yurizoku,* or "lily tribe," is a seldom-used term for lesbianism, and yet the majority of letters printed were from women who considered themselves to be heterosexual but had

Figure 4.5 Line drawing of beautiful boys. *Allan*, October 1980

a feeling of *akogare* or "yearning" toward homosexual men and used the column to seek out such men as marriage partners.[15] In response to this growing demand, in the 1980s *Barazoku* created a separate column entitled "Marriage corner" in which to place such ads (Lunsing 1995). Women's boy-love magazines like *Allan* sometimes ran articles about Japan's *homo* subculture, including descriptions of *homo* magazines and videos and where to buy them. One such article acknowledged that young women might feel embarrassed when making such purchases but assured them that they were not to worry, since many *homo* men would be similarly embarrassed (Kitazumi 1982). Surprisingly, perhaps, the crossover readership for male homosexual material that Itō had assumed would be impossible was established via heterosexual women's interest in male homosexuality, an interest that remains unabated even today.[16]

THE DEVELOPMENT OF A *HOMO* MARKET

Although undoubtedly the vision of one man, Itō Bungaku, ensured that Japan's first commercial homosexual magazine got off the ground when it did, the appearance of *Barazoku* at the beginning of the 1970s must also be understood in the context of the trend toward niche marketing that was taking place in other sex-related publications. It was at this time that the "perverse sexuality" paradigm apparent in publications since the war finally gave way to a hetero/homosexual division, where interest in one side of the divide was understood to preclude any interest in the other. Old-style magazines with an eclectic presentation of "perverse desire" like *Kitan kurabu* now gave way to more specifically heterosexual publications, such as *SM Select*. While lesbianism was still an important fantasy trope for these magazines, it was very much situated as a subgenre of SM, and the style of the magazines was oriented toward a male heterosexual readership. One example of this new genre was *Aien* (Love garden), describing itself as a "human sexuality magazine for the '70s," first published in October 1969. *Aien* was a larger, more lavishly produced venture than the earlier perverse magazines and opened with a special edition on lesbianism. The contents were generally more scholarly in tone than the earlier magazines and included many roundtable discussions between panels of (almost exclusively male) experts on a range of topics, including eroticism in art and the cinema. While early 1950s sex-customs magazines "for modern persons," such as *Ningen tankyū* and *Fūzoku zōshi*, had devoted many pages to illustrations of and discussions about male homosexuality, the topic was barely mentioned in *Aien* except in historical contexts.

Although mainstream erotic publications increasingly disavowed any interest in male homosexuality, under Itō's direction Dai ni shobō, the publisher of *Barazoku*, began to expand its range of publications catering to a niche market of homosexual men. As early as 1971, Dai ni shobō released a series of "homo porn" *(homo poruno)* titles including reprints of fiction originally published in the members-only magazines *Adonis* and *Bara* (Nishina 1971), a strategy that was clearly successful, as a new collection was released the next year (Nishina 1972a). Other titles included Japanese translations of American gay erotic fiction. Advertisements included in the back matter of these books offered to deliver copies of other titles direct from the publisher at a reduced price, thus avoiding any potential embarrassment when purchasing titles clearly emblazoned "homo porn" at the bookstore. Dai ni shobō went on to bring out numerous photo (Haga 1973; Nishina 1972b) and art collections as well as fiction directed at homosexual men, which greatly expanded the range of material available for this market.

As part of this trend toward increasing specialization, a few years after the publication of *Barazoku*, the *homo* press also began to diversify. *Adonisu bōi* (Adonis boy) was published in 1972 by Minami Teishirō, who was later to become an influential gay activist. Minami, who had been a frequent contributor to *Barazoku*, was at that time working on a trade journal for the motor industry and used his expertise to create the newspaper-style publication, which he delivered by hand to pornography bookshops and *homo* bars around Tokyo. *Adonisu bōi* was the first attempt to produce a tabloid-style homosexual newspaper in Japan and, having survived one year in publication, Minami was able to persuade a publishing company to bring the newspaper out in magazine format. In 1974 the publication's name was changed to *Adon*, and it was relaunched as a monthly magazine similar in format to *Barazoku*. The emergence of *Adon* as the first real competition to *Barazoku* reportedly made Itō so nervous that he also began to publish his magazine on a monthly basis (Aoki 2004: 67). More than any other *homo* magazine of the period, *Adon* addressed topics such as gay rights, and also it had a more practical focus than *Barazoku*, sometimes featuring discussions of sexually transmitted diseases and offering information on where to find understanding medical staff (*Adon* 1976).[17] Another of Minami's publishing initiatives later in the decade was the gay-lifestyle magazine *MLMW* (an acronym for My Life My Way, pronounced *murumu*), but this venture proved short-lived—as have all subsequent attempts to create more lifestyle-oriented publications for a Japanese gay audience (McLelland 2003a).

Adon (1974–1996), like *Barazoku*, ran to around 142 pages and contained the same mix of photos, stories and personals. Also similarly to *Barazoku*, *Adon* used *homo* and not *gei* as a referent for homosexual men. A popular feature in early issues was Japan's surviving *hadaka matsuri*, or "naked festivals," where village men clad only in loincloths *(fundoshi)* would compete with each other to capture a special charm blessed by the gods, or would undergo ritual Shinto ablutions, known as *misogi*, such as standing under freezing waterfalls in winter. However, neither *Barazoku* nor *Adon* discovered the erotic potential of these traditional homosocial activities, since the masochistic element of these festivals had already been widely discussed in the perverse press of the previous decades, as had many men's "mania" for wearing the *fundoshi* (*Fūzoku kitan* 1963b; Nishida 1962; Funayama 1959; Ohata 1955). (See figure 4.6.)

The *fundoshi*, a traditional undergarment worn by men, consisted of a length of white cloth six Japanese feet long looped through the legs and tied about the waist so as to restrain the genitals. Poor men, particularly in rural areas, often did not wear any other garment on their lower body.

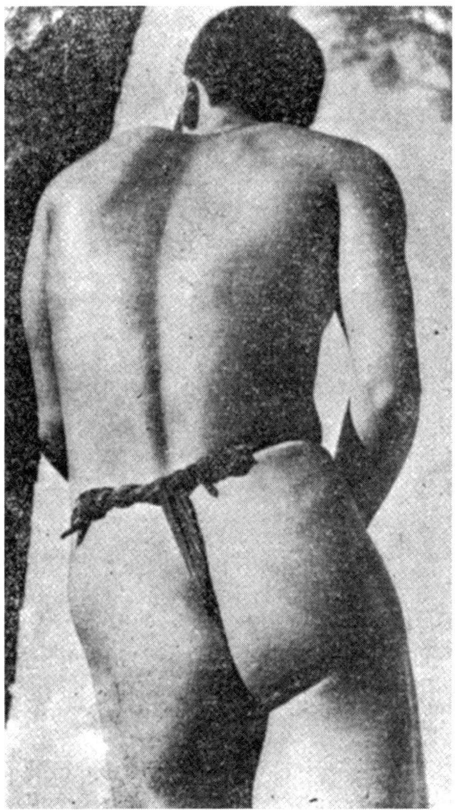

Figure 4.6 Rear view of male model in loincloth. *Fūzoku kagaku* (Sex-customs science), January 1954

In the post-Meiji period, as middle-class men rapidly adopted western styles of dress, *fundoshi* were replaced by western-style underclothes known as *pantsu* (pants) with an elasticized waist. However, a shortage of rubber during the war saw a return to the wearing of *fundoshi* by the armed forces, and the phrase *"kin kon ichiban"* (a tightly tied loincloth is number one) was an exhortation to observe proper self-discipline (Kan 1958).

In the postwar period, which saw the rise of the salaryman, it was only in ritual circumstances associated with local Shinto festivals or the performance of traditional sports like sumo wrestling that men would wear these loincloths (and little else). Consequently the association of the *fundoshi* with homosocial ritual and austerity, as well as its white color, led to its becoming a symbol of pure Japanese masculinity. For some men this led to a "fetish" surrounding the wearing of the *fundoshi,* and a voluble discourse took place in the perverse press on the topic of *konbi* (made up of *kon,* a variant reading for the character *fundoshi,* and the character *bi* or beauty), celebrating the aesthetics of the *fundoshi*-clad male form (see for example Yamaguchi 1954). The number of articles dedicated to this one garment was immense, with *Kitan kurabu* and *Fūzoku kitan* between them publishing nearly 200 discussions over the 20-year period from 1954 to 1974.

Author Mishima Yukio was one of a large number of intellectuals to show interest in the *fundoshi.* Mishima, who was fascinated by the homoeroticism of Japan's samurai past and had written about traditional masculine virtues in such nonfiction works as *Taiyō to tetsu* (Sun and steel; 1970 [1968]) and *Hagakure nyūmon* (Introduction to *Hagakure;* 1977 [1968]), had appeared pictured in a *fundoshi* in the collection *Barakei* (Ordeal by roses), in a photograph by Hosoe Eikō as early as 1963. The homosexual photographer Yatō Tamotsu,[18] who was a friend of Mishima's, also produced numerous studies of Japanese men in *fundoshi* in his photo collections *Taidō: Nippon no bodibirudātachi* (The way of the body: Japan's bodybuilders; 1966) and *Hadaka matsuri* (Naked festival; 1969).

The Japanese male figure clad only in a *fundoshi,* and often brandishing a sword, was to remain an icon of "traditional" masculinity in the pages of the gay press, often associated with right-wing crime gangs known as yakuza (Tagame 2003; McLelland 2000a: 133), and it is no surprise that both Mishima and Yatō had starred in gangster movies. These images, often imbricated with masochism, violence and death—particularly in Mishima Gō's illustrations for the *homo* magazine *Sabu* or the work of photographer Haga Kurō, who depicted scenes of *seppuku* (suicide by ritual disembowelment) in his 1973 photo collection *Bon*—were far removed from the more upbeat imagery current in anglophone gay magazines of the '70s (Tagame 2003: 16).

The fantasy types offered in *Barazoku, Adon, Sabu* and other magazines did not correspond to what Connell has described as "hegemonic masculinity" (2000: 11), which during this period was very much tied in with the image and role of the middle-class salaryman (Dasgupta 2000; Kinmonth 1981), who was more likely to be wearing Y-fronts than a loincloth under his business suit. In 1955 half of Japan's households were headed by salarymen, and by 1970 that number had risen to 75 percent (Roberson and Suzuki 2003: 7). Yet, despite often being depicted in the media as the "corporate warriors" of the new Japan, salarymen were dismissed by Mishima Yukio as "expense account aristocrats" who had been feminized as a result of "American democracy, 'ladies first,' and so forth" (1977: 18). The enduring popularity of the image of the *fundoshi*-clad Japanese male is no doubt related to Japanese men's problematic relationship to the men of western nations due to Japan's defeat and ensuing occupation by the Allies. Although western style in both fashion and work practices largely displaced traditional Japanese conventions in the postwar period, the wearing of the *fundoshi*—which, like a G-string, gives emphasis and definition to the genitalia and buttocks rather than obscuring them—can be read as a mode of resistance to western-derived "salaryman" masculinity, in which genitals were kept well out of sight.[19]

The *fundoshi* is more than just an undergarment; its association with Shinto ritual and Japan's samurai past enabled it to symbolize a mode of traditional Japanese masculinity untainted by modern conformist and consumerist values. Disdain for consumerism, modern life or even life itself was eloquently expressed by the numerous illustrations of men in *fundoshi* about to commit *seppuku* or otherwise prepared for death in the homosexual art of the period. None of the illustrations featured in Tagame's (2003) collection of Japanese gay erotic art from the 1950s, '60s or '70s, for instance, features models wearing anything other than *fundoshi*. One illustration, in particular, that associates the *fundoshi* both with Japanese masculinity and death is by Funayama Sanshi. The title of the (undated) line drawing can be rendered in English as "Going to the battle to die—anyone wishing to die with me, come to the front." It features a soldier wearing nothing but a cap, boots and a *fundoshi*. In this illustration, the soldier's *fundoshi*-clad loins are at the very center of the visual field, and his projectile-like genitalia, defined and highlighted by the *fundoshi*, are as much a signifier of Japanese masculinity as the phallic sword he is clasping. While it is difficult in the western context to see how choice in underwear could connote a "noble bearing" *(bitoku)*, it was precisely this quality of nobility to which writers drew attention when discussing the *fundoshi*, suggesting that during the 1950s the wearing of the *fundoshi* became not so much a fashion statement as a ritual act.

As the contemporary western gay scene became increasingly middle-class and consumer oriented, fantasy types tended to coalesce around images of tough, working-class men. These fantasies were associated with the kind of blue-collar workers who inspired the cropped-hair, jeans-clad image of the "gay clone" in the United States, personified by the '70s disco group the Village People, in their characters of the cop, the cowboy, the sailor and the construction worker. Japanese fantasy images were not class based but instead centered on the "tragic hero," often personified as a yakuza, described by Standish as emblematic of film representations of Japanese masculinity in the 1960s and '70s (2000: 5). To an extent, yakuza were represented in popular culture as inheritors of the *bushidō* spirit of the samurai,[20] a spirit expressed by screen idols such as Takakura Ken—himself often appearing on screen in a *fundoshi*—who starred in a series of yakuza roles throughout the 1960s and '70s. Such heroes performed a kind of "hard-liner" *(kōha)* masculinity characterized by a radical anti-establishment attitude, nostalgia for the past and a preference for the company of men over that of women. These images of "hard-line" masculinity were essentially nostalgic—encapsulated by models in loincloths who were able to draw upon the long tradition of homoeroticism originating in the samurai *nanshoku* code and the homosocial brotherhood of the past. Although in contemporary Japan the reader of the gay press is more likely to be confronted by models in Speedos than loincloths, the *fundoshi* has maintained a cult following. As the author of an essay extolling "the beauty of *fundoshi*-clad boys" commented in 1954, "saturated by a history of 2000 years, it will no doubt be difficult to replace this so-called Japanese beauty" (Yamaguchi 1954: 89).

CONCLUSION

The above discussion has shown a definite shift in the 1970s toward greater specialization in magazines dealing with sexual culture. The most significant separation was that of male homosexuality from other perverse interests like SM and "lesbianism" (the latter being conceived of as a genre of heterosexual male pornography or an activity that cross-dressed men might engage in with biological women). By this time, male homosexuality had been cast out of the family of "perverse desires" that were considered of interest to predominantly heterosexual men, and a new range of niche publications had developed to cater to a self-consciously homosexual market. These magazines expelled the transgender male body from their pages and, while giving a limited place to the more feminine charms of the "beautiful boy," pioneered strong, masculine, even hypermasculine images of the Japanese male body.

Like the United States and Europe in the 1970s, Japan saw a sudden boom in the production and consumption of published material aimed at a homosexual market, enabling the development of a specifically Japanese homosexual culture. However, it would be anachronistic to speak of Japanese *gay* culture at this time, since *gei* was still very much caught up with the figure of the *gei bōi,* whose role was that of performer within the entertainment world or *mizu shōbai*. The *gei bōi* was also a self-consciously trendy, modern figure, whereas the fantasy types aimed at the *homo* market were distinctly nostalgic and backward looking. During the 1970s, then, Japan had two quite distinct homosexual cultures, those of the masculine-identified *homo* and the transgendered *gei bōi,* neither of which had much interaction with the other or with the lesbian world. The *homo* press, substantial though it had become by the end of the decade, had comparatively little to say about homosexual activism or rights, and there was no organ, such as the American *Advocate* magazine, that addressed a broad coalition of sexual minorities.

Homo was to remain the main term signifying a more masculine-oriented homosexual culture throughout the 1980s. However, as outlined in the next chapter, the '80s saw the rise in profile of lesbian and gay organizations patterned along western lines alongside the decline in popularity of the term *gei bōi,* which was gradually displaced in the media by a new transgender category—*nyūhāfu*. The result was that by the beginning of the 1990s *homo* itself began to be displaced by *gei*—newly defined to refer to a more activist-oriented homosexual inclination without any transgender connotations. Accordingly, in the 1990s it became possible to talk of Japanese "gay culture" and to mean by this something closely approximating the connotations of that term in anglophone societies. However, as discussed in the next chapter, the newly invigorated category *gei* did not entirely replace earlier modes of homosexual identity and practice, and it is by no means as hegemonic among the denizens of *kono sekai* as gay has become on the "gay scene" in the west.

NOTES

1. As late as 1979 it was still possible to find general perverse magazines like *Black Cats,* which described itself as "an information magazine for general adult interaction," but this type of publication was now rare. The magazine featured submissions from a wide variety of readers: cross-dressers, homosexual men, "lesbian" women (in this case, biological women offering "lesbian play" for cross-dressed men) and the usual range of SM and fetish play advertised in other magazines for men.

2. See Joseph Hawkins's translation of sections from this discussion, available on the Web at academic.brooklyn.cuny.edu/education/jlemke/lavender/Hawkins_japanese_roundtables.htm (28 October 2002). The complete article was published in the December 1953 edition of *Fūzoku zōshi* as "Sodomia dai zadankai" (pp. 164–78).

3. Kenkyūkai means, simply, "research association." The advertisement appeared on page 83.

4. *"Sodomia yo, jishin o motte, anata wa hentai dewa nai no da."*

5. An unsigned letter published in a section entitled *sodomia tsūshin* (sodomy communication) on page 168 of the November 1953 edition of *Fūzoku kagaku,* for instance, complains that "the number of articles about homosexuality [*sodomii*] is extremely few, do you editors really think that homosexuals [*sodomiia*] are so scarce?"

6. Ōta Tenrei (1900–1985) was a researcher and popularizer of sexual knowledge whose career spanned the pre- and postwar periods. He was noted for his liberal views, such as the freedom of consenting adults to engage in premarital

sex, even during the 1930s. In the postwar period he wrote for several of the perverse magazines, including *Fūzoku kagaku,* where he published the preliminary results from a questionnaire administered to members of the FKK club in 1954 (Ōta 1954). For a discussion of Ōta's work see Fruhstuck (2003: 109, 181).

7. Joseph Hawkins tells me that he did encounter elderly Japanese gay men who recalled purchasing copies of *Adonis* but who, given their age, were vague on the details of when and where (personal communication)—perhaps from secondhand bookshops.

8. Examples include three black-and-white photographs in the November 1953 edition of *Fūzoku kagaku;* judging by their style they seem to be prewar, perhaps 1920s or earlier. The August 1954 edition, however, includes several photographs of a western model in a posing pouch, most probably from a postwar bodybuilding magazine. The magazine featuring the most blatant homoerotic artwork by Japanese artists was *Fūzoku kitan* (see Tagame 2003).

9. See for example the *dansei nūdo* illustrations in the December 1953 edition of *Fūzoku zōshi hizōhan* (pages unnumbered), which feature a naked Japanese man being tied and beaten.

10. *Adonis* letters page, issue 25, 1955, p. 9.

11. For a recent cinematic treatment of this theme, see Oshima Nagisa's 1999 movie *Gohatto,* released in the United States as *Taboo.*

12. Tom's first pictures appeared in *Physique Pictorial* in 1957. He was much influenced by the earlier Quaintance. For a discussion of their work and its place in nascent gay publishing of the '60s, see Ramakers (2000) and Hooven (1995; 1992).

13. The first edition of *Sabu,* published in November 1974, uses the term "sodom letters" *(sodomuretā)* for its correspondence page, although the preferred term for most men writing in is *homo.*

14. In 1978, in an attempt to cash in on the boom occasioned by the publication of *June,* Japan's first serial boy-love comic for women, *Barazoku*'s publisher, Dai ni shobō, brought out *Barazoku no kobeya* (*Barazoku*'s little room), a boy-love magazine aimed at girls. However, it failed to find a market and was discontinued after a few issues.

15. See for example a letter entitled "Contract a marriage with me" from a writer purporting to be a 20-year-old woman from Hokkaido, in *Barazoku* no. 47, December 1976, pp. 92–3.

16. Many gay men also appreciate women's boy-love manga. The monthly comic *June* (first published in 1978) is sold in gay bookstores, and the 1992 "Gay Present" edition of the popular magazine *Takarajima* includes a description of the top 40 boy-love manga enjoyed by gay men—practically all authored by women.

17. For a detailed discussion of the differing ethos between *Barazoku, Adon* and *Sabu,* see Aoki (2004).

18. For a discussion of Yatō's work with illustrations see www.rufusrufus.com/ty/index.html (18 November 2003).

19. Salaryman masculinity was, however, to emerge as a greater focus for erotic attention in the *homo* magazines of the 1980s, as Japan's economy burgeoned. At this time, military metaphors were deployed by the media to describe Japan's *kin-*

gyō senshi, or "corporate warriors." Conspicuously absent in Japanese homosexual pornography, however, have been representations of Japan's Self-Defense Forces.

20. Although, as Ian Buruma points out, these popular images "bear little resemblance to real members of Japan's highly organized criminal fraternity" (1984: 167).

5

Toward a Lesbian and Gay Consciousness

The previous two chapters looked at the development of two quite distinct homosexual subcultures in Japan—that of the transgender *gei bōi,* who lived and worked within the confines of the entertainment world, and the masculine-identified *homo,* who during the 1970s was catered to by a wide-ranging print and social culture. Although in the anglophone world the "gay community" was a broad church containing diverse individuals, from flamboyant drag queens and stone butches to more "gender normative" same-sex-loving men and women, in Japan as late as the mid-1980s the term *gei* was largely associated with the commercial category *gei bōi.* There were as yet no commonly used terms that could comfortably accommodate both masculine-identified and transgender homosexuals, let alone homosexual men and women; unlike in the United States, no magazines, community newspapers or organizations had developed that attempted to address a wide constituency of sex and gender nonconformists.

As Nancy Achilles points out, in the United States during the 1960s "the greatest sense of group cohesion in the homosexual community [was] expressed in reaction to the police," whose policies of persecution, harassment and entrapment galvanized many lesbians and gay men into action (1967: 235). Commenting on the turn toward radicalism among the homophile movement in the late 1960s, lesbian spokeswoman Barbara Gittings commented that "at that point we felt an identity as gay people, gay men, gay women, suffering from the same discrimination and needing to fight the same battles" (cited in Stein 2000: 278). Like blacks and women, who also faced entrenched discrimination, homosexuals were empowered by the emergence in the late 1960s of a counterculture that, as Humphreys notes, "was an essential condition for the gay revolution" (1972: 113). The late 1960s saw the rapid emergence of national and international alliances among homosexuals who had decided to fight back against the "statutory oppression" (Gould 1979), deriving from Judeo-Christian ethics, that underlay the civil codes of most western countries. By 1969, the concerns of "America's homophile community" were being voiced in such media as the *Los Angeles Advocate* and on university campuses across the country (Humphreys 1971).

In Japan, however, since neither cross-dressing nor homosexual sex was illegal, the police surveillance and harassment of sexual minorities, both male and female, that had proven such a binding factor in the United States was largely absent. Likewise, there was no powerful moral authority, such as the church, that singled out homosexuality as a particularly dangerous and heinous sin. It was therefore more difficult for different groups within *kono sekai* to imagine that they shared a common predicament, let alone an agenda for reform. On the whole, the 1960s radicalism that did so much to ignite lesbian and gay movements in the United States and Europe passed Japanese homosexual men and women by.

Japan was not, however, untouched by the counterculture movement. As elsewhere, feminism in Japan was revitalized in the late 1960s by the opposition to established authority that was sweeping societies throughout the world, focusing on opposition to the Vietnam War. In the 1970s a new generation of "fighting women" sought out alliances with other repressed groups within Japanese society, such as resident Koreans, the indigenous Ainu minority and the hereditary subcaste of Burakumin[1] (Mackie 2003). However, women's groups did not at this time attempt to reach out to sexual minorities, even within their own ranks. Indeed, the few lesbians who were out about their sexual orientation "felt marginalized from 'mainstream' feminist groups and activities" (Mackie 2003: 160). Although social groups of homosexual men were by this time well established, as were extensive *homo* print media, male homosexuals had little interest in establishing coalitions with lesbian women—not that such overtures would necessarily have been welcomed, since, as Mackie reports, lesbian groups considered homosexual men to be as sexist as their straight counterparts (1980: 108). Practically the only exception to this separation of worlds was Tōgō Ken's Zatsumin no Kai, or Miscellaneous People's Organization, very much a one-man show that failed to galvanize a broad range of interest groups.

Consequently, the 1970s in Japan did not see the birth of a lesbian and gay movement similar to that which in western nations agitated for the removal of antiquated laws governing homosexual association and practice. The Stonewall rebellion, that iconic event in which U.S. sexual minorities first glimpsed that they had the power to overturn the legal, medical and religious discrimination that sought to contain them, could not have eventuated in Japan, where the *gei bōi* was a public entertainer, not a subcultural pariah, and where regular masculine-identified homosexual men could carry on discreet sex lives largely ignored by the authorities.

The politicization of homosexuality did take place to a lesser extent, taking hold among lesbian women earlier than homosexual men, largely because of the politicizing influence of the women's movement and the fact that women were so obviously disenfranchised in Japanese society. However, the lack of interest of the mainstream women's movement in lesbian issues and the precarious financial and social situation of many lesbians meant that lesbian activism had little visibility or effect outside of specific communities in the 1970s. It was not until the mid-1980s that a new generation of "gay" men emerged and began to employ modes of organization and activism similar to those that had been pioneered by gay and lesbian organizations in the west, and that the mainstream media began to deal with lesbian and gay issues outside of the entertainment paradigm that had dominated the discussion in the postwar period.

However, these organizations, although successful in achieving small changes in specific areas, have never amounted to a combined "movement," and many members of sexual minorities in Japan feel ambivalent about organizations that purport to speak on their behalf. To an extent, this is due to the rise in the notion of the *tōjisha*—that is, the "person (directly) concerned"—as the final arbiter of truth and knowledge about the self. Originally a speaking position that grew up in the women's movement and later among activists for other disenfranchised groups, such as the disabled, the primacy of the *tōjisha* is now stressed by many members of sexual minority groups, particularly on the Internet, which has had a revolutionary impact upon gay, lesbian and transgender networking and visibility.

This chapter looks at a variety of factors that led to the development of a lesbian and gay consciousness in Japan, and argues that rather than having displaced earlier paradigms of sexual and gender diversity, this new consciousness lives alongside more traditional patterns and is sometimes in conflict with them.

EARLY ACTIVISM—*OKAMA* TŌGŌ KEN

In Japan 1960s radicalism did not encourage a broad coalition between sexual minorities and other disenfranchised groups. In the United States and Europe, homosexuality was still illegal in many jurisdictions, gay men in particular were harassed by the police and condemnation of lesbian and gay "lifestyles" by the psychiatric establishment, right-wing politicians and religious figures was routine; homophobia in Japan was less pronounced. In Japan, individuals were largely left alone to pursue their private gay lives; it was only if they insisted on making these lives public that they faced a barrage of discrimination. Lesbian and gay people, along with a wide range of other individuals, including unmarried cohabiting heterosexual couples and women who gave birth out of wedlock, were disadvantaged by their failure to conform to "commonsense" *(jōshiki)* notions of sex and gender roles (Lunsing 2001) but tended not to come in for the kind of religious and moral condemnation that faced sexual nonconformists in the west.

However, there was at least one activist who understood that a broad range of sexual nonconformists—both hetero- and homosexual—were similarly disadvantaged by Japanese social practices. In the mid-1960s Tōgō Ken (b. 1932), descended from a high-profile Japanese family, caused a scandal by resigning from his job in a bank, deserting his wife and children and openly proclaiming his homosexuality. Even today it would be remarkable for such an individual to come out in this manner; in the context of 1960s Japan, for a member of the elite to turn his back on the system was an extremely radical act. In fact, despite Tōgō's provocative actions, his wife has always refused to grant him a divorce, since she would then have to face the worse stigma of being a divorcée. Tōgō's actions are even more remarkable considering the extent to which he went out of his way to align himself with the stigmatized effeminate *okama* identity by opening a *gei* bar. Tōgō's radical politics were matched by his equally radical self-presentation—he began to wear makeup and to cross-dress. Of course, such behavior was expected of homosexual men working within the relatively safe confines of the *mizu shōbai,* but Tōgō was unusual in that he brought politics into the world of the *gei bōi* and the figure of the *gei bōi* into politics.

Despite the fact that Tōgō admitted to being influenced by lectures on Marxism he had heard during his university days, his rejection of the "family system" and adoption of a *gei* lifestyle was not at first the result of a heightened political awareness. When Japan, like many other nations, was swept by student protests in the late 1960s, Tōgō was already in his late thirties and making a comfortable living as the master of his gay bar, in Osaka. It was only through meeting and falling in love with a young student radical that Tōgō began to make the connection between the marginalization of homosexuals and other minority groups in Japanese society. It was at this time that he began to critique the Japanese concept of *jōshiki,* or "common sense," which underpinned most people's taken-for-granted ideas about how people should live their lives (Tōgō 2002).

Tōgō's burgeoning radicalism was evident in the manner in which he unapologetically identified with the feminized mode of homosexual performance that had long been prominent in Japanese tradition. Despite the fact that he came out at a time when there was a trend toward masculinization in Japan's homosexual subculture, Tōgō self-consciously appropriated the term *okama,* a slang term for the buttocks and a sly reference to anal sex that was used to objectify and denigrate effeminate homosexual men, and deployed it as a speaking position—"*Okama* Tōgō Ken" was to become his catchphrase (Tōgō 1986). Tōgō's reclamation of *okama* and his investing of the term with a more confrontational, political nuance came some 20 years before activists in the west were to perform similar recuperation on the English term "queer." Tōgō's style was quite distinct from that of the lesbian and gay activism that was beginning to emerge in the United States at this time. U.S. activism was characterized by its militancy and chauvinism, rejecting effeminate gender performance and "discredit[ing] camp and other evasive techniques" (Levine 1998: 26). On the contrary, Tōgō, through embracing the effeminate stereotype, was very much situated within Japan's postwar "perverse sexuality" paradigm. Furthermore, through embodying queerness in such a confrontational manner while also engaging in social critique, Tōgō was to develop in the early 1970s a mode of activism that was very close to contemporary queer positions.

Tōgō's positionality was queer in a number of ways. Rather than viewing mainstream society as repressing a small number of sexual minorities and calling for their liberation, Tōgō argued that society restricted the free sex and gender expression of all its members. He spoke of his desire to cross-dress as an expression less of his homosexuality than of a desire to change his body and thereby break free from the rigid gender norms that constrained all men. Cross-dressing for men could be a political act—a means of directly confronting society's "common sense" notions of how a man should comport himself. Arguing that the application of makeup and the wearing of women's clothes necessarily brought about a new way of experiencing the "male" body, Tōgō suggested that this was in fact an experience that would benefit a majority of men. As a result, Tōgō was opposed to sex-change operations by those working within the entertainment world, since he considered the tension created between the "male" anatomy and the "female" appearance a particularly productive site for personal transformation and social confrontation.

Tōgō was revolutionary in articulating the political nature of sex. The Japanese term for "politics" is *seiji,* written with a combination of two different characters meaning "government." Tōgō pointed out the way in which sexuality was also invested in politics and politics in sexuality by replacing the first character of *seiji* with the homophonous character *sei,* "sex." As he frequently argued, the Japanese family system, which requires one man and one woman to come together in a joint project to produce and manage children, is considered "normal" *(seijō)* simply because this is the form of family easiest to govern within the context of capitalist society.

Sophisticated language play was to be a mark of Tōgō's campaigning; he frequently made slight alterations to words in order to shift their meaning and produce arresting new definitions. For instance, he would change *sabetsu*, the term for "discrimination," made up of the characters "difference" and "separate," to *geibetsu*, designating the tendency for "normal" people to regard homosexuals as "other." Tōgō's language is important too in another respect, since his refusal to communicate in "standard" Japanese (understood as the Tokyo dialect) also signifies his outsider status. Born in Hyogo prefecture neighboring Osaka, Japan's second city and longtime commercial and cultural rival of Tokyo, Tōgō uses the dialect of his local Kansai region in both his spoken and written communication. His use of the Osaka way of speaking, which is considered more down-to-earth and forthright than that of Tokyo, also aligns Tōgō with the Kansai tradition of individualism, which has long adopted an oppositional stance toward the political culture imposed by Tokyo.

Particularly remarkable is Tōgō's playful use of the figure of the emperor in arguing for greater flexibility in Japanese conceptions of sexual and gender practice. Tōgō was often to point out how, in the period prior to Japan's defeat at the hands of the Allies in the Second World War, the emperor was unthinkingly regarded as divine. Indeed any questioning of the emperor's divine ancestry was considered treasonable and could lead to arrest and imprisonment. However, immediately after the war, under instruction from the Supreme Allied Commander, General Douglas MacArthur, the emperor made a proclamation that he was not in fact divine but a human being like every other citizen of Japan. If the Japanese people were able to accept the emperor's sudden change of status from god to human being with apparent equanimity, Tōgō argued, they surely should be able to come to terms with the different forms of love that exist between human beings or with, indeed, the relatively minor shift in a person's identity occasioned by a change of sex from man to woman.

Reference to the emperor's change in status was, in this context, an extremely radical intervention. In the prewar period, the emperor had been the supreme patriarch, a symbol both of heterosexual masculinity and of the subordination of women and children in a "family system" that made each male household head the sovereign of his own domain. After Japan's defeat, the emperor was enshrined in Japan's postwar constitution as a "symbol" of the Japanese people; he was and is treated by the popular press with a remarkable degree of deference, one that would be quite unthinkable with respect to European royalty. Invoking the figure of the emperor in a discussion of perverse sexuality is, then, in the Japanese context, extraordinarily provocative and was frequently to bring Tōgō into conflict with Japan's right-wing activists. To underline his ironic relationship to the emperor system, Tōgō named his female cat "Chin"—not, contrary to expectation, a sly reference to the penis *(chinchin)* but the Japanese version of the "royal 'we,'" a plural pronoun reserved exclusively to the emperor (Oikawa 2001: 28). Indeed, one of Tōgō's election slogans played on the homophony of these terms: "If the symbol of Japan is the Emperor's royal we [*chin*], then I prefer the symbol of a man—his penis [*chinchin*]."

Between 1971 and 1995 Tōgō ran more than ten times in national elections as an openly homosexual candidate. His support group, the Zatsumin no Kai (Organization of Miscellaneous People), is not, however, an exclusively homosexual organization but a wider assemblage of sexual nonconformists, including sex workers. He also addresses his message to divorced people, unmarried mistresses of rich men and people born out of wedlock, who all also face discrimination in Japan by failing to fit into "commonsense" notions governing family life. Tōgō addressed his manifesto to a broad range of *sogai sareta monotachi*—that is, "people who are alienated" both by and from the Japanese family system. In so doing, Tōgō adopted a position close to contemporary queer politics, which, unlike identity-centered lesbian and gay activism, does not rely upon normative notions of sameness to galvanize group identity. Instead, Tōgō stressed the importance of developing a shared agenda between people who, despite their many differences, were adversely affected by the same power structures.

Yet despite Tōgō's pioneering efforts and the controversial nature of his views, which kept him often in the news, his influence on Japan's developing homosexual subculture was minimal, for a variety of reasons. Whatever his Marxist sympathies, Tōgō's elite background is evident in his conviction that social and sexual change is not to come from the downtrodden masses, who are too preoccupied earning a living, but from the intelligentsia *(interi)*, among whom he certainly numbered himself. The association of intellectuals with perverse sexuality was, of course, nothing new. The early 1950s perverse magazines had been consciously marketed to an audience of "cultured persons," suggesting that such readers were able to look beyond the commonsense notions about human sexuality that governed those less well informed. Tōgō, despite the community-oriented nature of many of his activities (for instance, he organized one of the first call services for the discussion of problems concerning homosexuality), has often been perceived as egotistic. He named his first magazine *Za Ken* (The Ken), a reference to his own given name, and as if naming the magazine after himself were not sufficient, the contents page went on to describe *Za Ken* as "a sexual-love documentary magazine edited by Tōgō Ken."[2] The magazine was in the late 1970s renamed *Za gei* (The gay)—one of the first political uses of this term—and, in keeping with Tōgō's radicalism, publishes photos, stories and articles that are much more graphic than those in other gay magazines, for which reason it must be sold via subscription or, when in stores, in plastic wrap, thus limiting its impact in a culture where standing and reading in the store (without purchase) is a common mode of consuming print culture. *Za gei*, which is the main channel for Tōgō's views, is a very queer mixture of pornography, erotic fiction, reportage and political commentary and is quite unlike any of Japan's other homosexual media.

Furthermore, as the 1970s progressed, Tōgō's effeminate *okama* persona increasingly fell out of sync with the wider homosexual community. As the understanding of "gay identity" became more masculine, homosexual men with an interest in gay activism were put off by Tōgō's embrace of effeminate stereotypes and the fact that he reached out to groups with whom most homosexual men felt they had little in common. At a meeting in 2002 held to discuss discriminatory language in the media, AIDS activist Hasegawa Hiroshi, for instance, spoke about his initial reaction to seeing Tōgō campaigning on television in the early 1970s: "The time I saw Tōgō-san appear on the television I remember thinking that although I liked men, I didn't want to become like that and I didn't want to be grouped together [with him]" (Fushimi et al. 2002: 53). Another participant in the meeting also spoke about how his first sighting of Tōgō resulted in "trauma"; he felt his own attraction to men had nothing to do with "looking like a woman and mincing about" (Fushimi et al. 2002: 70). Bar owner and activist Ōtsuka Takashi too has mentioned to me the alienating affect that seeing Tōgō on the television had upon him as a young man who was just beginning to come to terms with his sexual feelings for other men (personal communication). Tōgō's fearless reclamation of the category *okama* was not necessarily inspirational for masculine-identified young men who were keen to establish identities separate from the transgender paradigms of the bar and entertainment world.

Tōgō's rather patrician attitude also made others reluctant to join with him in group-oriented projects. Yet, despite never having won widespread support, Tōgō's activism has been unflagging. In 1987 he became embroiled in a dispute with Japanese customs when his baggage was searched upon returning from a trip to San Francisco. Tōgō had brought back with him various gay magazines and videos, the explicitness of which contravened Japanese obscenity laws. Tōgō was resigned to seeing this material confiscated, but he was also fined, for attempting to bring the material in to Japan with the possible purpose of redistribution—a charge Tōgō denied, claiming that the pornography was for purely personal use. In fact, incensed by this charge, Tōgō took the matter to court. He lost the original trial, the court ruling that as the editor of a gay magazine there was a high chance that he might have attempted to disseminate the imported material. The Tokyo High Court, however, overturned this ruling on appeal, accepting that the magazines and videos had been in Tōgō's private possession. However, Customs further appealed the case to the Supreme Court, which once again reversed the decision, finding in favor of Customs and ordering Tōgō to pay both the fine and the trial costs, which by this point were considerable.

Now in his 70s, he is still to be found nightly in his bar; he still edits his magazine and has published his second autobiography (Tōgō 2002). At the beginning of the twenty-first century, Tōgō suddenly found that he was in vogue, and, under the influence of new "queer" approaches to sexuality, there is a growing appreciation among other gay activists and intellectuals of Tōgō and his efforts. In many ways, then, Tōgō's perverse politics can be seen as an uncanny precursor to the "queer" activism that developed in anglophone societies in the late 1980s.

Unlike "gay" and "lesbian" identities, "queer" is not based on a shared (homo)sexual orientation that brings a number of disparate individuals together into a community founded on sameness. Rather, "queer" is an attitude or a lifestyle characterized by its opposition to the norm. If "normal" or "commonsense" sexuality is understood to comprise sexual acts taking place between opposite-sex partners who, if not necessarily married, are in "stable" relationships, then "queer" encompasses any sexual acts that are not "normal," even such heterosexual activities as sex work or sadomasochism. "Queer" is therefore not an identity so much as a positionality—that is, it can include anybody who is alienated or marginalized by the fact that his or her sexual practices and relationships are denied legitimacy by the wider society. Tōgō's broad-based political movement, which reached out to a variety of disenfranchised individuals irrespective of the gender of their sexual object choice, was certainly queer in the above sense.

Tōgō, although he was the most visible homosexual activist of the 1970s, was not the figure who had the most impact on developing notions of gay identity in Japan. Despite his tenacity, Tōgō's queer approach to activism never caught on; he appeared an anachronism to a new generation of gay activists who felt they had more in common with the masculine-identified gay movement of the United States and Europe. Indeed, by the end of the 1970s it becomes possible to begin to use the term "gay" in reference to homosexual subcultures in Japan in something like the sense that the term conveyed in anglophone cultures at this time. By this time, the use of *rezubian* (lesbian) was, however, already well established among some women's communities, as described below.

THE EMERGENCE OF LESBIAN CULTURE

In the 1970s Japanese lesbians were faced with problems very different from those confronting Japanese homosexual men. By 1971, Japanese *homo* already had a long tradition of organizations and publications to look back on, small-scale though they had been, and at least one nationally available commercial magazine reflected their interests. Tōgō Ken, if often a cause for consternation rather than a figure to emulate, was at least out in public about his homosexual identity and was just one of many male public figures (albeit all from the entertainment world) who openly discussed their same-sex preference in the media. The problem facing gay men attempting to come to terms with their homosexual identity was to differentiate themselves from the *gei bōi* of the entertainment world and to develop ways of expressing their homosexual desires outside the transgender paradigm with which homosexuality was so routinely conflated. Gay men's privileged economic position and the freedom with which they could move about public space, including the red-light districts where many *homo* bars were located, gave them much more freedom of association than was available to same-sex-desiring women, who were liable to be tied to the home and to have less time, money or confidence to venture forth in search of like-minded women.

In contrast to homosexual men, who had been a constant focus for media attention in the mainstream press, apart from a brief exposure in the perverse press of the mid-1950s, same-sex-desiring women had received very little media attention other than as objects of male pornographic fantasy. "Lesbians" were often written about but only in male magazines, especially those focusing on eroticism and pornography. For instance, the first edition of a new general-interest erotic magazine entitled *Erochika* (Erotica), published in July 1969, was dedicated to *rezubianizumu* (lesbianism) and featured an article by Akiyama Masami, the male author of *Lesbian Technique*. The fact that this new venture opened with a special edition on lesbianism is evidence of the wide appeal this topic had among heterosexual men. Akiyama's (1969) article, entitled "The art of mutual rubbing: lesbian technique," rehearsed standard male fantasies of lesbian practices among the women of middle-eastern seraglios and was illustrated with what appear to be stills from the film version of the male-authored lesbian novel *Manji*.[3]

These male-authored narratives, hardly of interest to lesbian women themselves, were actually counterproductive, associating as they did the term *rezubian* with the world of prostitution and pornography (Hattori 1999; Ishino and Wakabayashi 1996: 99–100; *Aien* 1969). Indeed, one article published in 1969 declared that the spurious interest in lesbianism apparent in the weekly magazines had an adverse effect upon the number of "real" lesbians in Tokyo, suggesting that there were only 50 "real cohabiting lesbian couples" (*Aien* 1969: 182). While the popular press had occasionally entertained stories about same-sex-desiring women, women's same-sex desire, like that of homosexual men, was conflated with transgenderism; women who loved other women *as women* were unlikely to feel at home in bars featuring female-to-male cross-dressers, even if they could have afforded the price of a drink in such exclusive establishments. This problem of invisibility, in addition to the disadvantaged economic and social position that Japanese lesbians faced vis-à-vis homosexual men, meant that it was much more difficult for women to gain the critical mass necessary for group mobilization or, particularly, the finances necessary to support the kind of publications that men's groups had achieved by the end of the 1970s. Itō Bungaku was able to depend upon the resources of his family's publishing firm and his wide experience of and contacts with Japan's publishing world when launching the *homo* magazine *Barazoku;* lesbians had neither an industry sponsor nor access to the commercial press. At a time before personal computers, printers, and cheap photocopying services, the production of small-scale lesbian magazines was to prove both labor-intensive and expensive (Izumo et al. 1997). Hence, the social and economic conditions that lesbians faced as women (Chalmers 2002: 31), very different from those facing homosexual men, in large part explain the difficulty that lesbian groups had in maintaining momentum (Hattori 1999). In addition, Japanese women's groups were initially indifferent to lesbian issues and concerns (Mackie 1980); also, feminist critique in Japan has tended to focus on the patriarchal family system and not on the compulsory nature of heterosexuality itself (Chalmers 2002: 33). Both factors contributed further to the marginalization of lesbian culture.

While it remains unclear whether attempts made via *Fūzoku kagaku* in the mid-1950s to found a social group for "female homos" resulted in any actual organization, the earliest documented lesbian group seems to have been Wakakusa no Kai (Young Grass Organization, sometimes also referred to in English as Fresh Green Club), founded in the early 1970s (Izumo et al. 1997). It was primarily a social club that organized all-women events, such as hiking trips, but it also acknowledged the need to publish newsletters advertising their activities so as to reach a wider audience. The group put out the newsletter *Subarashii onna* (Wonderful woman), which fell through after only a few issues because of lack of financial and personnel support. Mackie (1980) mentions other, smaller lesbian groups that formed during the 1970s, including Lavender Gangs, which ran a monthly lesbian dance at a women's center in Tokyo (attracting as many as 60 women to each event), and a women's karate club that welcomed lesbian members.

Given the fact that there were no commercial, widely available lesbian magazines, boy-love manga such as *June* (1978–present) and *Allan* (1980–1984), which could be bought in main-street stores and read without suspicion, were important organs for some lesbian readers (Mizoguchi 2003). Many women were able to identify with the androgynous figures that filled the pages of these manga; as one of Summerhawk et al.'s lesbian informants commented, the beautiful boys had "such shapely and delicate bodies that they didn't appear to be male. It was easy for me to project my feelings onto the characters in these stories" (1998: 24). Surprisingly, perhaps, the letters pages of the magazines began to be used by young women in search of relationships with like-minded readers (Welker in press; 2003). Although the mediation of lesbian desire by male homosexual images may seem odd to western observers, it is an understandable development in Japan, where "boy love" had achieved widespread popularity among women from the early 1970s (McLelland 2000a).

From the late '70s to the early '80s, various lesbian and bisexual women's groups would come together, found in-house magazines or *minikomi*, such as *Za daiku* (The dyke) and *Hikari guruma* (Shining car)—both published for a time during 1978—and then disband or fall apart as members either lost interest due to ideological differences over who exactly was to be included in the category "lesbian" or moved on to other groups. The most enduring of lesbian organizations has been Regumi, a group founded in the late 1980s as a loose alliance of lesbians, some from the bar world and others involved in feminist activities. The group's name was made up of *re,* which stood for *rezubian,* and the character *gumi,* or group. *Regumi tsūshin* (Regumi news) is its newsletter, published from 1985; it prints information about lesbian literature, various support and discussion groups and a telephone information line. Like many lesbian organizations, Regumi is staffed by a small volunteer force, which means that it is not possible for their office to be maintained as a "drop-in" space, as opening hours are determined by members' availability (Mizutani 2001: 26). However, in 1995, a group named Lesbians of Undeniable Drive (LOUD) set up a small drop-in center in Nakano, Tokyo, for lesbian and bisexual women. Running a variety of events, including a highly successful lesbian translation project (see Curran and Welker, in press), LOUD has continued to provide important, albeit limited, support to Tokyo's lesbian community.

In 1992, *LABYRIS,* a magazine targeting lesbian and bisexual women, was published and gained a readership of over 1,500 during the short time that it was in print. It was not until May 1995 that *Phryne (furiine),* the first commercial magazine aimed at lesbian and bisexual women, was released, by Sanwa Shuppan. Welker (2002: 16) mentions that *Phryne* was chosen as the magazine's title, by the male editor-in-chief of the publishing company, because it was thought to be the name of a powerful ancient Greek woman.[4] It was hoped that this choice would help the magazine appeal to a wider audience of feminist women than would other names that had been considered, including *Dyke*. However, *Phryne* folded in September after only its second issue. The next year saw another attempt at publishing a commercial magazine for lesbian and bisexual women—*Anise (aniizu)*—this time published by Terra Shuppan, the same company responsible for *Badi*, Japan's most popular gay magazine, at the time selling on average 40,000 copies a month. Seven issues were published between 1996 and 1997 before lack of funds led to the temporary suspension of publication. However, gradual sales of back numbers enabled the magazine to recommence publication in 2001 (*Aniisu* 2001: 34–37), and as of 2004 it is the longest-running commercial lesbian publication in Japan.

In July 2002 Potto shuppan, a publishing house that has developed an extensive lesbian and gay list, released the lesbian periodical *Carmilla*; as of April 2004, four issues have been published.[5] The magazine's title is a reference to a nineteenth-century lesbian-themed vampire novel by Joseph Sheridan Le Fanu. The tone of the magazine is playfully perverse, with a major emphasis on female eroticism, explored through photographs, manga illustrations and text narratives on such topics as masturbation, bondage, fetishism and sex toys. Indeed, volume three features a "taboo sex manual" complete with detailed instructions on various kinds of bondage techniques. Printed in bold, eye-catching colors such as pink, purple, black and red, *Carmilla* takes a pop-culture approach to female sexuality. Its style is clearly influenced by Japan's manga culture—particularly the sexual explicitness (as well as the perversity) of the "ladies comics" genre. Many of the themes dealt with in the magazine are the same as those commonly represented in the perverse press of the 1950s, suggesting that these early stories may well have been of interest to female readers of an older generation. However, unlike the perverse press, *Carmilla* is very much under the editorial control of women and is conceived and presented as "an erotic book for girls on girls." Whether this new pop-culture approach to lesbian sex will catch on, however, remains to be seen.

JAPAN'S FIRST GAY CELEBRITY—ŌTSUKA TAKASHI

While there were many prominent entertainers in Japan dating from the '50s and '60s whose homosexuality was far from secret, none used their public visibility to challenge stereotypes and prejudices against sexual minorities. Located firmly within an entertainment paradigm, figures like

Miwa Akihiro and Peter capitalized on their gender and sexual nonconformity as part of their performance, reinforcing the elision of *gei* as homosexual into *gei* as artistic performer. Tōgō too, emerging as he did from the bar world and identifying with, rather than rejecting, the term *okama,* also presented to the public the effeminate face of homosexuality. It was not until 1979 that an openly gay public *tarento,* or "talent," appeared on Japan's entertainment scene choosing a gender performance that challenged rather than conformed to well-established paradigms of what it meant to be *gei.*

Ōtsuka Takashi[6] was an artist, who, after graduating from design school in the early 1970s, began to work in an editorial capacity on the first gay magazines, including *Barazoku* and *Adon.* This brought him to the attention of the mainstream press, and he began to write a column entitled "Tales of a thousand and one nights of a sister boy" for the magazine *Popeye.* In 1979 Ōtsuka was approached by Kuwahara Moichi, the producer of TBS radio's culturally radical *Snake Man Show.* The show, broadcast nightly at 10:45 PM, featured as DJs Kobayashi Katsuya and Ibu Masato, whose black humor and risqué conversation appealed to a large audience of disaffected youth. In keeping with the challenging nature of the show's contents, Ōtsuka was asked if he would appear once a week as an openly gay man. Sensing an opportunity to engage in a new kind of public discourse about homosexuality, Ōtsuka agreed, on the condition that he be allowed to write his own script and have some tenure on the show, not be dispensed with when the novelty of his homosexuality began to wane. Kuwahara readily agreed, and for a period of just over 18 months Ōtsuka appeared on the show every Wednesday, becoming famous for his opening line, "How are all you gays [*gei*] doing out there?"

Although gays were probably a minority of the show's audience, Ōtsuka's new exposure brought him to the attention of a wider variety of gay people than those in the gay bar scene. He used his exposure to promote "gay rap" *(geirappu),* which derived from the consciousness-raising discussions that were taking place among gay groups in the United States, where members met regularly to share and discuss their experiences. Numerous men wrote to the show asking to join such a group; this led to the formation of a small organization of about 30 or 40 members named OWC (Our Work Community). In addition to holding discussion meetings, this group brought out the small gay publication *Wednesday News.* However, the group drifted apart after two years, since many members were more interested in pursuing a social life in the bars of Shinjuku than in developing strategies for increasing gay visibility in the world at large (Ōtsuka 1996).

The late 1970s saw numerous small gay-liberation groups, many of which also brought out *minikomi.* In November 1976, the group Nihon

Dōseiai Kaihō Rengō (Association for the Liberation of Japan's Homosexuals) was founded by about ten gay men, and in March 1977 the group Front Runners[7] was founded by six men. The activity of both organizations was mainly limited to consciousness-raising meetings. In May 1977, another small gay organization, the Puratonika Club, released the first gay *minikomi,* entitled *Puratonika;* it ran for four issues before the group drifted apart. In March 1979 JGC (Japan Gay Center) was founded by several members of the by-then defunct Puratonika Club. This group published the magazine *GAY,* which produced eight issues, followed by *CHANGE,* which ran for only two (Purojiekuto G 1992: 60–1). Despite these early attempts to reclaim the term *gei* as an activist category and divest it of its transgender connotations, these groups had virtually no impact on or representation in the mainstream press. An article on "gay power" *(gei pawā)* published in the tabloid magazine *Jyabu* (Jab) in February 1980, for instance, while drawing attention to the radical nature of U.S. "homosexionalists" *(homosekushonaristu),* mentions only Tōgō Ken's activism in relation to Japan. However, it is not his radical agenda for social reform that was discussed but his "interesting" persona, which "combines camp speech with *gei* peculiarities." Contrary to expectations raised by the title, the article is not about the budding activism within a new kind of *gei* community but instead about the exotic lifestyle enjoyed by the staff of Japan's "thousands of gay bars." In this article *gei* as a sexual interest is once more conflated with *gei* as artistic performance.

As the short-term nature of these early alliances shows, despite the efforts of pioneers such as Tōgō Ken, Ōtsuka Takashi and later Minami Teishirō, the kind of mass mobilization of lesbians and gay men that was a conspicuous part of the social reform movements of the late 1960s and early 1970s in many western nations did not eventuate in Japan. This is not because Japan was unaffected by the radicalism that swept university campuses in Europe and America. The late 1960s and early 1970s in Japan were also a time of considerable social unrest, particularly surrounding the Vietnam War and the ratification of the joint U.S.-Japan defense treaty (Mackie 2003: 145–50). However, in Japan in the 1970s the concept of a social movement, or *undō,* centered on minority rights was mainly associated with the Burakumin antidiscrimination campaigns and with women's liberation *(uuman ribu),* and both had rather negative connotations. Burakumin organizations had developed the tactic of publicly humiliating individuals and institutions whom they considered to have made discriminatory statements, leading to a situation where people were extremely reluctant to make any reference at all to Burakumin issues. Some women's groups too had adopted the strategy of public shaming; for example, the radical Chūpiren (Alliance for Abortion and the Pill) publicly embarrassed men guilty of infidelity. However, their guerrilla tactics, which they undertook while wearing pink helmets, were ridiculed in the press and frequently backfired, alienating a majority of women as well as men (Mackie 2003: 167).

Also, the social situation facing gay men in Japan was very different from that in western societies, which had long traditions of religious, legal and medical oppression of sexual minorities. As outlined in chapter 2, the postwar period was a time of particularly harsh treatment of sexual minorities throughout the English-speaking world—homosexuals were branded sick by the medical establishment, sinful by the church and criminal by the legal system. In Japan, however, where *gei bōi* were allotted a role in society, where sex between men was not mentioned in the criminal code and where homophobic attack, whether on the streets or in the press, was less common, there was no pressing need for gay men to organize around specific issues. Knowing that discreet homosexual practice was overlooked by the wider society, many gay men had difficulty seeing a need for the kind of radical reorganization of society's sex and gender norms argued for by Tōgō and Ōtsuka. Organizing gay men in Japan was difficult, then, because compared with the treatment of homosexuals in western societies, discrimination in Japan was less intrusive and because no single issue, such as repeal of antihomosexual legislation, police harassment of lesbians and gays or the equalization of age-of-consent laws, presented itself as a catalyst. Many gay men and lesbians, once they had come out to a small group of friends, were more interested in pursuing social activities than in agitating for widespread reform—a situation that still largely exists today. However, two well-established gay and lesbian organizations in Japan have continued to challenge antihomosexual discrimination and agitate for more widespread social reform.

ILGA JAPAN AND OCCUR

Although by the late 1970s small local-based organizations like the one surrounding Ōtsuka Takashi had begun to utilize *gei* as an identity category, Japanese activists had few connections with gay and lesbian movements outside Japan. This is not surprising, since "gay" as a subject position *(shutai)* was only just beginning to be articulated in Japan at this time. OCCUR member Kawaguchi Kazuya (2003: 144–5), for instance, remembers that it was only as a consequence of discussion surrounding the controversial American movie *Cruising* (1980, dir. William Friedkin) that he became aware of the variety of the gay scene in the United States and the range of identities that could be expressed within it, from effeminate stereotypes to the "hard gay" world of the macho clones depicted in the movie. Needless to say, Kawaguchi did not find the film's "lurid and inarticulate depiction of gay life'' (Murray 1994: 393) very reassuring. He goes on to mention that

> at the beginning of the 1980s the requisite elements for being able to identify [*aidentifai*] as ''gay'' were comparatively few; of course today the number of people who identify themselves as ''gay'' is large but I think that 20 years ago, as you'd expect, it seems that almost no-one did so. Rather, most people around me claimed to be *''okama''* or *''homo'';* and if you asked older people about the word ''gay'' [they said] it connoted ''gay boys'' or ''those people who dress as women and work in the bar world,'' it seemed difficult to take on gay as an identity [*aidentiti*]. (2003: 146)

As Kawaguchi's use of the loanwords *aidentifai* and *aidentiti* show, the notion of ''identifying'' per se, let alone as a gay man, was not easily expressed using native vocabulary.

This situation began to change in 1983, when a Swedish journalist researching an article on homosexuality in Japan published an interview with Minami Teishirō, editor of the gay magazine *Adon*.[8] This brought Minami to the attention of the International Lesbian and Gay Association (ILGA). Primarily Europe-based, the International Gay Association (''Lesbian'' was added to the name only in 1987) had been founded in 1978. As well as offering support to developing lesbian and gay organizations around the world, it also lobbied national governments and international organizations, such as the UN, to ensure protection of lesbians' and gay people's rights. Despite its aspiration to be a truly international organization, however, it had no representatives in Asia in the early 1980s, and, concerned to establish a branch of ILGA in Japan, a representative contacted Minami while on a visit there in 1984.

In many ways, Minami was the most obvious point of contact in Japan for an overseas gay organization. His magazine, *Adon*, had long been the most vocal Japanese publication arguing for a more political conception of homosexual preference and identity. Also, as early as 1973 Minami had founded a ''unionist league of *homo* bars'' aimed at getting the *homo* leisure industry to adopt common standards and a common approach for dealing with the regulatory authorities (Aoki 2004: 86). Yet despite the success of these efforts, Minami was doubtful that a ''gay movement'' involving mass mobilization and demonstration by gay men and women was likely to eventuate in Japan. However, after discussing his concerns with ILGA, Minami began to feel that local grassroots activities, like meeting at members' homes for discussion or organizing regular events such as discos, could lead to community building and that the connections established thereby could act as a foundation for further activism. Bearing this in mind, Minami agreed to be the representative of ILGA in

Japan. When he managed to gather together 50 gay men for a Christmas party in Tokyo at the end of 1984, Minami began to think that there was the possibility for a more widespread mobilization of gay men. When Minami attended an ILGA conference held in Toronto in June 1985, he came into contact with a dynamic group of young Asian men who had founded the group Gay Asia Toronto. In consultation with them, he began to consider ways in which Japanese gay men could begin to engage in a more public kind of activism.

ILGA Japan's first public action took place in June the following year as part of the third International AIDS Candlelight Vigil. However, despite leafleting many of the numerous gay bars in the Shinjuku Ni-chōme area of Tokyo, only ten people participated. Many bars in the area had in fact refused even to accept leaflets, since the promotion of AIDS awareness was considered bad for business. The unwillingness to recognize the threat of AIDS by gay businesses in Japan was, of course, hardly confined to that society. U.S. gay magazines, for instance, had a very poor record of reporting AIDS-related news during the early years of the epidemic, and the owners of gay bars and bathhouses were similarly unenthusiastic about embracing an information campaign that associated homosexual practice with a deadly disease (Streitmatter 1995: 245). Given that Ni-chōme had the highest concentration of gay bars anywhere in Japan, ten people was an extremely low turnout, suggesting a strongly antipolitical mentality among Japanese gay men, a mentality that Minami needed to work against. In fact, the onset of AIDS, which did so much to reinvigorate American and European gay rights' activism in the early 1980s was not to have the same effect in Japan until much later. This was partly due to Japan's comparatively low infection rate[9] but also reflected a lack of community feeling among gay men. It was not until the mid-1990s that a new genre of gay magazines began to address AIDS awareness in a consistent manner and not until the end of the decade that gay community events in Tokyo, and later Osaka, made HIV a central concern (Hasegawa 2003: 137).

Minami found that gaining any kind of consensus among ILGA Japan's members on such issues as coming out, HIV prevention measures and the need for public activism was extremely difficult. As an older man and erring perhaps on the side of conservatism, Minami found that younger members were impatient of his leadership, and in 1986 an inevitable split took place, with younger members of the group leaving to found OCCUR, also known in Japanese as Ugoku Gei to Rezubian no Kai (Organization for Moving Gays and Lesbians). OCCUR has consistently taken a more proactive stance toward the media and professional and government organizations than earlier groups and has always included AIDS education as one of its key concerns. It has been involved in lobbying the

Japan Society of Psychology and Neurology to remove the classification of homosexuality as a mental illness and has lobbied the publishers of Japan's major dictionaries and encyclopedias to rewrite definitions of homosexuality in line with modern understandings of homosexuality as a *seiteki shikō*, or "sexual orientation" (Ishida and Murakami forthcoming). OCCUR has also worked with the Tokyo metropolitan government to have homosexuals included under the city's human rights charter. All these initiatives have proven successful. OCCUR has been the most successful of all Japanese gay organizations in gaining international attention, particularly through its participation in AIDS conferences. When sending delegates abroad, OCCUR often bills itself as "The Japan Association for the Lesbian and Gay Movement"—something of a misnomer, since it is just one of many organizations that represent the interests of lesbians and gay men in Japan.

The early 1990s saw a rapid proliferation of reporting about gay and lesbian issues in the mainstream media. Whereas previous reporting had tended to focus solely upon the transgender face of homosexuality as represented in the entertainment world, print media suddenly became interested in the new, more activist-oriented gay culture and identity. The women's magazine *CREA* is often credited with sparking what became known as the "gay boom" (actually Japan's second such boom—see chapter 3) when it ran an issue, its February 1991 number, entitled "Gay Renaissance," featuring a number of articles about and interviews with gay men. Other monthlies picked up on the boom, including the very popular journal *Takarajima*, which published in August 1992 a "Gay present" *(gei no okurimono)* special edition, with the English subtitle "Presented by Gay People for Everyone." Ōtsuka Takashi and Fushimi Noriaki (who was soon to emerge as Japan's leading gay critic and writer) edited the collection; contributors included many other prominent members of Japan's gay scene. The special edition proved so successful that another gay-themed issue was published in February 1994, this time edited by Ōtsuka Takashi and Ogura Tō (also known as the drag queen Margarette and later to become the editor of the magazine *Fabulous*). These publications were important not simply because they communicated information about Japan's gay culture to a wide and diverse audience of people who otherwise might not have thought much about the topic but also because they provided a point of first contact for many young gay men who had not yet come across gay magazines that, unlike *Takarajima*, were only sold in specialty stores.

While Japan's queer culture had always been written about, outside of the perverse press there had been little opportunity for sexual minorities to speak in their own voice. One of the important effects of the gay boom was the mainstreaming of gay and lesbian (and later, transgender) perspectives, through the inclusion of interviews, articles and fiction by sexual minorities in the popular press, as well as an increase in the number of books written from queer perspectives. Narrative accounts published by members of sexual minorities at this time included Fushimi Noriaki's *Puraibēto gei raifu* (Private gay life; 1991), Kakefuda Hiroko's *"Rezubian" de aru to iu koto* (On being "lesbian"; 1992) and Itō Satoru's *Otoko futarigurashi: boku no gei puraido sengen* (Two men living together: my gay pride declaration; 1993). These writers discussed English terms like "gay" *(gei),* "lesbian" *(rezubian),* "gay pride" *(gei puraido),* "homophobia" *(homofobia)* and "coming out" *(kamingu auto),*[10] and the interest created by their stories ensured that these English loanwords were widely reported in the media. A second boom in the late 1990s was to see interest in transgender phenomena increase, following on from the legalization of sex-change surgery in Japan in 1996 (McLelland 2004).

This new discourse of gay identity and gay rights was also promulgated in the media via a court case launched by OCCUR against the Tokyo metropolitan government, which had refused the group the use of public facilities for its residential seminars (Suganuma 2004). This controversy erupted in 1990, when OCCUR, which openly identified itself as a lesbian and gay organization, held an overnight seminar at a Tokyo youth activity center. Some members of the organization were harassed by other guests at the center, including members of a football team, but rather than take steps to counter this harassment the center's management decided not to allow OCCUR to use its facilities on future occasions. The somewhat spurious reasoning behind this decision was that a lesbian and gay group contravened the "single sex" principle of segregating guests by gender when assigning dormitories. This regulation, which was aimed at combating sexual and other "inappropriate" behavior among guests, was considered problematic in the case of homosexuals, who were attracted to the same gender. The confused logic of this position did not stand up in court, and OCCUR won both the original court case in 1994 and the appeal case in 1997 (Summerhawk et al. 1998: 206–11).

The gay boom of the early 1990s, along with increased media attention paid to gay rights organizations, ensured that notions of gay identity, rights and lifestyle were communicated far beyond the traditional confines of *kono sekai* and that gay and lesbian culture gained a new kind of prominence (as opposed to notoriety) in the mainstream press. While old-style *gei* culture had always been voyeuristically appreciated as a result of the touristization of the *gei* bars in the 1960s and the widely reported scandals associated with the *gei* world, the 1990s saw a broader demographic both producing and appreciating a new style of gay culture. Particularly successful have been the gay and lesbian film festivals held in Tokyo since 1990 (and more recently in other centers such as Osaka,

Nagoya and Kyoto). The first festival, held in Tokyo, attracted an audience of 1,000 and has continued to grow each year, with over 7,000 attending in 2000 (Fushimi 2002: 315). Japan has, in fact, been at the forefront in Asia in creating gay films, with works by openly gay directors such as Oki Hiroyuki and Hashiguchi Ryōsuke being shown regularly at international festivals. In 2002 Hashiguchi's film *Hush* was the first gay Japanese movie to break through into the mainstream, being screened widely in Japan and internationally.

Japanese gay and lesbian people have also become more visible in society. One of ILGA Japan's most conspicuous successes was the organization in August 1994 of the first Tokyo Lesbian and Gay Parade, which attracted over 1,000 participants. This success was repeated the next year, when participation more than doubled. However, participation in the 1996 parade fell back to just over 1,000, since many people were unhappy with the parade's organizers. Minami Teishirō, in particular, was criticized for dominating the organizing committee and attempting to control the dress and behavior of participants. Minami had apparently told marchers that they needed to present a "serious" *(majime)* face toward onlookers, instructing men not to wear clothing that revealed their buttocks or women their breasts (Lunsing 1999). This clash of ideologies over what it meant to be *gei*/gay is indicative that for many queer-identified Japanese, being queer was about being different. The parade offered some individuals the rare opportunity to be publicly different and to flaunt that difference; it offered a space in which to be "fabulous"—a term later taken up as the title of Japan's first gay lifestyle magazine.[11] Such arguments over proper decorum show that for many queers in Japan, as elsewhere, being queer is about "embodied relations rather than discursive ones" (Buckland 2002: 37), about conspicuously standing out, not "fitting in."

Since these disagreements were not easily resolved, attendance at the 1997 event was even worse, participation plummeting to less than a hundred; lesbians, who had felt they had been excluded from the decision-making process in earlier parades, refused to participate at all. Indeed, Lunsing reports that one lesbian, who had the temerity to jump the stage at the 1996 parade, was scolded by one of Minami's assistants: "What do you think you are doing, being merely lesbian?" (1999: 313). The implication of this comment was that in the eyes of the parade's gay male organizers, lesbians were not full participants. The collapse of the parade in the late 1990s illustrates the difficulty of building a community based on normative ideas of gay and lesbian identity. It was not until 2000 that a new, more queer-friendly and inclusive organizing committee was founded to stage that year's parade. According to the commemorative book based on the event, it attracted 2,500 participants (Sunagawa 2001:

13), few of whom seemed intent on making a "serious" impression. However, post-event, the same factionalism reasserted itself, and the success of the 2000 parade has not subsequently been repeated. Indeed, the 2003 and 2004 parades failed to get beyond the planning stage because of infighting.

OCCUR's tactic of presenting lesbians and gay men as "normal" in their interactions with official bodies, such as the law courts and government agencies, has resulted in alienating broad sections of the queer community. OCCUR member Niimi Hiroshi's testament that he was "completely male" *(kanzenna otoko)* in a 1991 interview with the women's magazine *Josei sebun* (Lunsing 1999: 312), while understandable given the transgender connotations that *gei* had long held, did little to recommend that organization to Japan's large transgender community, let alone to senior figures like Tōgō Ken who continue to identify with the indigenous category of *okama* and embody queer desire in a much more confronting manner than the salaryman persona adopted by more recent gay activists. OCCUR's constant referencing of U.S. models of gay and lesbian activism (Suganuma 2004) as well as its lack of interest in indigenous Japanese modes of queer identity and community have also proven alienating to many. In a recent pamphlet, for instance, OCCUR states, "The Japanese lesbian and gay movement did not begin in any real sense until the late 1980's, more than fifteen years after Stonewall" (cited in Mizutani 2001: 21), thus discounting the important contributions made by earlier activists Tōgō and Ōtsuka and completely ignoring the lesbian groups of the 1970s and '80s.

Organizations that, like ILGA Japan and OCCUR, have taken a prescriptive, "hard-line" approach to gay and lesbian identity can be seen as promoting a mode of "homonormativity" (Duggan 2003) that is at odds with Japan's well-established queer community, within which transgender identity and performance has a long history. Indeed, arguments over indigenous versus foreign identity categories, lifestyles and modes of activism have been conspicuous in recent years and make it impossible for one organization to represent Japan's diverse queer community.

THE *SHŪKAN KINYŌBI* DISCRIMINATING EXPRESSION CASE

The often tense relationship between what Lunsing (1998) has termed the "hard" and "soft" approaches taken by different lesbian and gay organizations and activists in Japan is well illustrated by a very public controversy that erupted over Tōgō Ken's self-designation as an *okama* in 2001. In June of that year, the left-leaning current affairs magazine *Shūkan kiny-*

ōbi (Weekly Friday) published an interview with Tōgō entitled *"Densetsu no okama: aiyoku to hangyaku ni moetagiru"* (Oikawa 2002). The title, which translates as "The legendary *okama*: burning with lust and rebellion," despite its apparently sensational tone, headed what is in fact a highly appreciative interview in which Tōgō speaks at length about his personal history, political career and ideas about the emperor system and sexual and gender identity. Tōgō was actually the fifth person to be interviewed in a series entitled "Living individually"; in keeping with the magazine's politics, the purpose of the article was not to sensationalize Tōgō's life but to give voice to one of the most vehement, if idiosyncratic, critics of postwar Japanese society.

The day after the article appeared, Itō Satoru, a prominent gay activist and director of Sukotan Project,[12] an influential team of gay educators and activists, complained to the magazine's editors that the use of the term *okama* in the title was "discriminatory" and that the definition of the term given in the article was "incorrect" and showed that the journalist responsible had "insufficiently studied" the issues involved. Itō was further incensed that despite having run a workshop for the magazine's editors sometime previously on how the media should treat the topic of homosexuality, they had gone ahead and used a discriminatory term. Itō, in making these accusations, was following the similarly prescriptive stance adopted by OCCUR toward homosexual nomenclature in its media guidebook *Dōseiai hōdō no tebiki* (Handbook for media reports on homosexuality), released in 1993. The handbook urged the media not to use terms such as *homo* and *okama*, because of their "discriminatory nuance." The fact that these terms were very often deployed by sexual minorities themselves went unmentioned.

Shūkan kinyōbi's editors replied that while in general terms such as *okama*, which were felt to be discriminatory by many, should be avoided in print, in the present context the use of the term was not only warranted but unavoidable. Tōgō Ken had, after all, been publicly identifying himself as an *okama* for over 30 years. As for the dispute over the meaning of the term *okama*, the definition offered was Tōgō's and not that of the journalist who interviewed him. In the article, Tōgō asserts that he likes the term *okama* because it is derived from the Sanskrit *kāma*, meaning "love" (as in the *Kāma Sutra*). As outlined in chapter 2, the term most probably dates from the Edo period, when it was used as a designation for the buttocks and thereby a reference to anal sex, but references to the *kāma* derivation are also common (see for example *Hyakuman nin no yoru* 1963a: 146). Though Tōgō was almost certainly aware of both derivations, many people felt that it was up to him to decide how to use the term and that it was quite proper for him to "reclaim" *okama* by stressing its connection with "love," no matter how dubious that claim might be.

In its publicity materials the Sukotan Project emphasizes that it is a gay organization made up of *tōjisha*—that is, "individuals [directly] concerned" with the topic—namely, homosexuals themselves. Given the paternalistic manner in which Japanese authorities have tended to deal with individuals who do not fit into "normal" society (Stibbe 2004: 22; Nakanishi and Ueno 2003: 13), the notion of listening to the "people concerned" had become a focus, particularly among feminist organizations fighting for women's rights and citizens' groups supporting the disabled and the mentally ill in the early 1980s.[13] In the 1990s the notion of the *tōjisha* emerged as an important authenticating device for stories about personal trauma, victimization, marginalization or disability and is now widely claimed as an authentic speaking position by gay men and lesbians—particularly on the Internet. Gay people are not alone in adopting this strategy, but, as Nakanishi and Ueno (2003) and Ishida and Murakami (forthcoming) point out, they are part of a general "*tōjisha* movement" that is gathering pace among minority groups. Whereas previously it had been considered appropriate for such third-party "experts" as doctors, psychiatrists, social workers and politicians to determine (or ignore) the rights of minority groups, since the 1990s a new discourse of *tōjisha shūken,* or the "sovereignty of the people concerned," has considerably empowered minority rights activists and is part of the general trend toward the "insurrection of subjugated knowledges" identified by Foucault as characteristic of late-twentieth-century social critique (2003: 7). The Internet has played an important role in this process, enabling greater networking between individuals and groups and also providing an opportunity to disseminate their ideas more widely.

Via the "media watch" section of the Sukotan website, Itō is constantly on the lookout for representations of gay men and lesbians that he considers to be discriminatory and, using tactics developed by the earlier Burakumin movement, is keen to challenge the authors or sponsors of these misrepresentations through accusing them of breaching human rights. However, in publicly challenging *Shūkan kinyōbi*'s motivation for using such an eye-catching headline, Itō found himself embroiled in a very public debate about nomenclature with Tōgō, himself a *tōjisha* of considerable seniority and a prominent spokesperson on gay issues.

To discuss the issues raised in this debate, Fushimi Noriaki, author of the seminal book *Private Gay Life* (1991) and editor of the periodical *Queer Japan,* organized a *zadankai,* or symposium, that was advertised in newsletters such as *Japan Gay News* and on the Internet. Although both Tōgō and Itō declined invitations to attend, Oikawa Kenji, the article's author, as well as *Shūkan kinyōbi*'s general editor Kurokawa Nobuyuki, were grateful for the opportunity to canvass a wider range of opinions on the contentious topic of speaking and writing about gay people in Japan. The consensus from the ensuing discussion, which was later published by Fushimi et al. (2002) as *Okama wa sabetsu ka* (Is *okama* a discriminatory term?), was that individuals had to be allowed to identify themselves in whatever way they chose and that it was always the context *(bummyaku)* and not specific terms themselves that should be used to judge whether a particular usage was discriminatory. Indeed, over 80 percent of men surveyed by gay magazine *Badi* felt that *okama* could still be used "depending on the circumstances" (Fushimi et al. 2002: 9).

Furthermore, as many people pointed out during the discussion, Itō's own preferred terms for discussing male homosexuals, *gei* and *dōseiaisha*, were themselves contentious, given the long association of *gei* with the *gei bōi* stereotype of the entertainment world and the history of *dōseiaisha* as a medical category signifying perversion. It was concluded that the right of *tōjisha* themselves to choose their own self-designations was paramount and that it was unhelpful to be too prescriptive about designating "correct" and "incorrect" nomenclature.

The "*Shūkan kinyōbi* discriminatory expression case" was widely discussed in Japan's gay world and on the Internet, showing that the problems associated with ideology and identification besetting lesbian and gay organizations in Japan (and elsewhere) over the past several decades will not be resolved easily. The continued presence of old-style activists such as Tōgō alongside more recent campaigners like Itō Satoru and the members of OCCUR suggest that a lesbian and gay consciousness has not so much displaced older paradigms of identity as now sits alongside them. It is not then surprising that "hard" groups such as Sukotan Project, ILGA Japan and OCCUR have met with opposition from a wide range of queer-identified individuals in Japan who feel that the prescriptive tone that these groups have sometimes taken, not only with "straight" society but also with members of their own community, is unhelpful and ultimately self-defeating. The "soft" groups, on the other hand, represented by people such as Tōgō, Ōtsuka and Fushimi, seem to have more in common with earlier paradigms of queer inclusiveness and to have been more successful in stimulating dialogue.

Indeed, the move toward championing the rights of the *tōjisha*, which establishes the individual as the final arbiter of truth about the self, is difficult to reconcile with a prescriptive, identity-based politics. Since each individual is unique and different, it is problematic when organizations seek to speak on behalf of widespread identity categories such as "homosexuals," because not all people will feel comfortable with the chosen terminology or sense that their needs or individual differences are being respected. This plurality of Japanese queer culture has been underlined by one recent development—the arrival and sudden escalation in the use of computer-mediated communications systems like the Internet. The queer presence on Japan's Net is enormous and diverse and has had a significant impact on *kono sekai*.

JAPAN'S GAY NET

The scope of the Japanese Internet is vast. Already by 1998 the amount of data in Japanese on the Internet had exceeded the total number of printed characters reproduced in all Japanese magazines and newspapers in an entire year (Gottlieb and McLelland 2003: 5); in that year Japanese was, after English, the most prevalent language on the Net, although it has subsequently lost that place to Chinese and Spanish. The Web contains tens of thousands of Japanese gay sites comprising personal homepages, chat rooms, bulletin boards and special "consultation" *(sōdan)* spaces where men can discuss such topics as how to "live as a gay" *(gei toshite ikiru)* and the meaning of "gay life" *(gei no jinsei)* (McLelland 2003a; 2003b; 2002; 2001; 2000b).[14]

Given the emphasis in earlier chapters on the plurality of sexual-identity categories and the difficulty of translating them into English, the most striking aspect of many websites is that they unequivocally use the terms *gei*/gay. Indeed, many are prefaced by a warning page that alerts browsers to the fact that they are about to enter a "gay space" *(gei supēsu)*. The entrance to the site *LUST*,[15] for example, contains the word "Oops!!" (in English), followed by the explanation: "This site has been made for gays (GAY *de aru tame*) and contains gay related stories and expressions. Gay people or people who understand about gays *(gei ni go-rikai no aru kata)*, please proceed. Other people can use the exit to go to Yahoo." Other sites, such as *MEN's NET JAPAN*,[16] are more exclusive. On its entrance page is printed "WARNING" (in English), followed by the explanation, "Since this page is a place used by gay people [*gei no kata gata*] to communicate with male companions, the following cannot use it: men not interested in homosexuality and women."

It is apparent that *gei*/gay is now established as the main term designating male-male sexuality on the parts of the Net used by "gay men" themselves. This provides a clear linguistic connection between Japanese and western "gays," for despite the fact that *gei* is usually (but not always) written in katakana, the pronunciation is identical. Indeed some sites address foreign gay men on their entrance pages. *MEN's NET*, for instance, states in English: "Welcome to MEN's NET JAPAN homepage. This homepage is written in Japanese. This site is GAY men only." The Internet itself is not responsible for this shift in terminology. As detailed in chapter 3, *gei bōi*, as the most visible (effeminate) face of male homosexuality, had already begun to disappear in mainstream media during the

1980s, due to several factors. Firstly, a new term—*nyūhāfu*—arose in the early 1980s to signify transgender homosexual identity, and this was followed mid-decade by the establishment of the first gay and lesbian organizations patterned on western models. Consequently, individuals who would previously have been described in the press as *gei bōi* were now being referred to as *nyūhāfu,* while a new, more political discourse of *gei* rights began to emerge. By the time of the "gay boom" of the early 1990s, *gei* had by and large won out over *homo* as the preferred self-designation for most, especially younger, homosexual men. With the demise of *homo* as a self-referent, the distinction between masculine *homo* and effeminate *gei* has also largely become redundant. Now *gei* can be used in a very broad sense to refer to a wide range of homosexual styles and identities, both masculine and feminine—just as it can in English, although many gays at the more feminine end of the spectrum prefer to use the traditional term *okama,* as does Tōgō Ken. However, despite this new breadth in usage, *gei* in Japanese is still distinctive, in that it is only used in relation to men and male gay culture. On the Internet, *rezubian* is the most common referent for same-sex-desiring women. Like gay sites, lesbian sites also include warnings on their entrance pages and request that men not enter. Consequently it is not possible to give an overview of lesbian networking on the Internet, but much of what is said below about gay men's use of computer-mediated communication is also true of women's uses.

The perverse press and later the *homo* magazines had always contained information about homosexual meeting spots and provided personals columns. However, the advent of online message boards and chat rooms has made it a fast and efficient matter to make contact with other gay men in one's city, locality or even school or workplace. Now that most gay bars have their own websites, it is easy to check them out online before plucking up the courage to go through their doors. Hence, much of the anxiety and arbitrariness associated with many individuals' debut in *kono sekai* has been resolved by the Internet, and this has contributed to a generation gap in gay consciousness. Sunagawa (2003: 30–1), for instance, notes a striking difference in the life stories of gay men under 25 and those who, like himself, are over 30. He finds that compared with more senior men, fewer young men are troubled by their "sexual orientation" *(seiteki shikō);* he puts this down to the fact that they came of age during the early 1990s—Japan's "gay boom," when information about Japan's gay culture was more widely dispersed through the media. Most significant, however, is the fact that many young men's debuts on the scene occur not in bars but via the Internet, a medium that not only gives access to an unlimited amount of information about the gay world but also, equally important, allows individuals to voice their own identities. On the Internet, young men are able to encounter the gay world and begin to communicate with others *as gay men* while still in their teens—something that was almost impossible previously. The Internet therefore offers space for what Miller and Slater (2001: 10) refer to as "expansive realisation," where "one can become what one thinks one really is," freed from many of the restrictions that condition offline identities.

On the entrance page of his website, gay activist and author Ishikawa Taiga reflects on the nature of the Internet in a way that seems to support Miller and Slater's observation:

> How did you come upon this page? Through a search engine? By Net surfing? Or. . . . Anyway, of all the home pages that you could have visited, I'm grateful for this unexpected opportunity to meet you. As you know, countless information exists in the world of the Internet. No doubt there are many people who discover completely fresh and surprising knowledge and information that they previously knew nothing about. I think that the Internet can be spoken of as a place where "new knowledge" can be encountered easily. When one encounters various sites with an open mind, from that point on one's life will doubtless become richer.[17]

Ishikawa goes on to describe the contents of his site and to talk about his positionality as a *tōjisha*. The space that the Internet has afforded gay *tōjisha*—that is, individuals who speak directly from a position of first-hand knowledge and experience of homosexual desire—to speak out about their experience *as gays* has enabled a significant shift in subjectivity. This function is in many ways as important as the ease of access to information that the Internet affords.

Of course, as discussed in previous chapters, postwar Japanese media have always contained spaces in which sexual minorities could write in and confront, challenge and modify the opinions of the "experts" by discoursing about their own experience. As early as 1954, ads for the FKK Club in *Fūzoku kagaku* were exhorting participants in the world of *sodomia* to stand firm and be proud: "You are not perverts." Early members-only magazines, such as *Adonis* and *Bara,* also provided the opportunity for *homo* to communicate and network with each other, a process that became easier in the 1970s with the advent of commercial, nationally distributed magazines like *Barazoku* and *Sabu*. However, none of these organs was able to approximate the range or scale of the Internet; the time lag between writing a letter or an article, seeing it published and receiving responses limited the extent to which these magazines could encourage the development of a homosexual speaking position. The Internet, whose advent came at a time when the notion of the primacy of the *tōjisha* was already being emphasized by a variety of pressure groups, has had an impact on Japanese gay culture that can only be described as revolutionary.

In an essay on gay men and the Internet, Kadoya Manabu points out, "For gay people, the most revolutionary event of the twentieth century wasn't Stonewall or the Mardi Gras Parade but . . . the birth of the Internet" (2003: 65). There is good reason to believe this true, especially in Japan. It is on the Internet that the voice of the *tōjisha* can be directly heard. As discussed in earlier chapters, many of the submissions to the perverse press were presented as "confessions" *(kokuhaku)*—indeed, Mishima Yukio's seminal homosexual novel, first published in 1951, was given the title *Kamen no kokuhaku*, or "Confessions of a mask." The confessional narrative has long been a part of the sexological tradition, going back to the case studies first collected by Krafft-Ebing and others in the nineteenth century. Confession is also a characteristic of many gay websites, yet these stories are increasingly framed as *kamingu auto* (coming out) narratives. As Ken Plummer points out in *Telling Sexual Stories*, "stories of 'homosexuality' have recently changed," increasingly focusing on "coming out," which he terms "a dominant narrative" (Plummer 1995: 81). He goes on to argue that coming out is now "a global story since many of the tales told criss-cross their way around the world" (Plummer 1995: 96). The term "come out" *(kamu auto)* is now ubiquitous on Japanese gay websites, turning up on personal homepages, problem pages, chat lines, and in personal ads. For instance, the online self-introduction form that readers filled out on the now defunct e-zine *gaywalker.com*[18] contained the question "Have you come out?" *(kamu auto shimashitaka)*. The choices provided were: "to everyone," "to friends only," "no answer" or "not yet," the latter implying that coming out was anticipated as a future event. Indeed, the Internet is brimming with personal homepages in which Japanese gay men come out and discourse about their positionality as gay men.

Writing on the radical shifts in black identity that came about in the United States as a consequence of the civil rights movement, Rainwater suggests that "each individual tries on identities that emerge from the cultural material available to him [*sic*] and tests them by making appropriate announcements" (1970: 375). The new authority of the *tōjisha*, the early '90s "gay boom" and the rise of the Internet have come together to establish *gei* as the most widespread male homosexual identity category in Japan, an identity that is increasingly constituted through "coming out." For many *gei* men, the Internet provides the stage for this announcement. Cheung (2000) has discussed the production of the self via online communication and notes how personal homepages encourage a self-reflexive mode of narrative—that is, they enable the owner to discourse about private issues that would be more difficult to communicate face-to-face. In his discussion, Cheung draws upon Goffman's theories of the presentation of the self, particularly the use of "dramaturgy." Indeed, many Japanese gay men's homepages feature a "dramatic" style of self-presentation, through the use of animation, eye-catching graphics and music; the narrative most frequently presented in this manner is the coming-out story.

Hence, one important function of computer-mediated communication is in "enabling us to extend our gender performances across space, to create spectacles of ourselves online in ways that can potentially be used for the purpose of extending our identities in our local and global daily lives" (Young 2004: 59). Although, no doubt, many gay men's online "out" persona may not be communicated to colleagues and family members in the offline world, cyberspace does provide the opportunity to experiment with different modes of self-presentation and may provide a conduit into "real life." For instance, one gay man explained on the *gaywalker* chat site that he had a novel way of coming out—when he felt comfortable with new acquaintances, he directed them to his homepage, where he had described his gay experiences. This enabled his friends to ask him various questions by e-mail that they might have felt too embarrassed or unable to bring up directly. This man clearly felt safer managing this disclosure online before dealing with it in face-to-face communication.

As Giddens (1992; 1991) has argued, modernity, in Japan as elsewhere, has seen the development and proliferation of "lifestyle sectors" that challenge "traditional" lifestyle patterns and gender roles. This has largely been an effect of media saturation, as the media continue to proliferate, diversify and niche market. The Internet, a classic example of media diversification, provides a window onto an enormous range of gay experience, a window that offers expansive potential and a space for trying out online identities that may then move into offline life. As more gay men encounter narratives of coming out on the Internet, they may well be encouraged to take this step in their daily lives. The sense of loneliness and isolation, of being the only one, that characterized the youth of many gay men prior to the days of the Internet will surely begin to disperse as an increasing number of teens find their way into gay chat rooms and discover the diversity of Japan's gay scene. Indeed, as *SindBad* states on its opening page, "Everyone, please make lots of friends and discoveries here," and then, in English, "We are not all alone!!" Likewise, the notions that homosexuality is unusual or associated with only a few character types will become increasingly untenable when confronted with the enormous variety of gay self-expression on the Internet.

CONCLUSION

The chapter opened with a discussion of various changes that took place in *kono sekai* during the 1970s. At the beginning of the decade, while Tōgō

Ken was arguing for the continued relevance of such long-standing Japanese terms as *okama*, a new, more masculine style of homosexual culture was developing around the term *homo*. This culture was, however, largely unaffected by the lesbian and gay rights' movement that proved so influential in the west, and it was only toward the end of the decade that Japanese understandings of the term *gei* began to expand to include the notion of political identity or rights. It was actually the term *rezubian*, not *gei*, that first took on political connotations, having been adopted by a number of Japanese same-sex-desiring women who, through their contact with second-wave feminist ideas, were developing radical critiques of the limitations of the female role in Japan. However, despite their greater radicalism, women's efforts were hampered by the failure of mainstream women's organizations to interest themselves in lesbian issues and by the disadvantaged social position that many lesbians found themselves in vis-à-vis men, whether gay or straight.

In the 1980s small organizations emerged that pioneered new understandings of the political ramifications of homosexuality. These perspectives were picked up and widely promulgated by the mainstream press during the gay boom of the early 1990s, which enabled many self-identified gay men and lesbians to publish narrative accounts of their lives outside of the entertainment paradigm that had previously structured such confessions. One result was that during the 1990s Japan developed a gay culture similar in many ways to that of anglophone societies and that both *gei* (gay) and *rezubian* (lesbian) are now commonly deployed as identity categories by Japanese homosexual men and women.

However, the hard-line approach taken toward "gay identity" by such groups as ILGA Japan and OCCUR and by activists like Itō Satoru has not been widely supported by Japan's queer community. As the *Shūkan kinyōbi* discrimination controversy shows, many sexually nonconformist individuals are aware of the very rapid manner in which terminology and attendant identities are changing in Japan, and it remains unwise to lay down rules about what terms individuals should or should not use to describe themselves or others or how they should present themselves to the general public. Ironically, the queer positionality developed by Tōgō Ken in the early 1970s—a positionality stressing queer *embodiment* as much as discursivity and attempting to establish a commonality based on alienation from "commonsense" ideas about gender, sexuality and lifestyle rather than on a shared identity—is now very much in vogue at the beginning of the new century.

Indeed, the rise in prominence of the *tōjisha*—that is, the person concerned—as the only arbiter of knowledge about the self, along with the rapid development of the Internet as a stage for the performance of individual identity, has accelerated this general queering effect on Japanese sexual subcultures. To the extent that everyone is different, it remains difficult for one individual, group or agency to represent the interests or demands of a wide range of others. This is particularly apparent in the context of Japan's transgender community, a constituency largely overlooked by Japan's established gay and lesbian organizations, and it is to a discussion of transgender lives in Japan that we now turn.

NOTES

1. Burakumin are a discriminated community whose ancestors constituted an untouchable class because of their "polluted" profession as butchers, leather workers and undertakers. Although this status was officially removed in the Meiji period, individuals whose family lines can be traced back to traditional Burakumin localities still face discrimination.

2. 1978, issue no. 4.

3. I thank James Welker for pointing this out to me.

4. Phryne was an Athenian courtesan famous for both her beauty and her wit. She amassed a considerable fortune and offered to rebuild the walls of Thebes, but only on condition that the words "destroyed by Alexander, restored by Phryne the courtesan" be inscribed upon them.

5. See *Carmilla*'s website for details of the contents: www.carmilla.jp/ (accessed 5 July 2004).

6. The information in this section is based on Ōtsuka's book *Ni-chōme no uroko,* as well as personal discussions with him. Further details of Ōtsuka's writings as well as his artwork can be found on his website: www.asahi-net.or.jp/~km5t-ootk/1taq.html (14 August 2003).

7. The name probably derives from the 1974 American novel *The Front Runner,* by Patricia Nell Warren, which details the trials faced by an openly gay athlete as he prepares to participate in the Olympics.

8. The information in this section is primarily based on the interview with Minami in *Queer Studies Japan 96*, pp. 172–81.

9. Hasegawa reports that as of 2003 there were 7,000 reported cases of HIV infection in Japan, among whom 4,000 were thought to be gay men (2003: 138). The population of Japan is just under 127 million. The UN AIDS Council estimates that at the end of 2003 as many as 1.2 million people were infected with HIV in North America.

10. The first instance of the use of *kamu auto* that I am aware of on Japanese TV occurred in the 1993 drama *Dōsōkai,* where it was glossed as *kokuhaku* (confession) and *sengen* (declaration) of sexual preference. In 1998, however, I heard the term used without qualification on MTV Japan in a news item about George Michael. James Welker (in press) mentions use of the term in the boy-love magazine *Allan* as early as 1981, but at that time "its use did not catch on."

11. The brainchild of Ōgura Tō (also known as the drag queen Margarette), *Fabulous* was published between 1999 and 2000 and saw four issues before finally going under.

12. For further information, see their website: www.sukotan.com (12 December 2003).

13. Stibbe (2003: 22) dates this change to the influence of the United Nation's International Year of Disabled Persons in 1981, which gave impetus to disabled activism in Japan.

14. In February 2004, the site *SindBad bookmarks*, just one of many Japanese links sites, had links to over 40,000 Japanese and overseas gay-related sites and was adding new ones at a rate of about 500 per week. Statistics available online: www.sindbadbookmarks.com (1 February 2004).

15. URL www.geocities.com/WestHollywood/Club/7266/ (8 January 2002).

16. URL www.mensnet.jp (8 January 2002).

17. URL www.taigaweb.jp/hajimete.htm (26 September 2003).

18. Site no longer active, formerly www.gaywalker.com (10 December 2000).

6

Transgender Lives

As outlined in earlier chapters, print sources in the period immediately after the war suggest an increase in both male and female transgender practice. In some cases economic necessity led women to pass as men in an attempt to gain greater social security, whereas some men, also for economic reasons, cross-dressed as women and worked as prostitutes. By the early 1950s, as the economic situation in Japan's cities began to stabilize, transgendered men could be found in a few bars centered in the old pleasure quarters of Tokyo and of other cities such as Osaka and Kyoto. The "gay boom" of the late 1950s led to a process of "touristization" that saw an increasing number of transgender bars, cabarets and clubs catering to a straight clientele. At this time bars featuring transgendered women also appeared in Tokyo, although their number was always few. The "blue-boy boom" of the 1960s led to a further increase in the entertainment value of transgender performance, and transgender entertainers like Miwa Akihiro, Carrousel Maki and Peter made the transition from subculture to mainstream, remaining influential figures on Japan's entertainment scene today. The *mizu shōbai*, Japan's enormous bar and entertainment world, has remained a hospitable environment for transgendered male and, to a lesser extent, female performers.

However, the limited space afforded some transgendered men and women in Japan's entertainment trade does not suit all, particularly individuals who resent having to put on performances in front of customers and clients. Not all men who like to cross-dress feel comfortable with the sexualized atmosphere that exists in the clubs and bars, and momentum has gathered for creating more purely social spaces in which men with transgender interests can be together during the daytime without the sexualized atmosphere and high expense characteristic of the *mizu shōbai*.

Still others in the transgender community consider themselves to be transsexual—that is, to be psychologically male or female but burdened with sexed bodies that are out of sync with their gender identities. Such individuals particularly dislike the spectacle that is made of the transgender experience in Japanese culture and want nothing more than to quietly undergo corrective surgery so as to be able to live as "ordinary" *(futsū)* men and women do.

In the late 1990s, when changes to legislation made sex-change surgery possible again in Japan after a 30-year hiatus, transsexual individuals began to come out in the media and receive more respectful treatment than the tabloid press had afforded transgender entertainers in earlier decades. The moral seriousness with which "gender identity disorder" *(sei dōitsusei shōgai)* is now treated in Japanese society has not, however, been welcomed by all transgender individuals, some of whom take exception to the notion that to fail to conform to stereotypical patterns of male or female identity and behavior is in some sense an illness. Social attitudes in Japan toward those considered "disabled" have until very recently been paternalistic and controlling; those failing to present as "normal" members of society often face ostracism and segregation (Stibbe 2004: 22). Hence, some transgenders are skeptical of the new sex-change arrangements that posit medical authorities as the "experts" in charge of giving assent to procedures while transgender individuals themselves *(tōjisha)*, who are the real experts on their condition, are relegated to the lay category of "patient." The traditional role of medical and psychiatric experts in Japan has been to assist those characterized as disabled "to work hard on their own to be as 'normal' as possible" (Stibbe 2004: 23), clearly an inappropriate strategy in relation to many transgenders who feel that the problem lies not in their own psychology but in a society that rigidly insists on assigning individuals to one or other side of a binary gender system.

The strict limitations that medical authorities place on sex-change procedures are particularly resented by those transgenders who do seek out and accept roles in the *mizu shōbai*. As outlined in chapter 3, there is a long tradition in Japan of male-to-female transgender entertainers undergoing medical procedures such as the injection of hormones, the removal of the testicles and the addition of implants in order to create a more commercially viable female image. More recently, some *onabe*—that is, female-to-male transgenders working in the bar world—have begun to take male hormones to induce beard growth and have had mastectomies (Lunsing in press; Longinetto 1996). Just as a fashion model might undergo surgery to "correct" a slightly misshapen nose or have collagen injections to create pouting lips, some transgenders wish to undergo surgery in order to create more feminine or masculine bodies, putting them into conflict with medical authorities who do not recognize such commercial "folk categories" *(minzoku hanchū)* as *gei bōi*, *onabe* or *nyūhāfu* as viable identities.

This chapter looks at the changing nature of transgender experience in Japan from the 1960s to the present, highlighting the wide variety of identities and practices that are covered by the now widespread Japanized English term *toransujendā* (transgender).

PRO AND SEMI-PRO TRANSGENDER LIVES

As outlined earlier, by the 1970s transgender cabarets and bars could be found all over Japan, even in relatively small cities. These bars were quite unlike the drag bars described by Esther Newton (1979) that proliferated in the United States throughout the 1960s and '70s. The American bars tended to be large and to feature a stage on which transgender entertainers would perform a variety of acts. The female impersonators who worked in these clubs, although most of them were also homosexual, saw themselves as professional entertainers and resented demands by the management that they mingle with the audience between acts and encourage the purchase of expensive alcoholic drinks. Also, given the widespread existence of "sodomy" statutes in different U.S. states and regulations against cross-dressing, which could be judged obscene behavior, any performer who mingled with the crowd while still in drag risked arrest. Newton points out that while it was unusual for a cabaret catering to a largely straight clientele to be raided by the police, gay bars that featured drag acts were common targets, which meant that spending time in such bars was not, for many men, a particularly relaxing experience. Indeed, as Nancy Achilles comments regarding the United States, "It is in large part due to the police that the homosexual can . . . regard himself as a member of an unfairly treated minority group" (1967: 235). In Japan, however, there was no police harassment of bars featuring transgender performers, and bars were never raided simply because homosexual men were known to gather there.

Although Tokyo, Osaka and other large cities did house large bars and cabarets catering to straight clienteles, most Japanese transgender bars were of a variety referred to as *sunakku*,[1] that is, tiny hole-in-the-wall places accommodating between ten and twenty regular customers. *Sunakku* are a common kind of bar in Japan; even the smallest towns have numerous different *sunakku* where male employees drop in nightly on their way home for a few drinks and to socialize with the other regulars. Many *sunakku* are run by husband-and-wife teams, whereas others employ small staffs of female hostesses to chat with the customers. Indeed, because *sunakku* rely upon the development of a regular customer base, it is particularly important that the hostesses develop personal relationships with the guests and create a "home away from home" atmosphere.

Japan also has numerous *sunakku* where both staff and clientele are transgender men. Some bars offer (for a membership fee) the use of a backroom where customers who arrive at the bar in male attire can change their clothes and apply makeup, either with or without assistance from the bar's staff. Such *sunakku* offered the chance for a wider community of "amateur" *(amachua)* cross-dressers to interact with each other and also with male customers who are interested in or admire transgenders *(josō aikō dansei)*. Most of these bars have a dual charge system whereby the gender-normative men who come seeking companionship pay substantially higher charges for tables and drinks than do cross-dressed men.

Unlike the staff of *gei bā*, who are "professionals" *(puro gei bōi)* living full-time in their transgender persona and deriving their livelihood exclusively from the entertainment world, transgenders who work in *sunakku* bars are sometimes referred to as "semi-professional" *(semi puro)*, in that they may gain auxiliary income from serving in the bars a few nights a week while also maintaining day jobs as men. Indeed, Kamo Kozue, the mama of Kozue bar, worked as a regular salaryman during the daytime, closing the bar at 3:00 AM and taking a taxi home to catch what sleep she could before leaving for her office job (as a salaryman) at the *Yomiuri* newspaper (Sugiura 2001: 32–3). However, the divisions between customer and staff and amateur and semi-professional can become quite blurred, as amateur cross-dressers may work in a part-time capacity at the bars through encouraging the male patrons to consume (or buy for them) more drinks, helping out men new to the cross-dressing world with dress and makeup tips and in some cases selling sexual favors in return for tips from male clients. The difference between semi-professional and professional transgenders is, however, clear to the extent that professional transgenders do not engage in any employment other than their entertainment work. Matsuba Yukari, for instance, who worked as a cross-dressed hostess in a variety of *sunakku* in the '60s and '70s and who also worked for a time as a *danshō* (or cross-dressing) male prostitute, did not regard herself as a "professional" cross-dresser, since throughout this period she also maintained a day job as a man and lived with her family (Sugiura 2001).

Other *sunakku* exist that, though run by transgender mama-sans, do not cater to clienteles of cross-dressers but to regular customers. One such bar, which became something of a tourist attraction in the 1970s, was Blue Night, located in the small town of Tendoshi in Yamagata prefecture on Japan's northeastern seaboard.[2] The bar was the creation of Nanjō Masami, who had started work as a *gei bōi* in Osaka clubs in the early 1960s and, showing considerable organizational ability, had become the manager of two different clubs while still in her early twenties. However, after a disastrous love affair with a man who could not accept the fact that she had a penis, in a drunken fit Nanjō cut her penis off with a Japanese sword. Had she not been discovered by a bartender only minutes later, she would certainly have bled to death. In the late 1960s, after recovering from this ordeal, Nanjō moved to the small town of Tendoshi, where, along with a new male lover, she opened her own bar.

Nanjō's experience testifies to an important difference between Japan and the United States and other anglophone societies with regard to the reception of transgender people. While the terrible story of her self-castration shows the lengths of desperation that some transgender men were driven to in the wake of the Blue Boy Trial (see chapter 3), the supportive environment that the *mizu shōbai* could offer should not be overlooked. Wanting to put the past behind her, Nanjō decided to leave the big city and recuperate in the less-demanding atmosphere of a small town. The fact that she could so easily open a bar and be seen about town with her much younger male lover points to the degree of license that Japanese society affords individuals who live and work in the *mizu shōbai*. Indeed, Nanjō quickly became an important person in town affairs, becoming a member of the organizing committee for the town's annual Cherry Festival (Sakuranbo Matsuri) and the star of many of the dramatic performances that took place during the festival period. Nanjō and her bar were proudly mentioned in the town's promotional literature as a tourist attraction.

Nanjō's story evidences both the potential and the constraints that Japanese society affords some transgender people. Bar and entertainment work, while not reputable in the sense that working for a bank or a major corporation is, can offer a relatively safe space for transgender people to live and work; it even has its own career structure, with talented individuals able to move from performance into management and establish their own bars. This space need not be a primarily urban one, as it almost always is in anglophone societies, but even the supposedly conservative, less cosmopolitan countryside can offer scope for a transgender lifestyle, particularly hot-spring spa towns, which have long been associated with recreational sexuality.

So long as the basic constraints of the *mizu shōbai* world are respected, many transgenders have found it hospitable. The *mizu shōbai*, or "water trade," is by its nature fickle, unstable and quite unlike the hard, dry nature of ordinary life, with its relentless family and work commitments. Operating mostly at night, these businesses cater to a primarily male clientele who stop by after work—that is, after the real business of the day is over—and expect to be entertained, pampered and taken care of. For them it is a time for play. Although the workers in the *mizu shōbai* may lack the moral seriousness that comes from shouldering the family and work responsibilities of the majority, they are nevertheless afforded a place in society, or perhaps a place beyond society, that not only permits but encourages differences of a kind that would not be tolerated in the "real world" of everyday life.

Stories such as Nanjō Masami's are by no means uncommon in Japan's transgender community, and in some respects their condition is better than that of transgenders in much of the west. Indeed, in the early 1980s a series of media events led toward yet another "boom" in interest in transgender performance, resulting in the further expansion of possibilities for Japan's transgenders.

THE *NYŪHĀFU* BOOM

As discussed in chapter 3, *gei bōi* remained the most prominent term for describing transgendered men working in the entertainment industry until the early 1980s. At this time two new Japanese-English neologisms appeared, "newhalf" *(nyūhāfu)* and "Mr. Lady" (Mr. *redi*), which designated entertainers who had gone beyond the wearing of women's clothes, makeup and hairstyles to develop breasts, through the use of hormones or implants. The term *nyūhāfu* dates back to 1981 and in most accounts is attributed to Betty, the mama of the Osaka show pub Betty's Mayonnaise, who said, "I'm half man and woman so I'm a new half" *(otoko to onna no hāfu dakara nyūhāfu)*. "Half," or *hāfu* in Japanese, is a term used to refer to individuals of mixed race, usually Japanese and Caucasian. The "new half" referred to by Betty was therefore another indeterminate figure, not of mixed race but of mixed gender.[3]

This term might not have gained such wide currency had it not been picked up by the media. But on 14 April 1981 the tabloid sports newspaper *Supōtsu Nippon* ran an article citing Betty's comment, entitled "Gay singer named Betty is called a *nyūhāfu*." However, it was the massive media attention given to "Roppongi girl" Matsubara Rumiko in May of that year that ensured the new term became widespread. Matsubara, hiding her biological status as a man, had won a beauty promotion staged by businesses in Roppongi (a popular upscale nightlife area in Tokyo), becoming the cover girl for a poster campaign promoting the area's clubs and bars. Once her transgender status was revealed, she was quickly elevated to idol status—posing seminude in men's magazine *Heibon panchi* on 8 June 1981, releasing an album of songs entitled *Nyūhāfu* in September 1981 and acting in the movie *Kura no naka* (In the storehouse; dir. Yokomizu Seishi, 1981).

"Mr. Lady," another term that is often used in the popular press interchangeably with *nyūhāfu*,[4] first featured in the Japanese title of the French-Italian movie *La cage aux folles* (originally released in Japan in 1978 under the title *Misutā redi misutā madamu*) but did not gain widespread currency until 1988. At this time, the popular lunchtime "wide show" (live general-interest TV program) *Waratte ii tomo* (It's OK to laugh)[5] introduced a regular segment entitled "Mr. Lady" featuring transgender beauty contests and guessing games, thus providing opportunities for some transgenders from the show-pub scene to develop media careers and bringing the transgender world to the attention of the wider public.

One of the most prominent of this new generation of transgendered talents was Asakawa Hikaru, who had appeared as a teen idol on the show-pub circuit with the song-and-dance troupe *Beru Popinsu* before being discovered by Fuji TV. She appeared on late-night shows, becoming famous for the gag that her top half (i.e., her breasts) resembled her mother's but her lower half (still) resembled her father's. Asakawa's gag is an example of a common practice in discourse surrounding *nyūhāfu*, which draws attention to their intersexual as opposed to transsexual nature. This is made explicit on websites belonging to *nyūhāfu* salons offering sexual services, where the state of the *nyūhāfu* companions' genitalia is always made explicit (usually *sao tsuki*—literally "has a shaft" or *sao nashi*—"has no shaft") (McLelland 2002: 171–2).

Nyūhāfu is a complex category that covers a range of sexual identities and practices—but not lifestyles. It is used to designate transgendered men who live and work in the sex and entertainment world. Komatsu's collection of *nyūhāfu* life stories *Nyūhāfu ga kimeta "watashi" rashii ikikata* (On deciding to be a *nyūhāfu* and living like "myself") features seven individuals who are all to some extent involved in the sex-trade or bar world. However, they display a range of transgender attributes, some having developed breasts through the use of hormones and some through implants. *Nyūhāfu* also differ regarding their attitudes toward their male genitalia, some having undergone castration only, others having had complete sex-change operations and yet others declaring a sense of identification with their penises. Cherry, for instance, says "I love my well-shaped penis" (2000: 126), which she is happy to use for penetrative purposes with her clients while rejecting the notion that she might use it to penetrate her boyfriend. Interviews with *nyūhāfu* in SM magazines also stress the fact that many choose to have their testicles removed but prefer to keep their penises, either because they appreciate the pleasure and convenience that a penis can supply or because keeping their penis is an advantage in their work. SM mistress Shanon no Mama tells one interviewer, "I won't have it cut off, in this line of work most people agree that it's better to keep it" (MISTRESS 1990: 141). Eve, in a separate interview, points out that "people feel differently about it but there are those who tell me its better to keep it and besides, it feels good" (HIP PRESS 1990: 103).

A brief look at *Nyūhāfu Net*'s[6] photo personals page also shows that *nyūhāfu* and their admirers are interested in a range of sexual interactions, including "lesbian relationships" *(rezu na kankei)*. *Nyūhāfu* represent what Valentine and Wilchins have termed "disruptive bodies," since they destabilize the "coherence between gender, sexual practices, and somatic makeup" that characterizes medical discussion about transsexualism (1997: 215). It is not possible, then, to collapse *nyūhāfu* into the category transsexual; *nyūhāfu* are best understood as a category of male-to-female transgendered entertainers and sex workers who are primarily, but not exclusively, sexually interested in gender-normative men. *Nyūhāfu* are a Japanese example of what Boellstorff terms "'ethnolocalized homosexual or transvestite professional' (ETP) subject positions." He goes on to argue that "it is a misnomer to speak of ETPs as *sexualities*, as that term is understood in the 'West,' since they are above all professions, not categories of selfhood organized around sexual desire" (2003: 231; emphasis in original).

The impossibility of ascribing a fixed sexuality to *nyūhāfu* is further underlined by the facts that *nyūhāfu* are sometimes represented as an intersexual category and that while they are generally presented as feminine in their gender performance, their phallic potential is not denied. In *nyūhāfu* sex work, it is important that clients know in advance the status of the *nyūhāfu* companions' genitalia—whether or not they have a "shaft" *(sao)* or "balls" *(tama)*—since a popular item mentioned on all *nyūhāfu* "health menus" is *gyaku* A or "reverse" A(nal), where the *nyūhāfu* companion anally penetrates the client with her penis. The fact that AF, or "anal fuck," in which the client penetrates the *nyūhāfu* with his penis, remains unmodified suggests that this is the default position, a notion in line with traditional understandings of the sexually active role played by the "normal" male and the passivity of the transgender partner.

This latter point brings up the issue of the status of *nyūhāfu* clients and their own sex and gender identities. Significantly, a guide to Tokyo's sex scene (Altbooks 1998) that is exhaustive in describing the kinds of establishments and services available in red-light districts such as Kabuki-chō does not offer information about *nyūhāfu* venues, despite their large number. Since gay clubs and services are also excluded from the collection, it appears that the guide is directed at a heterosexual audience and that interest in *nyūhāfu* falls outside this constituency. This is reinforced by the guidebook's discussion of cross-dressing *(josō)* clubs, where men can rent women's clothes and dress up with the assistance of professional female beauticians. Some venues also offer sexual services to their male clients, who can engage in "lesbian play" *(rezu purei)* with the club's biological women. The guidebook is clear about differentiating these clubs from those staffed by *okama* and *nyūhāfu,* who, as we have seen, are also characterized by cross-dressing. *Okama,* for instance, are described as "male homosexuals *(dansei dōseiaisha)* who like to cross-dress" (1998: 167) and who live in an "*okama* world" *(okama no sekai)* separate from the clubs under discussion. *Nyūhāfu,* on the other hand, are designated "male homosexuals who have undergone a sex-change operation," a definition that, curiously, excludes the very large number of *nyūhāfu* who elect to keep their male genitalia and, moreover, use them. This excision of *nyūhāfu's* male genitalia is significant given the dominant paradigm for viewing homosexuality in Japan as a gender transgression in which men take on a woman's "passive" role in sex.

That transgender men might be actively engaged in penetrative acts with other men is, however, sometimes noted in the press. For instance, on 19 September 2000 the tabloid *Nikkan supōtsu* ran the headline "*Okama ga kama horu Gotanda no NH deri SM,*" which plays on the polyvalence of the term *okama*—which can mean both "effeminate homosexual" and "backside." *Horu* means "to dig" and as a slang term is used for "fuck"—hence the headline could be translated as "Gotanda's *nyūhāfu* SM delivery service where *okama* fuck backsides." Gotanda, an area of downtown Tokyo centering on the train station, is home to numerous sex-related establishments, including several salons specializing in "*nyūhāfu* companions." "*Deri*" here is a contraction of "delivery health," "health" being a common sex-world euphemism for a variety of sexual services. While many clients visit the various salons and massage parlors in search of companionship, the Internet, particularly the mobile *i-mode* function popular in Japan, has made "delivery" services in which *nyūhāfu* companions visit clients' homes or hotels very common. The September 2000 article concerned a *nyūhāfu* "SM queen" *(SM no joōsama)* who anally penetrated her clients as part of her service. The phrase "*okama ga kama horu*" is a pun on the oxymoronic notion of an *okama,* defined by the notion that he takes it up the backside, penetrating another man's backside, and suggests that *nyūhāfu,* despite having emerged as a distinct transgender category in the early 1980s, has not entirely escaped from the traditional category of *okama* in which male homosexuality, transgenderism and "passive" sex were conflated.

Indeed, *nyūhāfu* clubs themselves tend to confuse *nyūhāfu* with the more general term *okama* in their promotional material. A 1991 promotion for the Osaka club Betty's Mayonnaise (which, as we have seen, was reportedly the birthplace of the term *nyūhāfu*) encourages customers to "Come and celebrate with us on *Okama* Day" (*Shūkan jitsuwa* 1991). The latter festival, which is not an official holiday, takes place on 4 April, a date that falls between the celebration of Hina Matsuri (or the Doll Festival, celebrating the birth of girl children, which falls on 3 March) and Kodomo no Hi (or Children's Day, where male children are celebrated, which falls on 5 May). In this advertisement Betty's club is referred to as a *gei bā*, suggesting that this term still had widespread currency even ten years after the creation of the term *nyūhāfu*. Several years later, however, a similar promotional feature in *Shūkan taishū* (1994) does not use the term *gei*, although it twice refers to the *nyūhāfu* entertainers with the diminutive *okama-chan*. This seems odd in that the text identifies the 17 *nyūhāfu* currently working at Betty's as having become "complete women" *(kanzen naru josei)*, describing them as "more feminine than real women" *(hon mono no josei ijō joseirashii)*. Given that the *okama* is usually a comic figure—that is, a man who attempts to pass as a woman but conspicuously fails—it seems a strange choice in a context where the transgender entertainers are described as "complete women."

The tabloids also enjoyed playing with the double entendre of *okama* when Carrousel Maki was involved in a car crash in 1998. As well as a designation for effeminate homosexuals and a slang term for the buttocks, *okama* can be used to refer to the back end of a car—*okama wo horareta* can mean "My back end was dug/crashed into"—hence the *Supōtsu nippon* headline of 18 March 1998 *"Karūseru Maki okama horareta."* In context the headline refers to the fact that her car was crashed into, but it also has a subsidiary meaning that would not have been lost on readers, that she was "fucked in the ass." It is an example of how earlier terms such as *okama* still live on and are used in parallel with more recent designations.

TRANSGENDER AND THE MEDIA

As outlined in earlier chapters, both mainstream and underground media in Japan have shown consistent interest in gender-variant behaviors and identities, especially those expressed within the entertainment world, and have discussed them largely without the censorious tone characteristic of anglophone reports. Indeed, the media have sought out, publicized and thereby helped in the proliferation of a range of commercial transgender identities—from Ueno Park's *danshō* in the immediate postwar period to the glitzy *gei bōi* of the 1960s and the *nyūhāfu* boom of the 1980s. Given the range and durability of this exposure, most Japanese would have been aware that transgender people existed and of where to go to find them. However, this kind of media treatment was sensationalistic and, focusing explicitly on transgender expression in the entertainment world, did little to foster a sense of identity or belonging among men interested in cross-dressing or other transgender behavior on a more personal or part-time basis. The perverse press of the 1950s and '60s did, however, largely fill this gap. Articles regularly reported on parks, bars and coffee shops where cross-dressers could be found and assignations made, and the personals columns provided opportunities for self-expression and the building of noncommercial networks. The most important magazine for men with an interest in cross-dressing was *Fūzoku kitan*, which ran a regular *josō aikō no heya* (room for lovers of cross-dressing) from 1961 until the magazine's demise in 1975. The contents of these pages (usually two per issue) were largely made up of reader contributions. From 1967 to 1974 *Fūzoku kitan* also featured a regular column entitled *Josō kōyū roku* (Cross-dressing friendship record), written by Kamo Kozue, the mama of the cross-dressers' bar Kozue.

Fūzoku kitan was also instrumental in helping set up a social organization for cross-dressers in the early 1960s. The club's name, Fūki (wealth and honor), was a reference to *Fūzoku kitan*, using characters with the same pronunciation as those in the magazine's title but with different meanings. The club operated out of a series of rented rooms mostly in the Shinjuku area, and as well as offering members a space in which to socialize it intermittently published a newsletter. The club was regularly advertised in *Fūzoku kitan*'s regular cross-dressing column,[7] with the result that by 1962 the club's secretary was receiving between 150 and 160 letters per month from men interested in its activities. Many of these inquirers seem to have mistaken the club for a dating agency the purpose of which was to arrange assignations with *gei bōi*, an assumption that group members vigorously rejected. Members were categorical that their club was for men who enjoyed cross-dressing as a *shumi*, or "taste," and that they were quite distinct both from the commercial transgender world and that occupied by male homosexuals (Saitō 1962: 128).

The Fūki Club was not, however, the earliest cross-dressing organization. The first such club to have left a record was the Engeki Kenkyūkai (Theatrical Society), which from 1955 to 1959 published 24 issues of the *Engeki hyōron* (Theatrical review), a magazine that was supposed to focus on cross-dressing in the theater but mainly included articles by members detailing their own cross-dressing experiences. The magazine, which ran to 24 pages, was handwritten onto a stencil and then mimeographed; it contained hand-pasted black-and-white photographs as well as hand-drawn illustrations, sometimes of an erotic nature. Such publications, albeit with limited circulations, were important because they gave voice to a wider community of cross-dressers and enabled the development of a less sexualized discourse about cross-dressing, establishing a space for transgender practice outside of the prostitution or entertainment-world paradigms.

However, the first commercial magazine dedicated to transgender issues was not published until 1980, when *Queen (Kuiin)* appeared. *Queen* was followed in 1987 by the privately circulated *Himawari* (Sunflower), which became a bimonthly commercial magazine in 1993. Both remain in publication today.[8] The early 1990s saw a rapid increase in the number of titles available, although several were short-lived. These included *Cross Dressing* (1991; folded after its second issue), *Shemale* (1992–), *Inner T.V.* (1994; folded after the third issue), *Josō tokuhon* (Cross-dressing reader; 1994–), *Nyūhāfu kurabu* (Newhalf club; 1995–), *Boku'tte KIREI* (You say I'm pretty; 1995, folded after its fifth issue) and *SheMale Love GOLD* (1996–).

Queen, closely associated with the Elizabeth chain of cross-dressing clubs, and *Himawari,* the brainchild of cross-dressing "talent" Candy Milky, are distinct from other magazines in focusing primarily on "amateur" cross-dressing as a "hobby." Consequently, they do not include pornography or advertisements for bars where gender-normative men go to meet transgender partners. Another important difference is that the other magazines choose as models only the most beautiful and sexy *nyūhāfu,* who already have careers in the commercial bar world, whereas *Queen* and *Himawari* offer the chance for "ordinary" nonpassing cross-dressers to share their photographs and experiences (Hagiwara 1997). Approximately half the magazines are devoted to articles and information aimed at men with an interest in cross-dressing, including detailed tips on how to apply makeup and dress appropriately, as well as advice on hormone injections for those who want to alter their bodies; the remainder provide space for cross-dressers and transgenders to send in their own tips, photographs and experiences. These magazines proved invaluable for people living in the provinces, where information about the transgender scene was more difficult to come by, and enabled the development of regional networks for men with an interest in transgender issues.

The other magazines have a variety of readers, including cross-dressers and men who are transgendered, transsexual, or who are interested in becoming so, as well as men who have an erotic interest in transgendered men *(josō aikō dansei)*. Most magazines thus contain articles directed at both audiences, including discussions of hormone therapy, fashion and cross-dressing accessories as well as pornographic fantasy stories, manga and erotic photographs. General-interest stories include a digest of what is being said about *nyūhāfu* in the media, reviews of books and films featuring transgender characters, readers' letters and a travel section highlighting transgender lives in other countries. Some articles in *Queen, Himawari* and *Nyūhāfu kurabu*[9] offer sophisticated reflections upon the history and philosophy behind cross-dressing in Japan, while others, such as *SheMale GOLD,* are more consistently pornographic. The magazines also carry a large amount of advertising, mainly for beauty salons (offering such services as electrolysis), bars, clubs and sex venues as well as mail-order catalogues for cross-dressing materials.

Although the print magazines are no doubt important in providing a medium for transgender expression, it is on the Internet that the majority of transgender networking takes place. Transgender individuals in Japan were among the first to establish a Net presence, even before the birth of the World Wide Web (Kuia sutadiizu heshu iinkai 1997: 33). EON, a BBS (bulletin-board system) for "transvestites and transsexuals," was established in 1990. (The name refers to the eighteenth-century cross-dressing diplomat Chevalier d'Eon, from whence "Eonism," an early term for transvestism, is derived).

The fallout from the Blue Boy Trial had made medical authorities extremely reluctant to involve themselves in any kind of transgender counseling or procedure and made it difficult to publish openly the names and details of doctors who were amenable to discussing sex-change procedures (whether out of personal sympathy or for financial gain). However, while full sex-change surgery was not available in Japan, there were doctors who would agree to the removal of the testicles; contact details for these practitioners were distributed via the BBS. EON also provided a suitable "underground" communications network that allowed transgender individuals to swap tips on hormone treatment and give pointers to others about how these drugs might be obtained and administered.

By 2000 there were hundreds of individual transgender websites as well as Web rings dedicated to providing information and contact services for transgender individuals and their admirers. In April 2000, the Web ring *Nyūhāfu Lady*[10] was one of the first to provide an *i-mode* service enabling browsers to surf and download material from the ring's websites via their mobile phones, thus helping close the digital divide between those with computer access and those without.[11] Today, most *nyūhāfu* clubs, bars and cabarets maintain websites, and there are now thousands of transgender sites offering advice about everything from new developments in hormone therapy to female fashions and news about transgender issues in Japan and abroad (McLelland 2002). One of the major impacts of the Internet upon Japan's transgender community is the degree to which it has enabled relationships with transgenders living overseas. It is very common to find overseas sites linked to Japanese sites and vice versa. However, perhaps the most important effect the Internet has had on the transgender community is the scope it has given both male and female transgenders to speak directly about their experience. As pointed out in chapter 5, *tōjisha,* originally a legal term meaning "concerned party," has a history in feminist and disabled rights movements going back to the early 1970s; it has recently emerged as an authenticating speaking position that challenges the right of the "experts" (doctors, government officials or others in positions of bureaucratic authority) to set the agenda within which transgender identities, experiences and issues are discussed (Nakanishi and Ueno 2003).

However, despite the fact that *nyūhāfu* and other transgenders have gained increased voice throughout the '80s and '90s through the development of niche publications and, increasingly, through the Internet, the respectable press in Japan has largely ignored them. The relative silence of the major dailies about the *nyūhāfu* phenomenon stands in contrast to the sensational interest shown by television and the tabloid press in transgender issues. Numerous articles about *nyūhāfu* or other transgender entertainers regularly appear in such magazines as *Takarajima, Focus, Shūkan hōseki, Nikkan supōtsu, Friday* and *Popeye,* and in the women's magazines *Josei sebun, Josei jishin* and *Fujin kōron,* while late-night television is full of discussion of transgender entertainers. In 2001, for instance, transgender Web mistress Metamo listed 99 television programs shown that year that had either featured transgender guests or discussed transgender topics.[12] The attention given to transgender issues in the popular media was, then, largely sensationalistic, promoting the familiar stereotype of transgender persons as entertainers and treating their lives voyeuristically. However, in 1996 this changed quite dramatically when the respectable media began to feature articles about a new kind of transgender identity—persons suffering from "gender identity disorder."[13]

REFORM OF SEX-CHANGE LEGISLATION

As noted earlier, information about sex-change operations was already widespread in the media in Japan in the 1960s and a number of high-profile castration and sex-change operations were performed on male entertainers, the first taking place as early as 1951. However, from 1965 to 1996, sex-change operations were suspended. Article 28 of the 1948 Eugenic Protection Law (Yūsei hogo hō), a reworking of the 1940 National Eugenic Law, stated, "No one shall, without cause, perform an operation or an X ray for the purpose of rendering reproduction impossible, other than in cases provided for in this law" (Norgren 2001: 152). As a result of the Blue Boy Trial, this article was interpreted in such a manner as to forbid surgery that interfered with otherwise properly functioning sexual organs even in the case of sex-change surgery (Lunsing 2003: 28; Ishida 2002; Mackie 2001: 187; Norgren 2001: 192, n. 168; Miyano 1978: 76–7). The result of this ruling was that Japanese doctors were reluctant to even counsel patients about sex-change procedures; individuals seeking sex-reassignment surgery had to travel abroad, initially to Morocco. Later, the United States and then Thailand emerged as preferred venues—although there was still no counseling available in Japan either before or after the operation.

However, in 1995 four doctors at the Saitama Medical College made an application to the ethics committee, asking that they be allowed to prescribe sex-reassignment surgery on behalf of two patients. In 1996 the ethics committee assented to this request but established strict guidelines for sex-change surgery, placing the decision to proceed with the treatment clearly in the hands of medical authorities. The guidelines, in order to comply with the stipulation in Article 28, needed to show that "gender identity disorder" was a medical condition for which sex-reassignment was the required "medical treatment" *(iryō)* (Ishida 2002). The first operation, a female-to-male procedure, was carried out in the hospital's gender clinic in October 1998.[14]

Female-to-male transsexuals have been particularly active in redefining transgenderism as a medical condition that impacts upon an individual's rights as a citizen and have been able to challenge long-standing public assumptions that transgenderism is primarily a male phenomenon restricted to the entertainment world. Torai Masae, a female-to-male transsexual who underwent sex-reassignment surgery in the United States in 1987, is the founder of the action group FTM Nippon, which circulates a newsletter about transgender issues. On 24 May 2001 Torai led a small group of transsexual plaintiffs who filed civil lawsuits to have their family register *(koseki)* details amended.

For Japanese people, the family register is the primary means for establishing their identity as citizens. It is a remnant of the prewar *ie seido*, or household system, whereby individuals were registered as belonging to a specific household under the authority of the family patriarch. The *koseki* is consequently a contentious document and has often been attacked, particularly by left-leaning intellectuals, since this form of registration denies people the right to be treated as individuals. A source of recent controversy concerning the *koseki* has been the requirement upon marriage of one spouse to "enter the register" *(nyūseki)* of the other. This means that one spouse must surrender her or his original surname and adopt the surname of the spouse whose register she or he enters. Although the law does not stipulate which spouse must surrender her or his name, in practice the vast majority of women surrender their surnames to take on the family name of their husbands, a practice that many women consider discriminatory (Lunsing 2001: 97–100).

The *koseki* records all the details of a family's life—the births, deaths, marriages and divorces of its members. Particularly troublesome for transgender individuals is the fact that the *koseki* not only records the birth sex of each individual but also lists the order of birth—that is, family members are registered as eldest son or daughter, second son or daughter, et cetera, so that a change in the sex of one family member would necessitate the reordering of the details of other family members. Since these changes would be clearly indicated on the *koseki*, it could lead to complications in the lives of other family members, who would have to account for their changed status when producing copies of the document for identification purposes.

Since production of the *koseki* is necessary for establishing personal identity when starting a new job, obtaining a mortgage, claiming medical insurance or renting a house, postoperative transsexuals and individuals who live in their newly assigned gender are often faced with awkward situations—especially at work. The result is that many transgender individuals who successfully pass try to avoid situations in which it is necessary to produce this identity document, but this often proves impossible. An example of the kind of problems that can occur when the family register is produced as "proof" of gender identity arose in September 2001 when Carrousel Maki was arrested for possession of drugs. Despite the fact that she had undergone a widely publicized sex change in Morocco in 1972, she was still listed in her family register as male and accordingly was detained in a male ward for 41 days.

Until 2004, the courts refused to permit change of sex on the family register, since such changes could only be endorsed when it was proven that a "factual error" had been made in the original entry. Such changes were occasionally permitted in the case of individuals born intersex (hermaphrodite)—that is, when an individual's "true" sex does not become apparent until the physical onset of puberty. One of the earliest such cases recorded in Japan took place in the Taisho period, when a young person, originally brought up as a girl, suddenly began to manifest signs of masculinization at age 20 and underwent surgery to make his genitalia more closely resemble those of other men. His entry in the family register was amended accordingly, in line with his sudden change in sex; he went on to be assessed for military service (he was found to be too short) and later married a woman (Sawada 1921). However, individuals not diagnosed as intersex were not covered by this provision. There is also the further problem that the *koseki* requires that individuals must be assigned to either the male or female gender, but as Lunsing (2003: 29–30) points out, there is a nascent movement of people born intersex who are refusing to accept classification as either men or women, preferring the designation *intāsekkusu* (see Hashimoto 1998).

Despite the traditional inflexibility of the *koseki* system, early in the new century there were signs of change in public sentiment that encouraged a more sympathetic and flexible response from legal agencies. For instance, on 20 June 2002 the Tokyo District Court ruled that a company that had sacked an employee when she changed sex from male to female had acted illegally and ordered that she be compensated for lost earnings. The judge decided that "it was not fully proven that the employee's presence would have damaged the standing of the company and its businesses" (*Japan Today* 23 October 2002). An employee at another company reached a negotiated settlement with her company when she expressed desire to transition from male to female. It was decided that she could keep her job but would be transferred to another department in a different city (*Asahi Shimbun News Service* 25 May 2002). The acceptance of the transsexual condition was also given a boost in 2002, when the Japan Speedboat Association changed its rules so that Andō Chinatsu, who had developed a reputation as a female racer, could continue to race as a man after undergoing sex-reassignment surgery and reentering competition as Andō Hiromasa. Another sign of transsexual acceptance was the recent election of Kamikawa Aya to the Setagaya local assembly, the first case of a transsexual elected to public office in Japan.[15] Finally, in July 2004, individuals who had been diagnosed as suffering from gender identity disorder and who had completed sex-reassignment surgery were granted permission to change their sex in the family *koseki*. However, married people and people with children were excluded (*Japan Times* 17 July 2004).

Since media response to transsexualism has centered on discussing legal changes necessary for transsexuals to fit back into the sex and gender system as "normal" representatives of their newly assigned genders, wider issues of how transgenderism might challenge taken-for-granted ideas about Japan's sex and gender system itself have been largely overlooked. However, there is growing militancy on the part of transgender individuals themselves, who are beginning to question the paternalism of both the state and medical authorities, who have undue influence upon their lives.

QUESTIONING THE MEDICAL MODEL

The medical model of transsexualism, popularly understood as a man or woman "trapped inside" a body of the wrong sex, is reminiscent of early postwar understandings of transgenderism that considered *danshō* and *gei bōi* to have "innate" feminine characteristics. But as Lunsing comments, "the various categories of transgender that a cultural discourse provides are never adequate to fully describe actual transgender experience" (2003: 21). Even in the postwar period, transgender individuals could not all be neatly explained in these terms, as the existence of unruly categories, such as the "reversibles" *(dondengaeshi)*, made clear. The more recent emergence of *nyūhāfu*, whose halfway status is often emphasized, has proven even more problematic for this model, but the media, in their new enthusiasm for discussing transsexual issues, have shown little interest in questioning whether binary categories such as "male" and "female" are natural or cultural.

Consequently, now that sex-change operations are once again being performed in Japan, there has been a shift both in the more respectable media and in popular understanding away from indigenous or "folk categories" *(minzoku hanchū)* like *gei bōi* and *nyūhāfu* to a more medical and arguably pathologizing discourse of "gender identity disorder" *(sei dōitsusei shōgai)* seeking to itemize and describe a series of discrete physical and psychological problems that can be detected and corrected by appropriate medical interventions (Ishida and Murakami forthcoming). Yet as Whittle points out, the designation gender identity *disorder* is problematic, in that a "disorder," at least according to the American Psychiatric Association, is associated with "present distress or a significantly increased risk of suffering, pain, death, disability, or an important loss of freedom" (2002: 20). This model clearly does not fit *all* transgender individuals, particularly those who are *not* traumatized by their transgender status, yet in order to qualify for treatment, "patients" need to conform to the medical model that expects to find significant signs of distress. The Japanese term *shōgai*, with its strong connotations of disability, is even more pathologizing than the English term (Ishida and Murakami forthcoming).

The increased visibility, acceptance and respect accorded transsexual people in Japan since the promulgation of the medical model of transgender in the late 1990s is clearly to be welcomed. However, according to Yamaushi Toshio, a psychiatrist at Saitama Medical School and head of the Japanese Society of Psychiatry and Neurology's special committee on gender identity disorder, less than 10 percent of the patients seeking treatment at the center wish to completely transform their bodies through surgery, instead preferring to live between the sexes (*Japan Times* 20 June 2001). While the designation of sexual identity disorder as a medical condition has undoubtedly proven enabling for some, in Japan as elsewhere "the transsexual discourses that medico-psychological practitioners have made available are too frequently applicable only to a small minority and are agenda-laden" (Cromwell 1999: 24). Many transgender individuals, especially those who locate themselves in the entertainment world, are more comfortable with the indigenous folk identities overlooked by the respectable press and medical authorities alike. For instance, Misaki, the Web mistress of *Trans Sexual Stars* and spokesperson on *nyūhāfu* issues, writes:

> Recently, the term "gender identity disorder" has popped up and it might be easy to think of this together with *nyūhāfu*, but this . . . is a separate issue. Among *nyūhāfu* there are also lesbians [*rezu*][16] and bisexuals [*bai*]. There are those who have no balls [*tama*] but have a penis [*sao*] remaining, there are also those who, although they want abundant breasts, want to keep their balls and penis.[17]

As a *tōjisha* or "person (directly) concerned" with the issue of transgender, Misaki is clearly disdainful of new medical categories like "gender identity disorder" that she notices have suddenly "popped up" in the media and that, though helpful for some, serve only to occlude other transgender identities. Misaki argues that the term *nyūhāfu* is more complex and ultimately more flexible than the term "transsexual," which is associated with pathologizing medical discourse. Unlike transsexuals who wish to have their outward appearance altered to correspond with their inner gender identity, the term *nyūhāfu* includes a wide range of individuals who, although starting off as biological men, employ a range of transgender techniques—some developing breasts through hormones, some through implants, some maintaining both their testicles and penis, others having their testicles removed and others having vaginas created. *Nyūhāfu* can also have a variety of sexual identities, not necessarily directed at men, including both lesbian and bisexual.

Longinetto's (1996) documentary *Shinjuku Boys* details a similarly complex range of identities among *onabe* who work in the entertainment world as female-to-male hosts and performers. As Maree (2003) notes, "*onabe* identify as non-female (sometimes identifying as men), sexually desire women (transgender women included), and typically cross-dress female to male (FTM). As *Shinjuku Boys* illustrates, self-identification as *onabe* does not presuppose identification as a man (or vice versa), nor does it imply exclusive sexual relations with female-born women." Hence, reductive medical models are clearly inadequate to describe the variety of lived experience of transgender people themselves.

The folk categories such as *nyūhāfu* that are considered problematic by the medical community work against the common assumption that gender and sexual orientation should reflect biological sex and that any asymmetrical relationship can and should be corrected through medical intervention. As Cromwell points out, "the goal for many transsexuals embedded in the ideology of the Euro-American sex and gender system is surgeries that will result in legally being seen as nontranssexual men or women" (1999: 20). It is not, then, surprising that Japanese society is increasingly accommodating transsexuals who, after gender reassignment, reenter society as a "normal" member of the other sex, thereby leaving the heteronormativity and gender polarity of the overall sex and gender system unchallenged.

Individuals who opt to develop intersexual or transgender characteristics, however, cause problems for this system through problematizing the supposed congruence between gender identity, genitalia and sexual orientation, since medical authorities have yet to recognize "transgender" as a diagnostic category (Cromwell 1999: 21). As Ishida (2002) points out, those transgender individuals who resist the "dominant story" that positions them as patients often come into conflict with medical gatekeepers who control access to such treatments as hormone therapy.

Nyūhāfu and other transgenders in Japan therefore have a fraught relationship with medical authorities: if sex-change surgery is conceived as a medical treatment for a diagnosed condition, then *nyūhāfu* and other transgenders who make selective use of medical technologies to construct bodies that refuse to fit into categories of male or female clearly fall outside the paradigm of "patient." As a consequence, a large number of transgender individuals in Japan are still denied access to safe medical treatment and live without the basic respect that is increasingly accorded Japan's transsexual community.

However, there is some sense that this situation is changing, given that the new emphasis on the primacy of the *tōjisha*, along with the development of multiple print and online media for the transgender community, is resulting in the "insurrection of subjugated knowledges." Foucault describes the emergence at the end of the twentieth century of a range of previously silenced or occluded ways of knowing and being in the world as "primarily, an insurrection against the centralizing power-effects that are bound up with the institutionalization and workings of any scientific discourse" (2003: 9). *Nyūhāfu* such as Misaki and others who occupy nonscientific "folk categories" are increasingly speaking back to medical authorities and looking for ways of sharing local knowledge so as to challenge, circumvent and displace the role that medical and other experts had previously played in their lives.

THE RISE OF AMATEUR TRANSGENDERISM

The increased visibility of transsexuals was one development in the 1990s that challenged the model that sought to relegate transgender people to the entertainment world. However, the 1990s also witnessed the rapid escalation of a much broader transgender consciousness that, through conceiving of transgender practice and experience outside the entertainment paradigm, exposed the limitations of this containment. This developing consciousness was in large part due to the increased networking facilitated by the Internet; however, it drew upon networks that had been established decades earlier.

By the early 1960s, there had already developed small groups of amateur cross-dressers who, unlike the *danshō* and *gei bōi,* did not seek to earn a living from their transgender interests. As mentioned earlier, one of the earliest of these groups, the Fūki Club, rented various rooms in Tokyo in the 1960s where men could meet, dress up and interact with one another. At these meetings an experienced group leader would induct more recent members into the arts of applying makeup, styling the hair and walking, moving and speaking with appropriate feminine decorum. Once the members were properly fitted out, photographs would be taken to record the session (Saitō 1962: 129). It was also possible for those members who were particularly accomplished at the skills of cross-dressing to arrange to go out on a date with a "male role" *(otoko yaku)* member of the club to a coffee shop, cabaret or the cinema. Regular men, most of whom were in their 40s and 50s, were free to join the club, although they were required to pay a membership fee twice that of the club's cross-dressing members (Sugiura 2001: 23). The dates followed the usual heterosexual pattern (with the male partner picking up the tab) and sometimes ending in a local love hotel. However, while the purpose of the dates was to enable the cross-dressers to experience being treated like a lady, not all members were prepared to go this far (Sugiura 2001: 25).

In 1975 Matsuba Yukari, who had been a member of the Fūki Club as well as a part-time staff member at the cross-dressing bar Kazue, founded Rouge, a club for cross-dressers in Shin Ōkubo, Tokyo. The club was housed in a regular apartment that had originally been rented by Matsuba and several cross-dressing friends as a venue to store their clothes and accessories and as a retreat from their family and work lives where they could relax while cross-dressed and hold parties and social events. Such was the interest shown in the apartment by people in their circle that it became clear they could earn some extra money by renting out clothes and offering makeup advice to inexperienced cross-dressers. Matsuba and her associates therefore placed advertisements in the tabloid press and recruited a small membership, which continued to meet until 1981, when Rouge, with its limited space and resources, found it could no longer compete with Elizabeth, a new chain of cross-dressing clubs (Sugiura 2001: 49–50).

Small social groups such as the Fūki Club and Rouge anticipated the larger, better-publicized commercial cross-dressing club—the Elizabeth chain—which opened its first branch in Tokyo in 1979. The first Elizabeth Club was not actually an innovation of the transgender community but grew out of a perfectly ordinary lingerie business whose owner was intrigued by the unusually large number of male customers visiting his store. He soon realized that many of the male customers were not buying presents for their wives or girlfriends but were interested in purchasing items for their own use. At this time, as a result of Japan's booming economy, men had plenty of extra cash to devote to their cross-dressing hobby, but there were no shops that catered explicitly to male tastes and sizes; in addition, other than the *sunakku* bars and tiny organizations such as Rouge, there were no venues where men could cross-dress and relax in a purely social setting. The Elizabeth shop was therefore remodeled to serve an exclusively male clientele, the second floor being turned into a social center where men could socialize while cross-dressed.

Unlike the Fūki Club, Rouge and the *sunakku* bars, Elizabeth did not allow access to men who did not cross-dress and did not permit the drinking of alcohol on premises or allow members to leave the club while cross-dressed in pursuit of adventure. This helped create a friendly, stress-free environment that allowed members to indulge in cross-dressing as a purely recreational activity *(shumi)*. The Elizabeth Club also refused to allow ''professional'' *(puro)* cross-dressers from the entertainment world to join, emphasizing that its facilities were for the ''amateur'' cross-dressing community (Sugiura 2001: 52). Matsuba Yukari, who joined Elizabeth in the early 1980s after the demise of her own club Rouge, noted a gradual change in the attitude of men who came to cross-dress at the club. She remarks that in the earlier clubs such as Fūki there had been considerable pressure placed on cross-dressers to ''pass'' successfully as women and that those less successful were discouraged from pursuing their transgender interests. In the early days at Elizabeth, too, more senior cross-dressers would criticize the makeup, dress and deportment of new members, scold them and demand they act in a more appropriately feminine manner. However, as paying clients,[18] many members resented this interference and insisted on their right to dress and behave in any manner they saw fit, without giving in to pressure to present an authentically feminine demeanor. Matsuba (who was herself heterosexually married to a woman) also noted a marked increase in the number of men whose ''love interests'' were women (Sugiura 2001: 58), and by the end of the decade heterosexual members were in the majority. Elizabeth's comfortable environment for recreational cross-dressing proved successful, and soon other Elizabeth clubs were opened in the Tokyo area and later in Nagoya and Osaka. These branches remain in business today.

Despite the media attention given to ''professional'' transgenders who have worked in the entertainment world as companions, hostesses, entertainers and sex workers, and more recently to sufferers of gender identity disorder, Japan's ''amateur cross-dressers'' *(amachua josō)* have largely been overlooked. Although networks of professional transgenders such as *kagema* and *danshō* clearly existed before the war, information indicating whether there were clubs or loose associations of men who met together to express their interest in cross-dressing and other transgender practices in noncommercial settings has yet to come to light. However, such organizations rapidly emerged in the early 1950s and have proliferated greatly in recent years due to the spread of the Internet. While "professional" transgender practice has been inexorably associated with sex, particularly homosexuality, because of its location in the sex and entertainment world, many of those expressing interest in part-time or amateur cross-dressing are insistent that their transgender practice is *not* about sex.

As mentioned, the Elizabeth Club was closely associated with the development of Japan's first commercial magazine dedicated to transgender issues, *Queen (Kuiin)*, which focuses on "amateur" cross-dressing as a "hobby" and does not include pornography or advertisements for bars where gender-normative men go to meet transgender partners. The development of *Queen* as a medium of communication between men with a nonsexual interest in transgender practices as well as the proliferation since the 1980s of cross-dressing social clubs that exclude "gender normative" males has provided a space for transgender practice outside of the exhibition mode of the entertainment world. Men who transgender themselves in these environments are, of course, aware of being observed by their peers, but their motivation is not to perform for an audience or to increase their earning potential. The designation *amachua* used to describe the transgender practices undertaken in these spaces signifies not so much part-time commitment or lack of ability as opposition to the term *puro*, which designates an identity built around a calculated transgender performance associated with the sex and entertainment world.

Although publications such as *Queen* and the development of recreational spaces like the Elizabeth and other clubs where men can meet together and explore transgender practices and identities have been important in widening the scope for transgender practice in Japan, the Internet has had an even greater impact on the variety of discourses surrounding transgender identities. As Miller and Slater point out, "The encounter with the expansive connections and possibilities of the Internet may enable one to envisage a quite novel vision of what one could be" (2001: 11).

Transgender individuals from both the professional and amateur worlds make use of Internet technology and most *nyūhāfu* clubs, bars and cabarets maintain websites promoting their services, as do individual transgender sex workers (McLelland 2003a; 2002), and there are thousands of other transgender sites offering advice about everything from new developments in hormone therapy and female fashions to news about transgender issues in Japan and abroad. In a few short years the Internet has developed an ever-expanding and practically inexhaustible databank of transgender culture and experience, which has impacted upon the range of expressions available for understanding transgender in all its forms. Through the medium of the Internet, it is possible to encounter a much wider range of transgender images and practices and to contribute one's own experience to the debate. Indeed, excellent online databases of Japanese transgender culture, such as *Metamorphosis,*[19] have made Japan's transgender history internationally accessible; links between Japanese and western transgender websites show that transgender collaboration is now worldwide.

The Internet has also been instrumental in promoting the visibility of a new kind of transgender personality—the transgender intellectual—who has entirely broken with the exhibition paradigm of the entertainment world. Mitsuhashi Junko is an adjunct university lecturer and amateur cross-dresser whose historical research into Japanese transgender practice regularly appears in *Nyūhāfu kurabu* magazine as well as on her website and, increasingly, in academic journals. Mitsuhashi is a married biological male who teaches gender studies at Tokyo's Chuo University dressed as a woman, while also lecturing in history at another Tokyo university dressed as a man (*Josei sebun* 2000). Media response to Mitsuhashi's innovative lecture courses has been largely positive, and she has been interviewed in several mainstream newspapers and magazines, and she has appeared on numerous television and radio programs, details of which are provided on her extremely well organized and informative website.[20]

Another high-profile transgender intellectual who has also made wide use of the Internet is also a heterosexually married father who in his "male mode" *(dansei mōdo)* teaches at high school and on the weekends, when in "female mode" *(josei mōdo),* becomes Miyazaki Rumiko, transgender activist, writer and lecturer, who, in addition to publishing her own books and writing for mainstream print media, has run a highly successful website dedicated to transgender issues since 1997.[21] Designating herself *sensei,* much as did writers for the perverse magazines half a century earlier, Miyazaki helps her readers understand the different forms that transgender expression may take, and yet in her analysis it is not transgender individuals themselves who have a "problem" but rather society as a whole that is amiss in enforcing a binary gender system on all its citizens. Miyazaki proposes a "gender free" society in which an individual's choice of dress, mode of communication, occupation and sexual orientation are decided not by birth sex but by personal preference and disposition. However, she is well aware that in order to normalize the transgender experience she must break down its abiding association with the entertainment world. As she says in the afterword to her book *Watashi wa toransujendā* (I am transgendered), "Up until now the word *nyūhāfu* has been well known. But so far the image of a person who works at night, singing, dancing and performing on a stage has remained strong. What I'd like the person reading this book to remember is that there are also transgendered people living beside you leading ordinary lives" (2000: 216). She goes on to comment that "*gender free* means living outside the narrowness of 'masculinity' and 'femininity,' it's a term, the importance of which is that you should live like yourself" (2000: 217–8).

The visibility that the Internet has afforded transgender intellectuals like Mitsuhashi is significant, given that Japan's universities have only recently begun to support innovative research and teaching in the field of gender studies. Mackie notes that teachers of women's studies tend to be part-time, casual or untenured and are "on the fringes of the academy" (2003: 163), although Tokyo's Ochanomizu University's long-standing Women's Studies Center has recently been transformed into the Institute for Gender Studies. Men's studies *(dansei gaku)* has also begun to further expand the range of gender theory on offer in Japanese institutions, but, like women's studies, in most institutions it tends to be offered as only part of wider social studies courses and is frequently available only at graduate level. Courses in lesbian and gay studies or in queer theory are still comparatively few, Tokyo's Chuo University being a rare example of an institution that supports a graduate seminar in transgender studies, largely due to the pioneering efforts of just one lecturer.[22] Queer studies, which grew exponentially out of the English departments of several major universities in the United States and the UK in the early 1990s, has not found a hospitable home in the more historically oriented literature departments of Japan (Ishida and Murakami forthcoming). Consequently, the widespread impact that queer theory has had on a range of academic disciplines in anglophone societies has not so far been seen in the Japanese academy. The Internet is therefore an invaluable forum for freelance researchers and intellectuals, of which Japan has many, and others only loosely affiliated with academic institutions in which to make their work available and to publicize those seminars and courses that do exist.

CONCLUSION

As outlined earlier, Japanese media have long provided space for the discussion of a variety of transgender and sexual practices. Yet the place for the enactment of these practices has overwhelmingly been the entertainment world—a situation that has worked against the development of fixed gender and sexual identities. While transgender individuals have certainly been discussed in terms stressing their "otherness," the kind of moral and social condemnation that at times has violently erupted in English-language media has been largely absent.

However, in the late 1990s the media exposure given to transsexual individuals and the widespread acceptance of "gender identity disorder" as a medical category with sex-reassignment surgery as its designated cure offered a forceful challenge to the entertainment paradigm, which had long contained transgender expression within the *mizu shōbai*. The moral seriousness afforded this condition by the endorsement of the medical community has enabled an increasing number of individuals to transition from one sex to the other and successfully carry on with their lives, even to the extent of being elected to public office. Yet a larger group of transgender individuals remains disenfranchised by this new ideology, which positions those who have failed to successfully embody gender identities in accord with their biological sex as the victims of a pathology or illness. But rather than simply acquiescing to the demands of the "dominant story" required by the medical authorities, a large number of transgender individuals are using the now numerous transgender print magazines and the Internet to speak back. As outlined above, transgender individuals, like other *tōjisha*, or "persons (directly) concerned," are increasingly challenging the right of "experts" to make decisions about their lives.

In the last decade, new technologies such as the Internet have provided further opportunities for transgender people to network and to challenge the sexualized images so prevalent in the mainstream press and argue for a greater range of gender expressions to be acknowledged in real life. The Internet has promoted the "insurrection of subjugated knowledges" and given power to the voices of the *tōjisha*—those who speak from direct experience of queer desire. Although the lives of many Japanese people are still very much constrained by hegemonic gender norms, there has been considerable movement in the last decade toward a more flexible society from which members of sexual minorities, in particular, have benefited. While there will always be resistance from some quarters to lifestyles and identities outside those traditionally endorsed, the proliferation of media and the power afforded minorities by new technologies like the Internet make the insistence upon one hegemonic mode of sex or gender identity less and less plausible. This is particularly the case in Japan, which lacks a tradition of religious fundamentalism and where conservative politicians do not orchestrate moral panics about a supposed "gay menace" in order to win votes. As Giddens (1992; 1991) has argued, modernity, in Japan as elsewhere, has seen the development and proliferation of "lifestyle sectors" that challenge "traditional" lifestyle patterns and gender roles. Increasingly, individuals with transgender interests are encountering diverse transgender practices on the Internet and, through participating in activities organized by the amateur cross-dressing clubs, are critically engaging with mainstream gender narratives. Like Mitsuhashi Junko and Miyazaki Rumiko, other transgenders are pioneering nonsexualized versions of transgender identity outside the entertainment world.

NOTES

1. *Sunakku* derives from the English "snack." While small items of food are served with the drinks, the emphasis in these bars is definitely on drinking, not eating.

2. The information in this section derives from an interview with Nanjō Masami in *The Ken*, issue 4, 1978, pp. 93–5.

3. Lunsing is incorrect when he says that "the terms half and *nyūhāfu* have nothing to do with each other" (2003: 34, n. 5)—he seems not to have heard the story about Betty.

4. Lunsing (2003: 26) reports contradictory responses when he inquired of his transgender informants about the difference between *nyūhāfu* and Mr. Lady. He concludes that "the fluidity between the various categories must be stressed" (2003: 27).

5. The show ran the Mr. Lady segment for one year, from 1988 to 1989.

6. URL www.nyuhafu.net/photo (26 November 2002).

7. See, for example, page 163 of the February issue of 1961.

8. Lunsing reports that the circulation of *Queen* is about 7,000 and *Himawari* 3,000–4,000 (2003: 22).

9. Since May 1998 (issue 24), *Nyūhāfu Club* has been running a series of essays by Mitsuhashi Junko on the history of cross-dressing in Japan, to which much of the material in this chapter is indebted.

10. URL www.nyūhāfu.com/nhl/ (18 May 2000).

11. For a discussion of the use of mobile phones for Internet access in Japan see Gottlieb and McLelland (2003: 7–8).

12. Online, available: metamo21.hp.infoseek.co.jp/tv/tv2001.html (30 July 2002).

13. According to Cromwell (1999: 20) and Whittle (2002: 20), the term "gender identity disorder" as a diagnostic category did not enter the American Psychiatric Association's *Diagnostic and Statistical Manual of Mental Disorders* until its fourth edition in 1994.

14. By the time the operation was carried out, the 1948 Eugenic Protection Law had been replaced by the 1996 Maternal Protection Law, but Article 28 of the previous law was carried over, becoming Article 9 of Chapter 5 in the new law (see Norgren 2001: 157).

15. Kamikawa won a seat on the Setagaya local assembly in 2003. See Kamikawa's website for details of the campaign and her platform: ah-yeah.com/index.html (16 May 2003).

16. Here Misaki is not referring to women-born lesbians but to *nyūhāfu* who are attracted both to biological women and to other *nyūhāfu*.

17. URL homepage1.nifty.com/Nyūhāfu/nyūhāfu.htm (29 July 2002).

18. In addition to an upfront membership fee, members also had to pay about $40 each time they visited the club. Many members also paid a monthly fee for lockers, in which they kept their women's clothes and accessories; for those without their own clothes, a further rental fee applied to make use of the club's wardrobe. Extra fees also applied for special events, such as the annual beauty contest, making membership a costly undertaking.

19. URL www.geocities.co.jp/Hollywood/4349/index2.html (19 February 2003).

20. URL www4.wisnet.ne.jp/~junko/index2.html (25 February 2003).

21. Miyazaki Rumiko's homepage: www4.justnet.ne.jp/~r.miyazaki/ (18 February 2003).

22. This is Chuo University's Sengo Nihon Toransujendā Shakaishi Kenkyūkai (Postwar Japan transgender social history research group), organized by Yajima Masami in the Faculty of Arts.

Afterword

As previous chapters have shown, by the final decade of the twentieth century there had emerged in Japan communities of gay men, lesbians and transgender individuals such as might be encountered in many large western cities. These communities are serviced by an extensive market, including online and print media, and by numerous community and commercial enterprises. This development of lesbian and gay media, particularly literature and film, as well as characteristically western modes promoting activism and visibility, such as LGBTQ (lesbian, gay, bisexual, transgender and queer) organizations, film festivals and parades in societies like Japan has been taken by some as evidence of a "global queering." As Dennis Altman, for instance, points out, "globalization has helped create an international gay/lesbian identity, which is by no means confined to the western world" (2001: 86).

However, as outlined, Japan was never a passive recipient of western influence. The Meiji period did not see the sidelining of original or authentic Japanese sexualities by new notions imported wholesale from the west. Rather, sexuality was constituted through a highly complex and contested process in which traditional terminologies were continually being overwritten by new meanings and in which foreign loanwords and ways of knowing were strategically redeployed to serve local uses. The Allied occupation following the end of the Second World War too was a time of great hybridity when the emerging American category "gay" was deployed alongside indigenous categories such as *okama*, historical terms such as *nanshoku* and late-nineteenth-century German notions such as *urning*—a term that had long since lost currency in Europe. The history outlined in these pages demonstrates, then, that in the realm of sexuality, globalization results in creative indigenization and cultural admixture much more than it does in any unilateral imposition of western sexual identities. As Martin Manalansan points out, we are right to be wary of "global" stories of lesbian and gay liberation in which "all same-sex phenomena are placed within a developmental and teleological matrix that ends with Western 'gay' identity'' (1995: 428). The reality, in Japan as elsewhere, is less tidy and more complex.

Given this background, it should come as no surprise to discover that contemporary Japanese notions of queer identity, despite some resemblance to western models, have their own distinct histories and trajectories, resulting as they do from a social context very different from that which produced the gay, lesbian and transgender liberation movements of the west. It is not the case that Japan is simply one among many sites for the elaboration of a kind of homogenized, international queer culture; rather, Japan is home to an alternative sexual modernity, a modernity produced by hybrid globalizing processes as much as by the continuation of identities, practices and mentalities inherited from the past.

The account given in these pages of Japan's postwar queer history has attempted to recover and give voice to local Japanese perspectives using archival material from the popular as well as the perverse press and from the Internet. These kinds of local knowledge, which are often overlooked in academic analyses, tend to be ignored because they are considered ''naïve knowledges, hierarchically inferior knowledges, knowledges that are below the required level of erudition or scientificity'' (Foucault 2003: 7). The perverse press, in particular, despite its wide range and longevity, is a genre that has been entirely overlooked by English-language scholarship on postwar Japan. Yet there are many more important stories buried in that archive that deserve to be told. Ethnographic work with members of Japan's queer communities, particularly the gathering of oral narratives, has barely begun as well, and it is imperative that people's local knowledge be preserved before this resource is lost to us. Websites also come and go; already much pioneering material placed on the Internet by sexual minorities in the early 1990s has been lost. If this book is to have any effect at all, I hope that it will be to encourage others to engage with *kono sekai* in multiple ways in search of other stories, other lives.

Bibliography

Achilles, Nancy. 1967. "The Development of the Homosexual Bar as an Institution." In John Gagnon and William Simon (eds.), *Sexual Deviance*. New York: Harper and Row.

Adon. 1976. "Seibyō no byōin'tte donna tokoro?" (What kind of places are sexual disease hospitals?). July, pp. 60–5.

Aien. 1969. "Taiyō no shita no resubian" (Lesbians under the sun). *AIEN: 70 nen no jinseishi* (Love garden: a human sexuality magazine for the '70s), no. 1, October, pp. 182–88.

Akasaka Tsuyoshi. 1952. "Senso to mazo" (War and masochism). *Kitan kurabu*, June, p. 69.

Akitomo Shingae. 2002. "The Birth of Gay Magazines in Post-War Japan." *SHARP News*, vol. 11, no. 2, pp. 5–6.

Akiyama Masami. 1970. *Beddo no ijiwaru* (Mischief in bed). Tokyo: Dai ni shobō.

———. 1969. "Sōgo masatsu no gijutsu: rezubian tekunikku" (The art of mutual rubbing: lesbian technique). *Erochika* vol. 1, no. 1, July 1969.

———. 1968a. *Resubian tekunikku* (Lesbian technique). Tokyo: Dai ni shobō.

———. 1968b. *Homo tekunikku* (Homo technique). Tokyo: Dai ni shobō.

———. 1967. *Pettingu no susume* (Advice on petting). Tokyo: Misaki shobō.

———. 1966. *Hitori bottchi no sei seikatsu* (A solitary sex life). Tokyo: Misaki shobō.

Altbooks. 1998. *SEX no arukikata: Tōkyō fūzoku kanzen gaido* (How to find your way around Tokyo's sex world: a complete guide). Tokyo: Mediawākusu.

Ambaras, David. 2004. "Juvenile Delinquency and the National Defense State: Policing Young Workers in Wartime Japan, 1937–1945." *Journal of Asian Studies*, vol. 63, no. 1, pp. 31–60.

Anderson, Benedict. 1983. *Imagined Communities: Reflections on the Origin and Spread of Nationalism*. London: Verso.

Angles, Jeffrey. 2003. "Writing the Love of Boys: Representations of Male-Male Desire in the Literature of Murayama Kaita and Edogawa Ranpo." Ph.D. diss., Ohio State University.

Aniisu. 2001. "Komyuniti no rekishi 1971–2001: nenpyō to intabyū de furikaeru" (Community history 1971–2001: reflecting back with timelines and interviews), no. 4, Summer, pp. 28–78.

Aoki, Darren. 2004. "The Rose Tribes: Sexual Solidarity and the Ethico-Aesthetics of Manliness in Japan in the Early 1970s." Ph.D. diss., University of Cambridge.

Aoyama Tomoko. In press. "Transgendering *Shōjo Shōsetsu*: Girls' Inter-text/sexuality." In Mark McLelland and Romit Dasgupta (eds.), *Genders, Transgenders and Sexualities in Japan*. London: Routledge.

Asahi geinō. 1964. "Burū bōi to koishita otoko no kokuhaku" (Confession of a man in love with a blue boy). 3 May, pp. 106–9.

Asakura Shirō. 1952. "Sensen ni okeru dōseiai" (Homosexuality on the battle front). *Kitan kurabu*, June, p. 137.

Ashidate Eikichi. 1960. "Otoko ni kuwaerareru seme" (Torture that was done to men). *Fūzoku kitan*, August, pp. 78–81.

Ashio Takami. 1953. "Sengo no sei hanzai ni miru byōheki" (Bad habits seen as postwar sex crimes). *Fūzoku zōshi*, July, pp. 111–5.

Bannon, Ann. 1999. "Foreword." In Jaye Zimet, *Strange Sisters: The Art of Lesbian Pulp Fiction, 1949–1969*. New York: Viking, pp. 9–15.

Bardsley, Jan. 1999. "Discourse on Women in Postwar Japan: The Housewife Debate of 1955." *US-Japan Women's Journal*, no. 16, pp. 3–47.

Benedict, Ruth. 1946. *The Chrysanthemum and the Sword: Patterns of Japanese Culture*. Cambridge: Riverside.

Berube, Allan. 1990. *Coming Out under Fire: The History of Gay Men and Women in World War Two*. New York: Free Press.

Bessatsu Taiyō (ed.). 1997. *Hakkinbon* (Banned books). Tokyo: Heibonsha.

———. 1995. *Takabatake Kashō: bishōnen, bishōjo* (Takabatake Kashō: beautiful boys, beautiful girls). Tokyo: Heibonsha.

Bessatsu Takarajima. 1991. *Hentai-san ga iku* (There goes Mr./Ms. Queer). Issue 146, December. Tokyo: Takarajimasha.

Blackwood, Evelyn, and Saskia Wieringa. 1999. "Sapphic Shadows: Challenging the Silence in the Study of Sexuality." In Evelyn Blackwood and Saskia Wieringa (eds.), *Female Desires: Same-Sex Relations and Transgender Practices across Cultures*. New York: Columbia University Press, pp. 39–66.

Boellstorff, Tom. 2003. "Dubbing Culture: Indonesian *Gay* and *Lesbi* Subjectivities and Ethnography in an Already Globalized World." *American Ethnologist*, vol. 30, no. 2, pp. 225–42.

Buckland, Fiona. 2002. *Impossible Dance: Club Culture and Queer World-Making*. Middletown, Conn.: Wesleyan University Press.

Buruma, Ian. 1984. *Behind the Mask: On Sexual Demons, Sacred Mothers, Transvestites, Gangsters and Other Japanese Cultural Heroes*. New York: Meridian Books.

Butler, Judith. 1990. *Gender Trouble: Feminism and the Subversion of Identity*. New York: Routledge.

Canaday, Margot. 2003. "'Who Is a Homosexual?' The Consolidation of Sexual Identities in Mid-Twentieth-Century American Immigration Law." *Law and Social Inquiry*, Spring, vol. 28, no. 2, pp. 351–86.

Chalmers, Sharon. 2002. *Emerging Lesbian Voices from Japan*. London: Routledge-Curzon.

Chamberlain, Basil. 1905. *Things Japanese*. London: Kelley and Walshe.

Chauncey, George. 1994. *Gay New York: The Making of the Gay Male World, 1890–1940*. London: Flamingo.

Cheung, Charles. 2000. "A Home on the Web: Presentations of Self on Personal Home Pages." In David Gauntlett (ed.), *Web.Studies: Rewriting Media Studies for the Digital Age*. London: Arnold, pp. 43–51.

Connell, R. W. 2000. *The Men and the Boys*. St. Leonards, NSW: Allen and Unwin.

Cory, Donald Webster. 1951. *The Homosexual in America: A Subjective Approach*. New York: Greenberg.

Cromwell, Jason. 1999. *Transmen and FTMs: Identities, Bodies, Genders and Sexualities*. Urbana: University of Illinois Press.

Cryle, Peter. 2001. *The Telling of the Act: Sexuality as Narrative in Eighteenth- and Nineteenth-Century France*. Newark: University of Delaware Press.

Curran, Beverly, and James Welker. In press. "From the Well of Loneliness to the *Akarui* Lesbian: Western Translations and Japanese Lesbian Identity." In Mark McLelland and Romit Dasgupta (eds.), *Genders, Transgenders and Sexualities in Japan*. London: Routledge.

Dasgupta, Romit. 2000. "Performing Masculinites? The 'Salaryman' at Work and Play." *Japanese Studies*, vol. 20, no. 2, pp. 189–200.

De Becker, Joseph. 1905. *The Nightless City or the History of the Yoshiwara Yukwaku*. London: Probsthain.

D'Emilio, John. 1992. "The Homosexual Menace: The Politics of Sexuality in Cold War America." In *Making Trouble: Essays on Gay History, Politics and the University by John D'Emilio*. New York: Routledge, pp. 57–73.

De Vos, George, with contributions by Hiroshi Wagatsuma, William Caudill, and Keiichi Mizushima. 1973. *Socialization for Achievement: Essays on the Cultural Psychology of the Japanese*. Berkeley: University of California Press.

Dikotter, Frank. 1995. *Sex, Culture and Modernity in China*. Honolulu: University of Hawaii Press.

Dore, R. P. 1999. *City Life in Japan: Study of a Tokyo Ward*. Richmond, Surrey: Japan Library.

Dow, Steve. 2001. *Gay*. Altona, Victoria: Common Ground.

Dower, John. 2000. *Embracing Defeat: Japan in the Wake of World War II*. New York: W. W. Norton.

Dowling, Linda. 1994. *Hellenism and Homosexuality in Victorian Oxford*. Ithaca, N.Y.: Cornell University Press.

Dudden, Alexis. 1999. "Japan's Engagement with International Terms." In Lydia Liu (ed.), *The Problem of Translation in Global Circulations*. Durham, N.C.: Duke University Press, pp. 165–91.

Duggan, Lisa, 2003. *The Twilight of Equality? Neoliberalism, Cultural Politics and the Attack on Democracy*. Boston: Beacon.

Duggan, Lisa, and Nan Hunter. 1995. "The Discipline Problem: Queer Theory Meets Lesbian and Gay History." In Lisa Duggan and Nan Hunter, *Sex Wars: Sexual Dissent and Political Culture*. London: Routledge, pp. 194–206.

Edogawa Ranpo. 1952. "Dōseiai bungakushi ni tsuite: Iwata Jun'ichi-kun no omoide" (On the history of homosexual literature: memories of Iwata Jun'ichi). *Ningen tankyū*, May, pp. 40–4.

Epstein, Steven. 1998. "Gay Politics, Ethnic Identity: The Limits of Social Constructionism." In Peter Nardi and Beth Schneider (eds.), *Social Perspectives in Lesbian and Gay Studies: A Reader*. London: Routledge.

Fabian, Johannes. 1983. *Time and the Other: How Anthropology Makes Its Object*. New York: Columbia University Press.

Faderman, Lillian. 1992. *Odd Girls and Twilight Lovers: A History of Lesbian Life in Twentieth-Century America*. New York: Penguin.

Faure, Bernard. 1998. *The Red Thread: Buddhist Approaches to Sexuality*. Princeton, N.J.: Princeton University Press.

Figal, Gerald. 1996. "How to *Jibunshi*: Making and Marketing Self-Histories of Showa among the Masses in Postwar Japan." *Journal of Asian Studies*, November, vol. 55, no. 4, pp. 902–33.

Foucault, Michel. 2003. *"Society Must Be Defended": Lectures at the Collège de France, 1975–76*. New York: Picador.

———. 1990. *The History of Sexuality Volume 1: an Introduction*. London: Penguin.

Fruhstuck, Sabine. 2003. *Colonizing Sex: Sexology and Social Control in Modern Japan*. Berkeley: University of California Press.

———. 2000. "Managing the Truth of Sex in Imperial Japan." *Journal of Asian Studies*, vol. 55, no. 2, pp. 332–58.

Fujii Akira. 1953. "Kantō, Kansai ni okeru dōseiaisha no shūgō chitai" (Homosexual meeting zones in the Tokyo and Osaka areas). *Fūzoku zōshi*, December, pp. 188–93.

Fukui T. 1953. "Kami no setsuri ni somuita boku" (I who have turned from God's grace). *Fūzoku kagaku*, November, p. 113.

Fukushima Jūrō. 1987. *Zasshi de miru sengoshi* (Postwar history seen through magazines). Tokyo: Ōtsuki shoten.

Funayama Akira. 1959. "Konbi zakki: boku ni mo hitokoto" (Miscellaneous jottings on the beauty of the loincloth: my say). *Kitan kurabu*, September, pp. 60–2.

Furuda Shigekazu. 1995. "Dōseiai senmonshi" (Homosexual specialty magazines). *Bessatsu Takarajima*, no. 240, December, pp. 96–102.

Furukawa Makoto. 1994. "The Changing Nature of Sexuality: The Three Codes Framing Homosexuality in Modern Japan." Trans. Angus Lockyer. *US-Japan Women's Journal English Supplement*, no. 7, pp. 98–127.

Furuta Haruo. 1954. "Sodomia wa anata no tonari ni iru" (Homosexuals are next to you). *Fūzoku kagaku*, March, pp. 160–5.

Fushimi Noriaki. 2003. *Hentai (kuia) nyūmon* (A hentai [queer] introduction). Tokyo: Chikuma bunko.

———. 2002. *"Gei" to iu keiken* (The experience called being "gay"). Tokyo: Potto shuppan.

———(ed.). 2000. "Hentai suru sarariiman" (Salarymen doing queer). *Queer Japan*, vol. 2, April. Tokyo: Keisō shobō.

———. 1991. *Puraibēto gei raifu* (Private gay life). Tokyo: Gakuyō shobō.

Fushimi Noriaki, Oikawa Kenji, Noguchi Katsuzo, Matsuzawa Kureichi, Kurokawa Nobuyuki and Yamanaka Toshiko (eds.). 2002. *Okama wa sabetsu ka: Shūkan kinyōbi no sabetsu hyōgen jiken* (Does *okama* have discriminatory connotations? The discriminating expression case in *Shūkan kinyōbi*). Tokyo: Potto shuppan.

Fūzoku kagaku. 1954a. "*Danshō* gakkō no seitai" (The *danshō* school mode of life). September, p. 111.

———. 1954b. "Musebi naku jotai: resubosu" (A sobbing woman's body: Lesbos). September, pp. 99–102.

Fūzoku kitan. 1963a. "Zenkoku homo no hattenba" (National homo cruise spots). April, pp. 124–5.

———. 1963b. "Zenkoku homo hattenba: fundoshi no maniya hattenba aru ki" (National homo cruise spots: a record of loincloth mania cruise spots). November, p. 59.

———. 1961a. "Geisha bōi no ryōtei wa daihanjō" (Geisha boy restaurants are flourishing). February, p. 63.

———. 1961b. "Dansei no 'josei' kashū omemie" (Debut of a male "female" singer). February, pp. 174–5.

Fūzoku zōshi. 1954. "Otoko to otoko no sekai: sodomii" (Male-male society: sodomy). September, pp. 102–4.

———. 1953a. "Sodomia dai zadankai" (Sodomia grand symposium). December, pp. 164–78.

———. 1953b. "Resubosu ai no shujusō" (Various phases of Lesbos love). December, p. 299.

Garon, Shelden. 1997. *Molding Japanese Minds: The State in Everyday Life*. Princeton, N.J.: Princeton University Press.

Giddens, Anthony. 1992. *The Transformation of Intimacy: Sexuality, Love and Eroticism in Modern Societies*. Cambridge: Polity.

———. 1991. *Modernity and Self-Identity: Self and Society in the Late Modern Age*. Cambridge: Polity.

Gluck, Carol. 1993. "The Past in the Present." In Andrew Gordon (ed.), *Postwar Japan as History*. Berkeley: University of California Press, pp. 64–95.

Gottlieb, Nanette, and Mark McLelland. 2003. "The Internet in Japan." In Nanette Gottlieb and Mark McLelland (eds.), *Japanese Cybercultures*. London: Routledge.

Gould, Meredith. 1979. "Statutory Oppression: An Overview of Legalized Homophobia." In Martin Levine (ed.), *Gay Men: The Sociology of Male Homosexuality*. New York: Harper and Row, pp. 51–67.

Greenberg, David. 1988. *The Construction of Homosexuality*. Chicago: Chicago University Press.

Greer, Germaine. 2003. *The Boy*. London: Thames and Hudson.

Haga Kurō. 1973. *Bon* (Purity). Tokyo: Dai ni shobō.

Hagiwara Miyoko. 1997. "Kyandi Mirukii-san to 'Himawari'" (Ms. Candy Milky and "Himawari"). *Ero hon no hon: ero hon no genzai*. Tokyo: Wani no ana, pp. 152–7.

Hall, Jonathan. 2000. "Japan's Progressive Sex: Male Homosexuality, National Competition and the Cinema." *Journal of Homosexuality*, vol. 39, nos. 3/4, pp. 31–82.

Hamura Kyōsuke. 1955. "Resubosu to kanchō" (Lesbos and enemas). *Kitan kurabu*, November, pp. 42–4.

Hanamura Emiko. 1954. "Resubosu no ki" (Lesbos diary). *Kitan kurabu*, December, pp. 165–8.

Hasegawa Hiroshi. 2003. "Eizu to gei komyuniti" (AIDS and the gay community). In Fushimi Noriaki (ed.), *Dōseiai nyūmon*. Tokyo: Potto shuppan, pp. 136–9.

Hashimoto Hideo. 1998. *Otoko demo onna demo nai sei: intāsekkusu (han-in'yō) wo ikiru* (A sex neither male nor female: living intersex [hermaphrodite]). Tokyo: Seiyūsha.

Hattori Ayako. 1999. "Heterosexism in Japan." *Off Our Backs*, vol. 29, no. 10, November, pp. 1–7.

Hentai shiryō. 1928. "Lesbische Liebe" (Lesbian love). Vol. 3, no. 1, January, p. 73.

HIP PRESS. 1990. "Nyūhāfu EVE intabyū: iroirona anaru purei wo keiken shitai" (Interview with newhalf EVE: I want to experience a variety of anal play). 15 November, pp. 102–5.

Hirano, T. 1947. "Gunpuku no danshōtachi" (*Danshō* in military uniform). *Shinsō jitsuwa*, May, pp. 114–47.

Honshi Chōsabu (Magazine Research Group). 1954. "Danshō no ijōseiai chōsa" (Research into the abnormal sexuality of *danshō*). *Fūzoku kurabu*, May, pp. 92–8.

Hooven, F. Valentine, III. 1995. *Beefcake: The Muscle Magazines of America 1950–1970*. Koln, Germany: Taschen.

———. 1992. *Tom of Finland: His Life and Times*. New York: St. Martin's.

Humphreys, Laud. 1972. *Out of the Closets: The Sociology of Homosexual Liberation*. Englewood Cliffs, N.J.: Prentice Hall.

———. 1971. "New Styles in Homosexual Manliness." *Trans Action*, vol. 8, nos. 5/6, March/April, pp. 38–46, 64–6.

Hyakuman nin no yoru. 1963a. "Nichijō no Y kaiwa" (Daily Y conversation). February, pp. 146–51.

———. 1963b. "Ware koso wa dansei biinasu no. 1" (We are indeed the no. 1 male Venuses). February, unnumbered photo section.

———. 1963c. "Sengo no ryūkōgo" (Popular postwar words). February, pp. 152–5.

———. 1963d. "Okama yōgo" (*Okama* terminology). February, pp. 157–9.

Igarashi Yoshikuni. 2000. *Narratives of War in Postwar Japanese Culture, 1945–1970*. Princeton, N.J.: Princeton University Press.

Ihara Saikaku. 1990. *The Great Mirror of Male Love*. Trans. Paul Schalow. Stanford, Calif.: Stanford University Press.

Ijyūin Shinobu. 1965. "Aru homo seinen no sōdan e no kotae" (Reply to a homo youth). *Fūzoku kitan*, May, pp. 140–41.

Ikegami Eiko. 1995. *The Taming of the Samurai: Honorific Individualism and the Making of Modern Japan*. Cambridge, Mass.: Harvard University Press.

Inagaki Taruho. 1993. *Shōnen'ai no bigaku* (The aesthetics of boy love). Tokyo: Kawade bunko.

Ishida Hitoshi and Murakami Takanori. Forthcoming. "A History of Queer Studies in Japan: From Hybridity to Variety." *Intersections: Gender, History, Culture in the Asian Context*, special "Queer Japan" issue.

Ishida Hitoshi. 2002. "Yomigaeru burūbōi saiban no 'seishin': seitenkan shujutsu to sono ihōsei ni kansuru zasshi media wo mochiita monogatarironteki gensetsu bunseki" (Revived blue-boy judgments' "spirit:" A discourse analysis of sex-change operations and their illegality in terms of the narrative model). *Hō to sekushuariti*, vol. 1, no. 1, pp. 85–117.

Ishino Sachiko and Wakabayashi Naeko. 1996. "Japan." In Rachel Rosenbloom (ed.), *Unspoken Rules: Sexual Orientation and Women's Rights*. London: Cassell.

Itō Bungaku. 2001. *Bara hiraku hi wo: Barazoku to tomo ni ayunda 30 nen* (Until the rose opens: 30 years walking alongside *Barazoku*). Tokyo: Kawade shobō.

Itō Satoru and Yanase Ryūta. 2000. *Coming Out in Japan*. Trans. Francis Conlan. Melbourne: TransPacific.

Itō Satoru. 1993. *Otoko futarigurashi: boku no gei puraido sengen* (Two men living together: my gay pride declaration). Tokyo: Tarōjirōsha.

Iwabuchi Koichi. 2002. *Recentering Globalization: Popular Culture and Japanese Transnationalism*. Durham, N.C.: Duke University Press.

Iwakura Tomohide. 1951. "Tensai to dōseiai" (Genius and homosexuality). *Ningen tankyū*, October, pp. 67–76.

Iwamoto Yoshio. 2002. "Ōe Kenzaburō's *Warera no jidai* (Our Generation): Sex, Power and the Other in Occupied Japan." *World Literature Today*, vol. 76, no. 1, Winter, pp. 43–51.

Izumo Marou, Hara Minako, Tsuzura Yoshiko, Ochiya Kumiko. 1997. "Nihon no rezubian mūbumento" (Japan's lesbian movement). *Gendai shisō*, May, pp. 58–83.

Jackson, Peter. 2003. "Gay Capitals in Global Gay History: Cities, Local Markets, and the Origins of Bangkok's Same-Sex Cultures." In Ryan Bishop, John Phillips and Wei-Wei Yeo (eds.), *Postcolonial Urbanism: Southeast Asian Cities and Global Processes*. New York: Routledge, pp. 151–63.

Jivani, Alkarim. 1997. *It's Not Unusual: A History of Lesbian and Gay Britain in the Twentieth Century*. London: Michael O'Mara Books.

Johnson, Mark, Peter Jackson and Gilbert Herdt. 2000. "Critical Regionalities and the Study of Gender and Sexual Diversity in South East and East Asia." *Culture, Health and Sexuality*, vol. 2, no. 4, October–December, pp. 361–75.

Josei sebun. 2000. "Junko sensei wa sei no ekkyōsha: Nippon hatsu! Wadai no Chūō Daigaku josō kōshi ga karada wo hatte oshieru 'otoko no karada de onna no kokoro' no shakaigaku" (Japan's first! Professor Junko transgresses sex: a cross-dressing Chuo University lecturer teaches sociology from the perspective of a woman's heart in a man's body). 30 November, pp. 55–7.

Jyabu. 1980. "Gei pawā wo chokuseyo" (Face up to gay power). February, pp. 56–60.

K. 1954. "Danshoku kissaten no jissō" (Actual facts about homosexual coffee shops). *Fūzoku kurabu*, March, p. 111.

Kabiya Kazuhiko. 1962a. "'Gei bā' to iu go no meimei sha" (The person who christened 'gay bars'). *Fūzoku kitan*, January, pp. 146.

———. 1962b. "Dōjin zasshi no danshoku shōsetsu" (Homosexual fiction clique magazine). *Fūzoku kitan*, February, pp. 146–7.

———. 1962c. "Homo kurabu L Kai no koto" (About the homo Club L). *Fūzoku kitan*, March, pp. 92.

———. 1962d. "Aru kawatta kaigō" (A different kind of get-together). *Fūzoku kitan*, March, p. 92.

———. 1962e. "Furuki sodomia no tegami" (An old homosexual letter). *Fūzoku kitan*, July, pp. 124–5.

———. 1962f. "Gei masutā kara kiita koto" (Things I heard from a gay bar owner). *Fūzoku kitan*, December, pp. 102–3.

———. 1955. "Geibā no seitai sono II" (The gay bar mode of life part II). *Amatoria,* July, pp. 38–46.

———. 1954a. "Danshoku kissaten" (Homosexual coffee shops). *Fūzoku zōshi,* January, pp. 146–51.

———. 1954b. "Sodomiya kōsaijutsu" (Homosexual interaction techniques). *Fūzoku zōshi,* June, pp. 236–41.

———. 1954c. "Homo no hanataba III: Dōseiai no hyakka jiten" (A homo bouquet III: a homosexual encyclopedia). *Fūzoku kagaku,* August, pp. 142–8.

———. 1953a. "Danshoku kissaten" (Homosexual coffee shops). *Fūzoku zōshi,* July, pp. 26–30.

———. 1953b. "Sodomia ni okeru kōjō no seitai" (Modes of intimacy among homosexuals). *Fūzoku zōshi.* December, pp. 268–73.

Kadoya Manabu. 2003. "Nettoraifu" (Net life). In Fushimi Noriaki (ed.), *Dōseiai nyūmon.* Tokyo: Potto shuppan.

Kaiser, Charles. 1997. *The Gay Metropolis.* Boston: Faber and Faber.

Kakefuda Hiroko. 1992. *"Rezubian" de aru to iu koto* (On being "lesbian"). Tokyo: Kawade shobō.

Kamiizumi Gō. 1972. "Rōtiin ai no jitsurei to mondai ten" (Examples and points of concern about low-teen love). *Barazoku,* August, pp. 62–73.

Kan Ryōta. 1958. "Dōkan: shōnen jidai no omoide" (Admiration for the loincloth: a recollection of boyhood). *Kitan kurabu,* November, pp. 75.

Kanō Mikiyo. 1993. "The Problem with the 'Comfort Women Problem.'" *AMPO Japan-Asia Quarterly Review,* vol. 24, no. 2, pp. 40–3.

Kawaguchi Kazuya. 2003. "Komento" (Comment). In Vera Mackie (ed.), *Gurōbaruka to jendā hyōshō* (Globalization and representations of gender). Tokyo: Ochanomizu shobō, pp. 139–52.

Kerkham, Eleanor. 2001. "Pleading for the Body: Tamura Tajirō's 1947 Korean Comfort Women Story, *Biography of a Prostitute.*" In Marlene Mayo and Thomas Rimer (eds.), *War, Occupation and Creativity: Japan and East Asia 1920–1960.* Honolulu: University of Hawaii Press, pp. 310–59.

Kingu gurafu tokushū. 1954. "Josei kara dansei e: sono go no Tsutsumi-san" (From woman to man: Tsutsumi-san's life after). June, p. 46.

Kinmonth, Earl. 1981. *The Self-Made Man in Meiji Japanese Thought: From Samurai to Salaryman.* Berkeley: University of California Press.

Kita Reiko. 1953. "Yawa hada wo semete" (Torture delicate skin). *Fūzoku zōshi.* August, pp. 131–5.

Kitahara Domu and Saotome Hiromi. 2003. *Kitan kurabu no hitobito* (The people of *Kitan kurabu*). Tokyo: Kawade bunko.

Kitazumi Izumi. 1982. "Homo shi go san ke wo kanzen dokuha" (A complete reading of three homo magazines). *Allan,* February, pp. 127–8.

Koga Takeshi. 1973. "Rikugun danshoku monogatari" (A tale of male eroticism in the army). *Fūzoku kitan,* November, pp. 168–72.

Kogure Genji. 1952. "Onna demo otoko demonai otoko: [danshō] okama dekameron" (Men who are neither women nor men: a [*danshō*] *okama Dekameron*). *Kibatsu kenkyū,* August, pp. 22–30.

Komatsu Anri. 2000. *Nyūhāfu ga kimeta "watashi" rashii ikikata* (On deciding to be a newhalf and living like "myself"). Tokyo: KK Ronguserāzu.

Kondō Kyō. 1954. "Danshoku henreki: aru sodomia no shuki" (A sojourn into male eroticism: sodomia notes). *Fūzoku kurabu*, May, pp. 143–9.

Kuia sutadiizu henshū iinkai (Queer studies editorial group). 1996. *Kuia sutadiizu '96* (Queer Studies '96). Tokyo: Nanatsumori shokan.

Kuia sutadiizu henshū iinkai (Queer studies editorial group). 1997. *Kuia sutadiizu '97* (Queer Studies '97). Tokyo: Nanatsumori shokan.

Kuno Yoshi. 1937. *Japanese Expansion on the Asiatic Continent: A Study in the History of Japan with Special Reference to Her International Relations with China, Korea and Russia*. Berkeley: University of California Press.

Kyōgaku Miki. 1959. "Hageshii onna" (Tempestuous woman). *Ura Mado*. February, pp. 204–13.

Leupp, Gary. 2003. *Interracial Intimacy in Japan: Western Men and Japanese Women 1543–1900*. London: Continuum.

———. 1998. "'The Floating World is Wide . . .': Some Suggested Approaches to Researching Female Homosexuality in Tokugawa Japan (1603–1868)." *Thamyris*, vol. 5, no. 1, Spring, pp. 1–40.

———. 1995. *Male Colors: The Construction of Homosexuality in Tokugawa Japan*. Berkeley: University of California Press.

Levine, Martin. 1998. *Gay Macho: The Life and Death of the Homosexual Clone*. New York: New York University Press.

Longinetto, Kim. 1996. *Shinjuku Boys*. BBC: Twentieth-Century Vixen (videocassette).

Low, Morris. 2003. "The Emperor's Sons Go to War: Competing Masculinities in Modern Japan." In Kam Louie and Morris Low (eds.), *Asian Masculinities: The Meaning and Practice of Manhood in China and Japan*. London: RoutledgeCurzon.

Lunsing, Wim. 2003. "What Masculinity? Transgender Practices among Japanese 'Men.'" In James Roberson and Nobue Suzuki (eds.), *Men and Masculinities in Contemporary Japan*. London: RoutledgeCurzon, pp. 20–36.

———. 2001. *Beyond Common Sense: Negotiating Gender and Sexuality in Japan*. London: Kegan Paul.

———. 1999. "Japan: Finding Its Way?" In Barry Adam (ed.), *The Global Emergence of Gay and Lesbian Politics: National Imprints of a Worldwide Movement*. Philadelphia: Temple University Press, pp. 293–325.

———. 1998. "Lesbian and Gay Movements: Between Hard and Soft." In Claudia Derichs and Anja Oziander (eds.), *Soziale Bewegungen in Japan*. Hamburg: Mitteilungen der Vereinigung für Natur und Volkenkunde, pp. 280–310.

———. 1997. "Gay Boom in Japan: Changing Views of Homosexuality?" *Thamyris*, vol. 4, no. 2, Autumn, pp. 267–93.

———. 1995. "Japanese Gay Magazines and Marriage Advertisements." In Gerald Sullivan (ed.), *Gays and Lesbians in Asia and the Pacific: Social and Human Services*. Binghamton, N.Y.: Haworth.

Mackie, Vera. 2003. *Feminism in Modern Japan*. Cambridge: Cambridge University Press.

———. 2001. "The Trans-Sexual Citizen: Queering Sameness and Difference." *Australian Feminist Studies*, vol. 16, no. 35, pp. 185–92.

———. 1980. "Women's Groups in Japan: An Overview of Major Groups." *Feminist International*, no. 2 (Asian Women '80), pp. 106–10.

McLelland, Mark. In press. "Salarymen Doing Queer: Gay Men and the Heterosexual Public Sphere in Japan." In Mark McLelland and Romit Dasgupta (eds.), *Genders, Transgenders and Sexualities in Japan*. London: Routledge.

———. 2004. "From the Stage to the Clinic: Changing Transgender Identities in Post-War Japan." *Japan Forum*, vol. 16, no. 1, pp. 1–20.

———. 2003a. "Gay Men, Masculinity and the Media in Japan." In Kam Louie and Morris Low (eds.), *Asian Masculinities: The Meaning and Practice of Manhood in China and Japan*. London: RoutledgeCurzon, pp. 59–78.

———. 2003b. "Private Acts/Public Spaces: Cruising for Gay Sex on the Japanese Internet." In Nanette Gottlieb and Mark McLelland (eds.), *Japanese Cybercultures*. London: Routledge, pp. 141–55.

———. 2002. "The Newhalf Net: Japan's 'Intermediate Sex' On Line." *International Journal of Sexuality and Gender Studies*, vol. 7, nos. 2/3, pp. 163–76.

———. 2001. "Local Meanings in Global Space: A Case Study of Women's 'Boy Love' Web Sites in Japanese and English." *Mots Pluriels*, no. 19, Special issue: *The Net: New Apprentices and Old Masters*, October. Available online: www.arts .uwa.edu.au/MotsPluriels/MP1901mcl.html (accessed 22 March 2004).

———. 2000a. *Male Homosexuality in Modern Japan: Cultural Myths and Social Realities*. London: RoutledgeCurzon.

———. 2000b."Out and About on Japan's Gay Net." *Convergence: The Journal of Research into New Media Technologies*, Special issue: *The Internet*, vol. 6, no. 3, September, pp. 16–33.

Maeda, Mariko. 1999. "Frailty Thy Name Is a Woman: Homefront Mobilization in Japan for World War II." Online, available: www.minpaku.ac.jp/jcas/nc/ firstworkshop.html (accessed 3 November 2003).

Manalansan, Martin. 1995. "In the Shadows of Stonewall: Examining Gay Transnational Politics and the Diaspora Dilemma." *GLQ: A Journal of Lesbian and Gay Studies*, vol. 2, pp. 425–38.

Maree, Claire. 2003. "*Ore wa ore dakara* ['Because I'm me']: A study of gender and language in the documentary *Shinjuku Boys*." *Intersections*, issue 9. Online, available: wwwsshe.murdoch.edu.au/intersections/issue9/maree.html#t3 (accessed 3 November 2003).

Mariposa Film Group. 1977. *Word Is Out*. New York: Adair Films.

Marlowe, Kenneth. 1964. *Mr. Madam: Confessions of a Male Madam*. Los Angeles: Sherbourne.

Martin, Bernd. 1995. *Japan and Germany in the Modern World*. Providence, R.I.: Berghahn Books.

Martin, Fran (trans.). 2003. *Angelwings: Contemporary Queer Fiction from Taiwan*. Honolulu: University of Hawai'i Press.

———. 2003. *Situating Sexualities: Queer Representation in Taiwanese Fiction, Film and Public Culture*. Hong Kong: Hong Kong University Press.

Maruo Chōken. 1966. "Burūbōi no seirigaku: Karūseru Maki ni okeru kōsatsu" (The physiology of blueboys: a consideration of Carrousel Maki). *Suriiesu*, March, pp. 62–6.

Matsuzawa Goichi. 1997. "Meiji, Taishō, Shōwa, kindai fūzoku shuppan no rekishi" (Meiji, Taisho, Showa, a history of modern sexual-customs publishing). In Wani no ana (ed.), *Ero no hon*. Tokyo: Wani no ana.

Mihalopoulos, Bill. 1993. "The Making of Prostitutes: The *Karayuki-san*." *Bulletin of Concerned Asian Scholars*, vol. 25, no. 1, pp. 41–56.

Miller, Daniel, and Don Slater. 2001. *The Internet: An Ethnographic Approach*. Oxford: Berg.

Miller, Laura. 2003. "Male Beauty Work in Japan." In James Roberson and Nobue Suzuki (eds.), *Men and Masculinities in Contemporary Japan: Dislocating the Salaryman Doxa*. London: Routledge.

Miller, Stephen (ed.). 1996. *Partings at Dawn: An Anthology of Japanese Gay Literature*. San Francisco: Gay Sunshine.

Mishima Yukio. 1977 (1968). *Yukio Mishima on Hagakure: The Samurai Ethic and Modern Japan*. Trans. Kathryn Sparling. New York: Basic Books.

———. 1973 (1951–53). *Zenshū* (Complete works), vol. 5, *Kinjiki*. Tokyo: Shinchōsha.

———. 1970 (1968). *Sun and Steel*. Trans. John Bester. Tokyo: Kodansha.

———. 1968 (1951–53). *Forbidden Colors*. Trans. Alfred H. Marks. Tokyo: Tuttle.

MISTRESS. 1990. "Nyūhāfu koso ga penisu no tsuita joōsama de aru" (The thing about newhalf is that they are queens with penises). Vol. 1, no. 1, 25 May, pp. 140–3.

Misushu Akira. 1951. "Onna ni haru wo utta otoko" (Men who sell sex to women). *Ningen tankyū*, October, pp. 46–9.

Mitchell, Richard. 1983. *Censorship in Imperial Japan*. Princeton, N.J.: Princeton University Press.

Mitsuhashi Junko. 2001. "Burūbōi no shōgeki" (The blue boy impact). *Nihon josō mukashibanashi* (Reminiscences about Japan's cross-dressers), part 8. *Nyūhāfu kurabu*, no. 31.

———. 1998. "Saisho no amachua josō shūdan" (The first amateur cross-dressing associations). *Nihon josō mukashibanashi* (Reminiscences about Japan's cross-dressers), part 2. *Nyūhāfu kurabu* no. 25.

Miyano Akira. 1978. "Seitōna iryō kōi: burūbōi jiken" (Justifiable medical procedures: the blue-boy incident). *Bessatsu juristo* no. 57, pp. 76–7.

Miyazaki Rumiko. 2000. *Watashi wa toransujendā* (I am transgendered). Tokyo: Neoraifu.

Miyazono Sanshirō. 1953. "Danshoku kandan" (Gossip about male eroticism). *Fūzoku kagaku*, August, pp. 74–9.

Mizoguchi Akiko. 2003. "Male-Male Romance by and for Women in Japan: A History of the Subgenre of YAOI Fictions." *US-Japan Women's Journal English Supplement*, no. 25, pp. 49–75.

Mizutani, Kristine. 2001. "Lesbian Tokyo: Identity, Sexuality and Community." M.A. thesis. California Institute of Integral Studies.

Mochizuki Mamoru. 1955. "M to W no shakaigaku" (The sociology of M and W). *Fujin kōron*, September, pp. 152–5.

Mohanty, Chandra Talpade. 1984. "Under Western Eyes: Feminist Scholarship and Colonial Discourses." *Boundary 2*, vol. 12, no. 3/vol. 13, no. 1, Spring/Fall, pp. 333–58.

Molasky, Michael. 2001. *The American Occupation of Japan and Okinawa: Literature and Memory*. London: Routledge.

Mori Ōgai. 1971. *Zenshū* (complete works), vol. 1, *Wita sekusuarisu*. Tokyo: Chikuma Shobō.

Morihara Taichi. 1953. "Ware ga guntai jidai no kaiko" (Reflections on my time in the army). *Kitan kurabu,* March, pp. 94–7.

Morii Akira. 1952. "Rikugun chūi jidai no kaisō" (Reminiscences of my time as an infantry officer). *Kitan kurabu,* August, pp. 128–32.

Murray, Raymond. 1994. *Images in the Dark: An Encyclopedia of Gay and Lesbian Film and Video*. Philadelphia: TLA.

Nakamura Daihachi. 1960. "Onna ni ubawareta 'otome'" (The "virgin" who was captivated by a woman). *Fūzoku kitan,* March, pp. 100–9.

Nakanishi Masamori and Ueno Chizuko. 2003. *Tōjisha no shuken* (The sovereignty of the *tōjisha*), Tokyo: Iwanami shinsho.

Nakano Masanao. 1951. "Bungei ni arawareta dansei no dōseiai" (Male homosexuality as it appears in the literary arts). *Amatoria,* September, pp. 82–6.

Namiki Sansaku. 1954. "Miniya karapa: sodomii no kazekaoru" (Coconut oil: a fragrant breeze of homosexuality). *Fūzoku kagaku*. May, pp. 152–9.

Narumi Giichirō. 1951. "Osorubeki kodomotachi: shōnen seihanzai" (Children to be afraid of: youth sex crimes). *Amatoria,* May, pp. 92–7.

Narushima Yaeko. 1954. "Onēsama no muchi no shita" (Under my elder sister's whip). *Fūzoku zōshi*. March, pp. 70–8.

Nealon, Christopher. 2001. *Foundlings: Lesbian and Gay Historical Emotion before Stonewall*. Durham, N.C.: Duke University Press.

Newton, Esther. 1979. *Mother Camp: Female Impersonators in America*. Chicago: University of Chicago Press.

Nishida Tatsuo. 1962. "Kokuhaku: fundoshi to hadaka matsuri" (Confession: loincloths and naked festivals). *Fūzoku kitan,* August, pp. 91–3.

Nishijima Minoru. 1953. "Dōseiai keikō no tsuma to seikan" (A wife with a tendency toward homosexuality and sexual feeling). *Amatoria,* December, pp. 98–101.

Nishina Shō. 1972a. *Shin bara no kairaku* (New rose ecstasy). Tokyo: Dai ni shobō.

———. 1972b. *STRIPPED GUYS shasshin shū: nuida otokotachi* (Stripped guys photo collection: naked men). Tokyo: Dai ni shobō.

———. 1971. *Bara no kairaku* (Rose ecstasy). Tokyo: Dai ni shobō.

Norgren, Tiana. 2001. *Abortion before Birth Control: The Politics of Reproduction in Postwar Japan*. Princeton, N.J.: Princeton University Press.

Ōgiya Afu. 1958. *Sodomia banka* (Elegy to homosexuality). Tokyo: Shineisha.

———. 1954. "F.K.K. dayori" (News about FKK). *Fūzoku kagaku,* September, pp. 84–5.

———. 1953. "Danshokusha to sono seiteki tokushitsu" (Male homosexuals and their sexual characteristics). *Fūzoku kagaku,* October, pp. 156–60.

Ohata Ichizō. 1955. "Fundoshi no miryoku wo saguru" (Looking for the attraction of the loincloth). *Fūzoku kagaku,* February, pp. 86–91.

Oikawa Kenji. 2001. "Densetsu no okama: aiyoku to hangyaku ni moetagiru" (The legendary *okama* burning with lust and rebellion). *Shūkan kinyōbi,* 15 June, pp. 34–9. Reproduced in Fushimi Noriaki (ed.), *Okama wa sabetsu ka: Shūkan kinyōbi no sabetsu hyōgen jiken* (Does *okama* have discriminatory connotations?

The discriminating expression case in *Shūkan kinyōbi*). 2002. Tokyo: Potto shuppan. pp. 16–32.

OK erosu ando suriru. 1949. "Mondai no kokuhaku: danshō zadankai" (Problem confession: *danshō* roundtable." Vol. 2, no.1, pp. 12–6.

Oka Masashirō. 1953. "Ryōsei dōbutsu: danshoku yobanashi" (Amphibious animals: night talks about male homosexuality). *Kitan kurabu*, October, pp. 100–2.

Oniyama Ayakazu. 1955. "Joshi puroresuringu zakkan" (Miscellaneous impressions of women's pro wrestling). *Kitan kurabu*, November, pp. 152–4.

Ōno Shigeru. 1972. "O-te wo furu GAY tachi" (Gays waving with outspread arms). *Barazoku*, November, pp. 98–9.

Osugi Sakae. 1992. *The Autobiography of Osugi Sakae*. Trans. Byron K. Marshall. Berkeley: University of California Press.

Ōta Tenrei (ed.). 1957. *Dai san no sei: sei no hōkai?* (The third sex: the breakdown of sex?). Tokyo: Myōki shuppan.

———. 1954. "Dōseiai no dōkō: chōsa daiikkai chūkan hōkoku" (Trends in homosexuality: a first interim report). *Fūzoku kagaku*, September, pp. 78–83.

Ōta Tenrei and Kabiya Kazuhiko. 1954. "Petting wa ryūkō suru" (Petting is popular). *Fūzoku kagaku*, March, pp. 79–83.

Ōtsuka Takashi. 1996. "Long Interview." *Adon*, February. Online, available: www.asahi-net.or.jp/~km5t-ootk/taqo_text/adon1.html (accessed 7 October 2003).

———. 1995. *Ni-chōme kara uroko: Shinjuku geisutoriito zakkichō* (Ni-chōme rediscovered: notes on Shinjuku's gay street). Tokyo: Shōeisha.

Pflugfelder, Gregory. 1999. *Cartographies of Desire: Male-Male Sexuality in Japanese Discourse, 1600–1950*. Berkeley: University of California Press.

Plant, Richard. 1986. *The Pink Triangle: The Nazi War against Homosexuals*. New York: Henry Holt.

Plummer, Ken. 1995. *Telling Sexual Stories: Power, Change and Social Worlds*. London: Routledge.

Purojekuto G. 1992. *Otoko no ko no tame no bōifurendo gei handobukku* (A gay boyfriend handbook for boys). Tokyo: Shōnensha.

QR. 1954. "Josei no dōseiai ni tsuite" (Concerning female same-sex love). *Fūzoku kagaku*. September, p. 65.

Rainwater, Lee. 1970. *Behind Ghetto Walls: Black Families in a Federal Slum*. Chicago: Aldine.

Ramakers, Micha. 2000. *Dirty Pictures: Tom of Finland, Masculinity and Homosexuality*. New York: St. Martin's.

Roberson, James and Nobue Suzuki. 2003. "Introduction." In James Roberson and Nobue Suzuki (eds.), *Men and Masculinities in Contemporary Japan: Dislocating the Salaryman Doxa*. London: RoutledgeCurzon.

Robertson, Jennifer. 2002. "Blood Talks: Eugenic Modernity and the Creation of New Japanese." *History and Anthropology*, vol. 13, no. 3, pp. 191–216.

———. 2001. "Japan's First Cyborg? Miss Nippon and Wartime Technologies of Beauty, Body and Blood." *Body and Society*, vol. 7, no. 1, pp. 1–34.

———. 1999. "Dying to Tell: Sexuality and Suicide in Imperial Japan." *Signs*, Autumn, vol. 25, pp. 1–36.

———. 1998. *Takarazuka: Sexual Politics and Popular Culture in Modern Japan*. Berkeley: University of California Press.

———. 1992. "The Politics of Androgyny in Japan: Sexuality and Subversion in the Theatre and Beyond." *American Ethnologist*, vol. 19, no. 3. pp. 419–42.

Robinson, Paul. 1999. *Gay Lives: Homosexual Autobiography from John Addington Symonds to Paul Monette*. Chicago: University of Chicago Press.

Roden, Donald. 1990. "Taisho Culture and the Problem of Gender Ambivalence." In J. Thomas Rimer (ed.), *Japanese Intellectuals during the Inter-War Years*. Princeton, N.J.: Princeton University Press.

———. 1980. *Schooldays in Imperial Japan: A Study in the Culture of a Student Elite*. Berkeley: University of California Press.

Rosenfeld, David. 2002. *Unhappy Soldier: Hino Ashihei and Japanese World War II Literature*. Lanham, Md.: Lexington Books.

Rubin, Gayle. 2002. "Studying Sexual Subcultures: Excavating the Ethnography of Gay Communities in Urban North America." In Ellen Lewin and William Leap (eds.), *Out in Theory: The Emergence of Lesbian and Gay Anthropology*. Urbana: University of Illinois Press.

Rubin, Jay. 1988. "The Impact of the Occupation on Literature or Lady Chatterley and Lt. Col. Verness." In Thomas W. Burkman (ed.), *The Occupation of Japan: Arts and Culture*. Norfolk, Va.: General Douglas MacArthur Foundation, pp. 167–74.

———. 1985. "From Wholesomeness to Decadence: The Censorship of Literature under the Allied Occupation." *Journal of Japanese Studies*, vol. 11, no. 1, pp. 71–103.

Ryūta Shinji. 1954. "Chigo heishi kanbu kōhosei" (The page-boy soldier who was a candidate for the management corps). *Kitan kurabu*, June, pp. 181–3.

Saijō Michio (chair). 1955. "Zadankai: Josei no homo makari tōru" (Roundtable: female homos here we go). *Fūzoku kagaku*, March, pp. 148–56.

Saitō Hifumi. 1959. "Otoko geisha nanbāwan ni naru made" (Before I became the number one male geisha). *Hyakuman nin no yoru*, September, pp. 151–6.

Saitō Tetsu. 1962. "Josō wo tanoshimu atashitachi" (We who enjoy cross-dressing). *Fūzoku kitan*, special edition, January/February, pp. 127–31.

Sakaguchi Ango. 1986. "Discourse on Decadence." *Review of Japanese Culture and Society*, vol. 1, no. 1, pp. 1–5.

Sakai, Naoki and Yukiko Hanawa. 2001. "Introduction." In Naoki Sakai and Yukiko Hanawa (eds.), *Specters of the West and the Politics of Translation: Traces, a Multilingual Journal of Theory and Translation*, vol. 1, pp. v–xiii.

Sakai, Naoki. 2001. "Dislocation of the West and the Status of the Humanities." In Naoki Sakai and Yukiko Hanawa (eds.), *Specters of the West and the Politics of Translation: Traces, a Multilingual Journal of Theory and Translation*, vol. 1, pp. 71–94.

Saotome Hiromi. 1998. "Homo zasshi wo hajimete sōkan shita Itō Bungaku" (Itō Bungaku: the first person to publish a homo magazine). *Sei no shigotoshita hitotachi*. Tokyo: Kawade bunko, pp. 192–9.

Satō Eisaku. 1960. "Bishōnen no ie: tanbōki" (Beautiful-boy houses: a report). *Fūzoku kitan*, August, pp. 58–63.

Sawada Bushō. 1921. "Onna ga shujutsu wo ukete otoko ni natta" (A woman who had an operation and became a man). *Fujin kōron*, August, pp. 59–68.

Sedgwick, Eve Kosofsky. 1990. *Epistemology of the Closet*. London: Penguin.

Seki Tamiko. 1980. *Edokōki no onnatachi* (Women in the late Edo period). Tokyo: Akishobo.

Shiba Fumiko. 1997. "Nemurenu yoru no tame ni" (For a sleepless night). *Aniisu* 4, Summer, pp. 110–1.

Shibata Tomo. 1999. "Japan's Wartime Mass-Rape Camps and Continuing Sexual Human-Rights Violations." *US-Japan Women's Journal English Supplement*, Number 16, pp. 48–86.

Shibukawa Tetsuo. 1953. "Sodomia hōrōki" (Ramblings about homosexuality). *Fūzoku zōshi*, October, pp. 71–7.

Shiga Yūji. 1956. "San nin no josō aikōsha" (Three lovers of cross-dressing). *Kappa*. August, pp. 190–3.

Shimokawa Kōshi. 1995a. *Nihon ero shashinshi* (History of Japan's erotic photographs). Tokyo: Shōkyūsha.

———. 1995b. "Hentai no sōgō depāto *Kitan kurabu* kara *SM serekuto* ga ubugoe wo agerumade" (From *Kitan kurabu*, perversity's general department, to *SM serekuto*'s first cry). *Bessatsu Takarajima*, "Sei media 50 nen," no. 240, December, pp. 48–55.

Shin Young-sook and Cho Hye-ran. 1996. "On the Characteristics and Special Nature of the Korean 'Military Comfort Women' under Japanese Rule." *Korea Journal*, Spring, pp. 50–78.

Shinagawa M. 1953. "Sodomii shumi ni ikin" (Sodomy interests live on). *Fūzoku kagaku*. November, p. 113.

Shiroyama Naoto. 1994. "Jūnisai no haru: sakura gari" (The twelfth spring: hunting for cherries). *Barazoku*, April, pp. 234–7.

Shōnen hantā. 1982. "Shōnen hantā zadankai" (Boy hunter roundtable). *Barazoku shōnen'ai shashinshū to zadankai*, April, pp. 12–29.

Shūkan bunshun. 1973. "Karūseru Maki jotai kaizō jūnen keikaku no owari" (Carrousel Maki: the end of a 10-year project to construct a woman's body). 17 December.

———. 1961. "'Yōroppa no yoru' wo utau seitenkan" (Sex-change sings "Europe by night"). 23 January, pp. 86–90.

Shūkan gendai. 1965. "Jūnin no 'onna' no taiken hōkoku" (A report on the experience of ten "women"). 28 October, p. 133.

Shūkan jitsuwa. 1991. "Shigatsu yokka wa okama no hi: issho ni o-iwaishitene" (April 4 is *okama* day, come and celebrate with us). 11 April.

Shūkan taishū. 1994. "Series: Nippon no bijotachi—Betii no mayonēzu, Kansai ichi no honkaku shō" (Series: Japan's beauties—Betty's Mayonnaise, Kansai's number one proper show). 12 December.

———. 1958. "5000nin no shitsugyōsha: gendai no kikeiji gei bōi no SOS" (5000 unemployed: an SOS from today's freaks of nature—gay boys). 18 August, pp. 24–7.

Simon, William and John Gagnon. 1967. "Homosexuality: The Formulation of a Sociological Perspective." *Journal of Health and Social Behavior*, vol. 8. no. 3, September, pp. 177–85.

Sonomura Keiko. 1954. "Resubosu tsūshin" (Lesbos communication). *Fūzoku zōshi*. August, pp. 86–91.

———. 1953a. "Resubosu tsūshin" (Lesbos communication). *Fūzoku zōshi*. July, pp. 127–9.

———. 1953b. "Resubosu tsūshin" (Lesbos communication). *Fūzoku zōshi*. September, pp. 120–4.

———. 1953c. "Resubosu tekuniiku" (Lesbos technique). *Fūzoku zōshi*. (expanded Autumn edition), December, pp. 214–8.

Spencer, Colin. 1995. *Homosexuality: A History*. London: Fourth Estate.

Standish, Isolde. 2000. *Myth and Masculinity in the Japanese Cinema: Towards a Political Reading of the "Tragic Hero."* Richmond, Surrey: Curzon.

Stein, Marc. 2000. *City of Sisterly and Brotherly Loves: Lesbian and Gay Philadelphia, 1945–1972*. Chicago: University of Chicago Press.

Steward, Samuel. 1981. *Chapters from an Autobiography*. San Francisco: Grey Fox.

Stibbe, Arran. 2004. "Disability, Gender and Power in Japanese Television Drama." *Japan Forum*, vol. 16, no. 1, pp. 21–36.

Streitmatter, Rodger. 1995. *Unspeakable: the Rise of the Gay and Lesbian Press in America*. Boston: Faber and Faber.

Sueyoshi, Amy. 2002. "'Love . . . by Buddha's Name': The Question of Same-Sex Love in Yone Noguchi." Paper presented at the Third AsiaPacifiQueer Conference, University of Melbourne, 8 December 2002.

Suganuma Katsuhiko. 2004. "Sexuality Politics in Contemporary Japanese Society in Relation to Anglo-American Queer Globalization." M.A. thesis, State University of New York at Albany.

Sugiura Ikuko. 2001. *Matsuba Yukari no raifuhisutorii* (Matsuba Yukari life history). Tokyo: Chūō Daigaku Sengo Nippon Toransujendā Shakaishi Kenkyūkai.

Sumi Tatsuya. 1949. *Danshō no mori* (Forest of male prostitutes). Tokyo: Hibiya shuppan.

Summerhawk, Barbara, Cheiron McMahill and Darren McDonald (eds.). 1998. *Queer Japan: Personal Stories of Japanese Lesbians, Gays, Bisexuals and Transsexuals*. Norwich, Vt.: New Victoria.

Sunagawa Hideki. 2003. "Nihon no gei no rekishi" (Japan's gay history). In Fushimi Noriaki (ed.), *Dōseiai nyūmon*. Tokyo: Potto shuppan, pp. 44–47.

———(ed.). 2001. *Parēdo: Tōkyō rezubian and gei parēdo 2000 no kiroku* (Parade: a record of Tokyo's lesbian and gay parade 2000). Tokyo: Potto shuppan.

Suzuki Masahiro. 2001. "Senso ni okeru dansei sekushuariti" (Men's sexuality during war). In Asai Haruo, Itō Satoru and Murase Yukihiro (eds.), *Nihon no otoko wa doko kara kite doko e iku?* Tokyo: Jūgatsusha, pp. 98–119.

Tagame Gengoroh. 2003. *Gay Erotic Art in Japan* Volume 1: Artists from the Time of the Birth of Gay Magazines. Tokyo: Potto shuppan.

Takahashi Tetsu. 1954. "Kitai dōseiai dan" (Talk about strange homosexuality). *Fūzoku zōshi*, January, pp. 74–82.

Takahashi Tetsu and Richard Lane. 1952. "Nichibei seiai mondō" (Questions and answers about Japanese-American sexual love). *Ningen tankyū*, April, pp. 38–51.

Tanaka Sumio (chair). 1954. "Dai ni zadankai: Ōsaka—Tōkyō wo kataru" (Second roundtable: talking about Osaka and Tokyo). *Adonis* no. 17, pp. 17–20.

Tanaka Yuki. 2002. *Japan's Comfort Women: Sexual Slavery and Prostitution during World War II and the U.S. Occupation*. London: Routledge.

Tanizaki Jun'ichirō. 1988. *Childhood Years: A Memoir*. Trans. Paul McCarthy. Tokyo: Kodansha International.

Tōgō Ken. 2002. *Jōshiki wo koete: okama no michi 70 nen* (Overcoming common sense: 70 years on the *okama* path). Tokyo: Potto shuppan.

———. 1986. "'Okama no Tōgō Ken' no kyacchifurēzu de watashi ga hontō ni iitakatta koto soshite 'minzoku no heya' ni tsuite" (What I really wanted to say with the catchphrase "*Okama* Tōgō Ken" and also about the "people's room"). *The Gay*, July, pp. 38–49.

Tomita Eizō. 1958. *Gei* (Gay). Tokyo: Tōkyō shobō.

Tomita Sodomiia. 1953. "Dansei nūdo wo tanomu" (Request for male nudes). *Fūzoku kagaku*. November, p. 113.

Toyama Hitomi. 1999. *Miss Dandy: Otoko toshite ikiru joseitachi* (Miss Dandy: women living as men). Tokyo: Shinchōsha.

Ueno Chizuko. 1996. "The Making of a History of Feminism in Japan." *Asia-Japan Women's Studies*, vol. 2, pp. 170–91.

Ujiie Mikito. 1995. *Bushidō to erosu* (The way of the warrior and eros). Tokyo: Kōdansha.

Valentine, David, and Riki Anne Wilchins. 1997. "One-Percent of the Burn Chart: Gender, Genitals and Hermaphrodites with Attitude." *Social Text*, vol. 15, nos. 3 and 4, pp. 215–22.

Vaporis, Constantine Nomikos. 1994. *Breaking Barriers: Travel and the State in Early Modern Japan*. Cambridge, Mass.: Harvard University Press.

Wada Isamu. 1953. "Aru yoru no keiken" (My experience one night). *Kitan kurabu*, January, p. 145.

Warren, Carol. 1979. "Women among Men: Females in the Male Homosexual Community." In Martin Levine (ed.), *Gay Men: The Sociology of Male Homosexuality*. New York: Harper and Row, pp. 222–38.

Watanabe Tsuneo and Jun'ichi Iwata. 1989. *The Love of the Samurai: A Thousand Years of Japanese Homosexuality*. Trans. D. R. Roberts. London: GMP.

Weisenfeld, Gennifer. 2002. *Mavo: Japanese Artists and the Avant-Garde, 1905–1931*. Berkeley: University of California Press.

Weissman, Aerlyn and Lynne Fernie (dirs). 1992. *Forbidden Love: The Unashamed Stories of Lesbian Lives*. National Film Board of Canada.

Welker, James. In press. "Lilies on the Margin: Beautiful Boys and Lesbian Identities." In Peter Jackson, Mark McLelland, Fran Martin and Audrey Yue (eds.), *AsiaPacifiQueer: Rethinking Gender and Sexuality in Asia*. Champaign: University of Illinois Press.

———. 2003. "Borrowed or Border Identities: Altered States of Lesbian Cultural Production in Japan/Asia." Presentation given at International Convention of Asia Scholars, Singapore, 19–22 August.

———. 2002. "Telling Herstory: The Japanese Lesbian Community 1971–2001." M.A. thesis, University of Sheffield.

Westwood, Gordon. 1960. *A Report on the Life of the Male Homosexual in Great Britain*. London: Longmans.

Whittle, Stephen. 2002. *Respect and Equality: Transsexual and Transgender Rights*. London: Cavendish.

Wotherspoon, Gary. 1991. *City of the Plain: History of a Gay Subculture*. Sydney: Hale and Iremonger.

———. 1986. *Being Different: Nine Gay Men Remember*. Sydney: Hale and Iremonger.

Wu, Peichen. 2002. "Performing Gender along the Lesbian Continuum: The Politics of Sexual Identity in the Seitō Society." *US-Japan Women's Journal English Supplement*, no. 22, pp. 64–86.

XYZ. 1955. *"Danshoku kissaten/sakaba no Tōkyō chizu"* (Map of Tokyo male-eroticism coffee shops and bars). *Fūzoku kagaku*, February, pp. 72–8.

Yajima Masami (ed.). 2000. *Okama dō wo iku: Yatsuse Yumi no kenkyū* (On the *okama* road: Yatsuse Yumi's research). Tokyo: Chūō Daigaku Sengo Nihon Toransujendā Shakaishi Kenkyūkai.

———. 1997. *Dansei dōseiaisha no raifuhisutorii* (Male homosexuals' life histories). Tokyo: Gakubunsha.

Yamaguchi Kōichi. 1954. "Shōnen no konbi ni tsuite" (Concerning the beauty of boys in loincloths). *Kitan kurabu*, October, pp. 86–9.

Yamamoto Akira. 1976. *Kasutori zasshi kenkyū: shinboru ni miru fūzokushi* (Kasutori magazine research: sex-customs seen as symbols). Tokyo: Shuppan nyūsusha.

Yamamoto Akira and Ozawa Shōichi. 1975. "Kisu wo suru koto minshushugi no shinboru da" (Kissing is a symbol of democracy). In Nippon shuppansha (ed.), *Kasutori fukkokuhan*. Tokyo: Nippon shuppansha.

Yanagiya Wataru. 1953. "Gaikokujin no danshoku: ikoku shudō dangi" (Male eroticism among foreigners: a lecture on the way of boys in foreign countries). *Fūzoku zōshi*, December, pp. 300–4.

Yatō Tamotsu. 1969. *Hadaka matsuri* (Naked festival). Tokyo: Bijutsu shuppansha.

———. 1966. *Taidō: Nippon no bodiibirudātachi* (The way of the body: Japan's bodybuilders). Tokyo: Weatherhill.

Yokota-Murakami, Takayuki. 1998. *Don Juan East/West: On the Problematics of Comparative Literature*. Albany: State University of New York Press.

Yoneyama, Lisa. 1999. "Habits of Knowing Cultural Differences: *Chrysanthemum and the Sword* in the U.S. Liberal Multiculturalism." *Topoi* 18, pp. 71–80.

Young, Greg. 2004. "From Broadcasting to Narrowcasting to 'Mycasting': A Newfound Celebrity in Queer Internet Communities." *Continuum*, vol. 18, no. 1, March 2004, pp. 43–62.

Yume Miruko. 1955. "Josei homo no kai" (Female homo organization). *Fūzoku kagaku*, February, p. 37.

Zimet, Jaye. 1999. *Strange Sisters: The Art of Lesbian Pulp Fiction, 1949–1969*. New York: Viking.

Index

About the Author

Mark McLelland is research fellow in the Centre for Critical and Cultural Studies at the University of Queensland. His numerous publications include *Male Homosexuality in Modern Japan* (2000) and the edited collections *Japanese Cybercultures* (2003) and *Genders, Transgenders and Sexualities in Japan* (2005). He is currently working on a queer history of Tokyo.

ASIAN VOICES
Series Editor: Mark Selden

Tales of Tibet: Sky Burials, Prayer Wheels, and Wind Horses
edited and translated by Herbert Batt, foreword by Tsering Shakya

Voicing Concerns: Contemporary Chinese Critical Inquiry
edited by Gloria Davies, conclusion by Geremie Barmé

Peasants, Rebels, Women, and Outcastes: The Underside of Modern Japan
by Mikiso Hane

Comfort Woman: A Filipina's Story of Prostitution and Slavery under the Japanese Military
by Maria Rosa Henson, introduction by Yuki Tanaka

Japan's Past, Japan's Future: One Historian's Odyssey
by Ienaga Saburō, translated and introduced by Richard H. Minear

Sisters and Lovers: Women and Desire in Bali
by Megan Jennaway

Moral Politics in a South Chinese Village: Responsibility, Reciprocity, and Resistance
by Hok Bun Ku

Growing Up Untouchable in India: A Dalit Autobiography
by Vasant Moon, translated by Gail Omvedt, introduction by Eleanor Zelliot

Rowing the Eternal Sea: The Life of a Minamata Fisherman
by Oiwa Keibo, narrated by Ogata Masato, translated by Karen Colligan-Taylor

Red Is Not the Only Color: Contemporary Chinese Fiction on Love and Sex between Women, Collected Stories
edited by Patricia Sieber

Sweet and Sour: Life-Worlds of Taipei Women Entrepreneurs
by Scott Simon

Dear General MacArthur: Letters from the Japanese during the American Occupation
by Sodei Rinjirō, edited by John Junkerman, translated by Shizue Matsuda, foreword by John W. Dower

Unbroken Spirits: Nineteen Years in South Korea's Gulag
by Suh Sung, translated by Jean Inglis, foreword by James Palais